TAX CREDITS FOR LOW INCOME HOUSING

New Opportunities for Developers, Non-Profits, and Communities Under the 1986 and 1988 Tax Acts

FOURTH EDITION

Joseph Guggenheim

SIMON PUBLICATIONS
Washington, D.C.

Fourth Edition

ISBN 0-941239-02-0

Published by:

SIMON PUBLICATIONS
P.O. BOX 70425 Southwest Station
WASHINGTON, D.C. 20024-0425

Library of Congress Catalogue Card Number 88-92725

DISCLAIMER

Every reasonable effort has been made to insure that the information in the publication is correct. However, there may be mistakes, both typographical and in content. Numerous judgements of a subjective nature have been made by the author. Some unbiased students of the matter may arrive at different interpretations or assessments of various provisions and the overall program. In certain instances, intricate and complex details have been summarized and minor matters omitted. More definitive further interpretations of the statute will be rendered in future regulations and issuances of the Internal Revenue Service. As in all complex matters of this sort, specific professional advice and legal opinion may be required by potential users of the tax credits.

The author and publisher do not assume liability for any cost, damage, or inconvenience resulting from use of this book.

ACKNOWLEDGEMENTS

I am indebted to various people for their assistance and encouragement in producing this book. In the first two editions, Douglas Diamond of the National Association of Home Builders; Chuck Edson of the Kelley, Drye, & Warren law firm and an editor-in-chief of Housing and Development Reporter; Frank Frantz of Preservation Reports, publisher of Urban Conservation Report; Rick Goldstein of the Kelley, Drye, & Warren law firm; John Muller, formerly of the Boasberg and Norton law firm; Glenn Petherick of Housing and Development Reporter; Drew Lyon of the University of Maryland, formerly with the Joint Committee on Taxation of the U.S. Congress; and Tom White of the Federal National Mortgage Association read major portions of the manuscript and made invaluable suggestions. Byron Fielding, editor of Housing Affairs and Community Development Digest for CD Publications, edited key chapters, and he and his wife Jane made helpful suggestions.

Chuck Edson, Drew Lyon, and Glenn Petherick reviewed and commented on most of the revisions contained in the third edition.

Glenn Petherick and David Reznick did yeoman work in reviewing the detailed changes in the Fourth Edition, and made numerous helpful suggestions. Tony Freedman and Jerry Breed of the Powell, Goldstein, Frazer & Murphy law firm provided excellent advice on a few difficult issues addressed in this edition.

Donna Young, Chris Wilson and John Metras of the U.S. Internal Revenue Service answered many questions and provided additional information. The National Council of State Housing Agencies (NCSHA) and the Florida Housing Finance Agency provided needed information and data. Ronne Thielen of NCSHA was particularly helpful in this regard. The publication Housing and Development Reporter graciously permitted use of their compilation of Section 42 of the Internal Revenue Code.

Timely advice and assistance in understanding intricacies in the 1986 Tax Reform Act was provided by Tom Coughlin of the Boasberg and Norton law firm, and Frank Cantrel of the Senate Finance Committee. Joe Riley, Ray Kahn and Dave Shenk of the Division of Economic Market Analysis, Office of Economic Affairs, U.S. Department of Housing and Urban Development, provided the voluminous statistics on median and maximum incomes and additional assistance in working with the data.

Bob Dumouchel, author of Government Assistance Almanac and publisher of Foggy Bottom Publications, provided invaluable advice and encouragement about publishing.

Kay and Don Watson of the D. L. Watson Company performed excellent word processing and computer work in earlier editions, and produced the computerized tables on income and rent levels in Appendix 1 in all four editions. Sylvia Barak provided competent clerical assistance in a timely manner.

The people at John M. Mertens and Associates and Donna M. Watson and Associates competently performed the word processing and computer work that produced the copy for the Fourth Edition. Particularly, Claudia Blake of the Donna M. Watson firm did excellent work in producing the final copy that looks so well on the pages that follow.

My wife Shelly provided editorial assistance and encouragement and understanding when it was needed. My son Simon selected the color for the cover of the Fourth Edition, and provided lots of inspiration.

Finally, this book would not have been possible without the relentless efforts of the many dedicated persons and organizations who lobbied successfully to see the tax credit program with all its promises and defects enacted into law, and who continue to work to improve the program and extend its existence.

Joe Guggenheim

FOR SHELLY AND SIMON

TABLE OF CONTENTS

Table of Contents (cont.)

Table of Contents (cont.)

Table of Contents (Cont.)

Table of Contents (cont.)

Table of Contents (cont.)

LIST OF TABLES

1

INTRODUCTION

Following a period of retrenchment and reduction of Federal support for low income housing, the Congress of the United States produced as part of the Tax Reform Act of 1986 an innovative and seemingly generous program called "Tax Credit for Low-Income Rental Housing."

It is "the most generous tax credit in history," according to a Congressional staff person who participated in its creation. "The intent of the credit is to provide a sufficient incentive so that there will be a supply of low income housing," according to another involved Congressional staffer.

The dollar allocations provided by the program amount to a potential of close to $10 billion worth of funding aiding over 300,000 units of low income housing over a three-year period.

The program can aid more types of low income rental housing than any one program has addressed previously -- new construction, substantial rehabilitation, moderate rehabilitation, simple acquisition of existing properties, and repairs by existing owners. It can cover a modest, existing one-unit rental property or a development with hundreds of units of new construction.

Incongruously, it is a tax benefit approach to low income housing that was included in the 1986 tax reform act along with severe restrictions on existing and future tax benefits for rental real estate that were described by some critics as the death knell for rental housing production in the United States.

This action followed a period of intense Congressional criticism of real estate tax provisions generally, and a charge that the existing tax benefit system for low income housing was not providing much housing for needy low income persons.

This new version of low income housing tax benefits improves considerably on the targeting of tax benefits in prior law. It requires that the housing be geared to incomes at 50 or 60 percent of area median income, rather than 80 percent of median income. In addition, the amount of tax credits is directly based on the number of qualified low income units where both the rent levels and the incomes of the occupants meet the targeting requirements.

The tax credits are a complex program that is part of a larger, even more intricate set of related tax code provisions governing individual and corporate taxation, investment, and tax-exempt financing by state and local government. Some minimal understanding of all of these subjects is necessary in order to use the financial largesse that the tax credits offer.

* * * * * *

This publication explains in understandable language the provisions of this new program and the basics of other relevant portions of the tax reform act, and analyzes their impact and significance as well. This is done in Chapters Two and Three. Chapter Four, "Will the Tax Credit Work?", answers the question by using model pro forma budgets to analyze the financial impact of the tax credit on various types of projects at a range of median income levels representative of metropolitan areas across the country.

Chapter Five discusses various aspects of working with the credits, including strategies for coordinating with other forms of government aid for low income housing and strategies for maximizing the amount of credits earned in individual projects. This chapter also includes suggestions as to how state and local government agencies can work effectively with the tax credit program. Chapter Six deals with the problem of raising investment capital through syndication and the formation of limited partnerships. It includes a list of syndicators who have experience in low income housing and are already involved in syndicating tax credit projects.

The final chapter, Seven, summarizes the author's conclusions and overall judgment of the program based on material in earlier chapters as well as his experience with the program for more than two years. It also analyzes the conclusions of the Congressionally-appointed Mitchell-Danforth Task Force which studied the tax credit and made recommendations with respect to its continuation after 1989.

The appendixes include data tables showing estimated maximum incomes and qualifying rent levels for various household sizes for each metropolitan area in the United States and for the rural balance of each state at the 60 percent of median income level for 1989; the outline of a possible program to enable existing owners of low income rental properties to use the tax credit to make needed repairs without having to bring in outside investors; a special pro-forma analysis of a rural new construction project with tax credits; a list of the tax credit allocation agencies and contact persons; the text of the low income housing tax credit statute after the 1988 amendments; Congressional explanations of the tax credit provisions; IRS regulations, notices, and issuances governing the tax credit; IRS tax forms for the tax credit; and the Executive Summary of the report of the Mitchell-Danforth Task Force on the low income housing tax credit.

THE LOW INCOME HOUSING TAX CREDIT

is a credit or reduction in tax liability each year for 10 years for owners and investors in low income rental housing that is based on the costs of development and the number of qualified low income units.

The tax credit rate in 1987 was 4 percent for acquisition costs, and 9 percent for rehabilitation and new construction costs, but only 4 percent if a project has federal subsidies or tax-exempt financing. Credit rates in subsequent years will be based on monthly prevailing interest rates to provide a "present value" credit of 30 percent and 70 percent respectively over 10 years.

The annual credit amount is the credit rate multiplied by average eligible costs for the number of low income units where tenant incomes and rents are below stated maximums. Non-depreciable costs, such as land, and the amount of any grants are excluded from eligible costs. Additional units that qualify after the first year earn two-thirds of the annual credit amount for the balance of the 15-year compliance period.

Eligibility: A project must have a minimum of either 20 percent of its units occupied by low income households with incomes under 50 percent of area median income, or 40 percent of its units occupied by low income households with incomes under 60 percent of area median income. Income limits are adjusted for various household sizes, and in certain unusually high or low housing cost areas.

Rents for low income units cannot be greater than 30 percent of the maximum income for each household size. Tenant-paid utilities are counted as part of the rent.

Limit on volume: States can allocate tax credits up to a total value of $1.25 per resident each year. Only the first year of ten years of tax credits is counted against the limit. In addition, projects with tax-exempt financing which are subject to a separate volume limitation automatically receive tax credits if they are completed by the end of 1989.

State and/or local agencies select projects under a state adopted plan. An agency can assign a lower amount of credits than the project is eligible for.

Recapture of some credits can occur if the number of qualified low income units is not maintained for 15 years. Household income can increase up to 40 percent (70 percent in special circumstances) above the current eligibility level and the unit can remain qualified.

Non-profit organizations are allocated a minimum of 10 percent of total credits in each state each year.

Three-year program began January 1, 1987 and ends December 31, 1989. Projects can be completed up to two years after the end of 1988 and 1989 allocation years, if 10 percent of project costs are spent by the end of the allocation year.

The amount of credits an investor may effectively use is limited due to passive losses restrictions and alternative minimum tax provisions.

2

THE LOW INCOME HOUSING TAX CREDIT PROVISIONS: EXPLANATION AND ANALYSIS

TAX CREDIT BASICS

The "Tax Credit for Low Income Rental Housing" is a three-year program to provide tax credits for owners and investors in low income rental housing. The tax credit is a fixed percentage of certain costs of development or property acquisition. An annual tax credit amount is provided for a project each year for 10 years.

Under the federal income tax code a credit is a dollar-for-dollar reduction in the tax liability or tax bill for the property owner or investor. A credit is subtracted after the amount of taxes is calculated. It differs from a deduction or adjustment to income, which is subtracted from income before the tax rate is applied and the amount of taxes is calculated. A dollar of tax credit is generally worth a dollar in the taxpayer's pocket, while the value of a deduction is a fraction of each dollar equal to the taxpayer's marginal tax rate. However, the use of tax credits can be limited by the application of the passive losses provision or the alternative minimum tax. These limitations will be discussed in Chapter 3.

Low income housing benefits from the tax credit primarily when the owners of a project, either profit-motivated or non-profit, "sell" the tax credits to limited partner investors who contribute equity to the development in exchange for the use of the tax credits and other economic benefits. These equity contributions, which can be substantial under this program, reduce the amount of other financing needed to acquire or develop the project. Or they could be used to add an income stream during the years of the project's operation, and thereby reduce the amount of rent the tenants have to pay for the project to operate successfully.

The annual tax credit percentages for calendar year 1987 are specified directly in the statute. For 1988 and 1989, the additional two years under the three-year program, the annual tax credit percentage is calculated monthly by the Treasury Department, using a complex formula which is intended to provide a tax credit with a "present value" of either 70 percent or 30 percent of the qualified development costs of the housing project.

A "present value" of 70 percent means, in this case, a constant percentage amount each year for 10 years that provides a real current value of 70 percent. The percentage amount in years two through ten is "discounted" or reduced mathematically to take into account the loss in the real value of the money over time. The discount factor used is the prevailing level of interest rates on an after-tax basis. This represents a "real" loss in value because the money is not available to earn interest for the owner.

THE TYPES OF TAX CREDITS

Four separate and distinct tax credits are provided:

1. New construction. The credit for each year of the 10 years is 9 percent of qualified development costs for low income housing units for a newly constructed building or project that is "placed in service" -- completed and available for occupancy -- in 1987. For buildings placed in service after 1987, the annual credit percentage for new construction will be based on a "present value" of 70 percent over the 10-year period.

2. Rehabilitation, where total rehabilitation and related expenditures over a 24-month period must be $2,000 or greater per unit. The credit is the same as for new construction: 9 percent of qualified rehabilitation costs for low income units placed in service in 1987, and in subsequent years, an annual credit percentage calculated to provide a present value of 70 percent of qualified costs related to rehabilitation.

3. Acquisition of an existing building, including any minor rehabilitation expenditures of under $2,000 per unit incurred through the end of the first year the credit is taken. The acquisition of an existing building earns a tax credit of 4 percent each year for 10 years if the building is placed in service in 1987. (For acquisition of a building in use, placed in service is when ownership is transferred.) If it is placed in service after 1987, the annual tax credit percentage will provide a present value of 30 percent over the 10-year period.

4. Projects which receive a federal subsidy. A federal subsidy is an obligation or loan of federal funds provided directly by a federal agency or indirectly by a local or state governmental unit where the interest rate on the loan or obligation is less than prevailing Treasury interest rates. This is measured by the Applicable Federal Rate (AFR) which is also used to determine the tax credit amount after 1987. Any type of tax-exempt financing provided by state or local governments, the interest on which is exempt from federal taxation under the Internal Revenue Code, is also considered a federal subsidy. Farmers Home Administration Section 515 loans are also federal subsidies.

The qualified development costs against which the tax credit percentage is applied is the owner's depreciable basis in the property under the tax code. The tax credits do not apply to development costs which cannot be depreciated, such as the cost or value of land.

CREDIT AMOUNTS FOR PROJECTS WITH FEDERAL SUBSIDIES OR GRANTS

If a project benefits from a federal subsidy (a loan with an interest rate below the AFR on the date the loan is made), then the tax credit for the entire property is 4 percent per year for 10 years if the project is placed in service in 1987. If placed in service in subsequent years, the annual credit is based on providing a present value of 30 percent of qualified basis or costs.

A grant of federal funds where there is no obligation to repay is treated differently. Tax credits cannot be obtained for project costs financed by a federal grant. The amount of any federal grant is not included in the qualified basis or eligible costs against which the tax credit percentage is applied.

The higher 9 percent (70 percent present value) tax credit for new construction or rehabilitation is not available if federal subsidies are used to pay for the new construction or rehabilitation work. Only the 4 percent credit is available in this situation.

A federally subsidized construction loan that is entirely paid off before a building is placed in service will not reduce the tax credit to the 4 percent level.

A 4 percent tax credit cannot be converted to a 9 percent credit by subsequently paying off a federal subsidy that was in effect any time after the placed in service date.

In order to determine if a federal loan is a federal subsidy, the Applicable Federal Rate (AFR) for the corresponding loan duration is used. Loans with a duration in excess of 9 years would be compared to the Long-Term AFR; loans of from 3 to 9 years would be compared to the Mid-Term AFR; and loans of less than 3 years would be compared to the Short-Term AFR. If the interest rate on the loan is less than the corresponding AFR, then it is considered a federal subsidy, and the 4 percent (30 percent present value) tax credit applies.

The statute provides one exception to the rule regarding federal subsidies, however. The owners of a property receiving a federal subsidy have the option of treating the subsidy amount as if it were a federal grant and deducting the amount of the subsidy from the eligible basis or costs against which the amount of the credit is calculated.

> ***Owners should opt to exclude the amount of a subsidy from basis if it is less than 57.1 percent of new construction or rehabilitation costs eligible for a 9 percent (70 percent present value) tax credit. The tax credit is larger using a 70 percent present value tax credit for 42.9 percent of development costs (57.1 percent excluded) than using a 30 percent present value tax credit for all 100 percent of development costs.***

TABLE 1
THE AMOUNTS OF THE TAX CREDITS FOR LOW INCOME HOUSING

In 1987:	Annual Tax Credit
New construction	9 percent
Rehabilitation	9 percent
Building acquisition and related minor rehabilitation	4 percent
"Federally subsidized" new construction or rehabilitation	4 percent
Subsequent to 1987:	**Present Value Tax Credit**
New construction	70 percent
Rehabilitation	70 percent
Building acquisition and related minor rehabilitation	30 percent
"Federally subsidized" new construction or rehabilitation	30 percent

TAX CREDITS FOR REHABILITATION

The tax credit for rehabilitation — 9 percent in 1987 and a 70 percent present value credit in subsequent years — can either be obtained by an existing owner, or by a new owner/developer in combination with the separate tax credit for building acquisition. Both improvements to privately owned buildings by existing landlords and new projects by profit-motivated developers or non-profit sponsors can benefit from this tax credit. In either case, rehabilitation and related expenses must be equal to at least $2,000 per unit in the building. There is a 24-month period over which the rehab expenses can be made, and the expenses are considered to be "placed in service" at the end of the 24-month period, or earlier if so elected.

In determining the amount of the credit, all rehab expenditures on a building are allocated to all the units in the building. There is no advantage in doing rehabilitation only in units that will be occupied by eligible low income households. The amount of the credit is based on the total amount of rehab work done on the building and the percentage of the building occupied by eligible low income tenants at qualifying rent levels.

Rehabilitation expenditures include all amounts incurred in connection with short-term work which are chargeable to capital account for purposes of depreciation. Thus, they include "soft" costs such as engineering studies, architectural specifications, fees connected with short-term financing, relocation expenses, construction period interest, performance bonds, and general contractor fees. Any rehab expenditures written off over a 5 year period under prior sec. 167(k) of the tax code are not eligible for the tax credit.

The use of federal subsidies in the acquisition of a building, whether a prior loan assumed by a new owner or a new subsidy loan to aid in the acquisition, will not reduce the credit for the subsequent rehabilitation work on the building from a 9 percent credit to a 4 percent credit. The rehab element is treated separately from the acquisition element.

> *Whenever possible, federal subsidies (and federal grants) should be used for acquisition costs rather than rehab costs so as to maximize the amount of eligible tax credits.*

In addition to the 9 percent tax credit for rehabilitation work of at least $2,000 per unit, an owner can claim a 4 percent credit for rehab expenditures of less than $2,000 per unit in connection with an eligible building acquisition. Expenditures made through the end of the first year of the 10 year credit period can earn tax credits. This first year can either be the year in which the building is acquired or the subsequent year. This compares to the 24-month period available for aggregating the larger rehab tax credit. These lesser rehab expenditures would be considered as part of the acquisition tax credit.

> *Any owner contemplating spending about $1,400 per unit for rehab work in connection with an eligible acquisition should look for other improvements to bring this rehab and related costs up to $2,000 per unit. With a 9 percent credit available for $2,000 of work per unit, compared to a 4 percent credit for lesser amounts of work, the <u>net costs</u> to the owners (after subtracting the extra value of the larger 9 percent credit) is the same for $1,400 of work with a 4 percent credit as it is for $2,000 of work with a 9 percent credit. Additional depreciation benefits also would be available. And under the 9 percent credit, there is additional time to complete the work.*

TAX CREDITS FOR BUILDING ACQUISITION

The 4 percent tax credit for acquiring existing buildings can be used regardless of whether or not the building qualifies for a rehabilitation tax credit. Minor rehabilitation expenditures of under $2,000 per unit can be a part of this acquisition tax credit.

The acquisition tax credit normally can only be used if: (a) the ownership of a building in active use has not changed in the last 10 years; (b) rehabilitation work greater than 25 percent of the building's adjusted basis has not been performed in the last 10 years; (c) the building has not previously received a low income housing tax credit for which the 15-year compliance period is still in effect; and (d) the building was not acquired from the same owner or a related party.

The costs of land acquisition, or the imputed value of the land underlying an existing structure, are excluded from the basis or the costs that qualify for a tax credit.

Under IRS rules governing property acquisition from a related person, an individual owner can sell his/her property to a new partnership and hold up to a 10 percent interest in the new partnership without jeopardizing the use of tax credits and depreciation writeoffs based on the sales price to the new partnership.

A building that is boarded up and not in use for more than 10 years can qualify as not "placed in service" in the last 10 years even if it was sold and ownership changed hands during that period.

A building that does not qualify for the acquisition tax credit might still qualify for the rehabilitation tax credit, however.

DISTRESSED FEDERALLY ASSISTED PROPERTIES CAN BE EXEMPT FROM THE TEN YEAR PREVIOUS OWNERSHIP REQUIREMENT

The Treasury Secretary can waive this 10-year disqualification period to help rescue any distressed property where federal mortgage funds are at risk. This applies to projects that are federally assisted under HUD sections 8, 221(d)(3), 221(d)(4), 223(f), or 236, or the Farmers Home Administration section 515 program. The Treasury Secretary will grant a waiver upon an application from an owner if this is necessary to avert an assignment of the mortgage to HUD or the Farmers Home Administration, or to avert a claim against a federal mortgage insurance fund.

In order to demonstrate that federal mortgage funds are at risk, HUD or the Farmers Home Administration must indicate that it intends to either accept a mortgage assignment, accept conveyance of the property after foreclosure, take possession of the property as a consequence of a default, or designate the project as "troubled" based on a review of the project's financial condition and its history of financial distress and mortgage defaults.

The factors that HUD would look at to determine if a project is "troubled" include high vacancy rates, negative cash flow, major physical deficiencies, inadequate reserve funds, unauthorized cash distributions, past defaults, poor management practices, and serious tenant complaints.

An owner can apply to the IRS for the waiver of the 10 year disqualification period for the acquisition tax credit if he/she has acquired the property in the past year or has a binding contract to acquire it in the future. The procedures that an owner must follow to request the waiver, and the information that must be provided are outlined in the IRS regulations on this subject (see Appendix 9).

OTHER EXEMPTIONS FROM THE TEN YEAR PREVIOUS OWNERSHIP REQUIREMENT FOR QUALIFYING FOR THE TAX CREDIT FOR ACQUISITION

The law provides other exemptions from the 10-year change of ownership limitation. There is no disqualification for a transfer of ownership that was a non-taxable exchange of property, or for a non-taxable contribution of property into a partnership, in which a new owner "stepped into the shoes" of a previous owner, and in which the new basis for depreciation was based on the adjusted basis of the previous owner.

Additional ownership changes occuring during the previous ten years that would not disqualify an owner from earning an acquisition tax credit include: a) a transfer of ownership due to death of an owner; b) acquisition by a governmental, quasi-governmental, or non-profit organization; and c) a transfer of ownership as the result of a foreclosure of a mortgage where the building is subsequently sold within 12 months after the transfer.

In any case, there must be a new acquisition of a building by the owner seeking the tax credits, and there must not be any other disqualifying ownership changes during the last 10 years.

HIGHER QUALITY IN NON-LOW INCOME UNITS CAN RESULT IN FEWER CREDITS

In mixed income developments, there can be severe penalties if the units occupied by eligible low income tenants are of a lesser quality than units occupied by non-eligible higher income tenants. If the "average quality standard" of the low income units is significantly lower than that for the non-low income units, then the entire "eligible basis" or tax credit value of the non-low income units with the higher quality is deducted in computing the amount of the credits. The low income percentage stays the same but is applied against a lower basis or project value.

The "average quality standard" is measured by costs per square foot, unless the Treasury Secretary by regulation adopts a different measure. If the differential between the square foot cost for any non-low income unit and the average square foot cost for all low income units in the building is not more than 15 percent, then only the costs representing the differential amount are excluded from the eligible basis, if the owner elects to do this on IRS form 8609. If this square foot cost differential is greater than 15 percent, then the entire cost of the non-low income unit is excluded from eligible basis.

MAXIMUM INCOME AND RENT LEVELS GOVERN PROJECT ELIGIBILITY AND THE AMOUNT OF THE TAX CREDITS; COMPLIANCE PERIOD IS 15 YEARS

Both the overall eligibility for particular projects and the qualification for individual units as low income units receiving tax credits involve three elements: (a) maximum income levels, (b) maximum rent levels, and (c) a 15-year compliance period.

All projects must, for a 15-year period beginning when tax credits are first claimed, have a minimum number of qualified low income units. These units must be occupied by families who both have incomes and pay gross rents below specified maximum levels.

The maximum income and rent levels are based on median family income statistics that are updated annually by the U.S. Department of Housing and Urban Development for each metropolitan area and for each county outside a metropolitan area in the United States. Separate income and rent maximums are set for each household size (one-person household, two-person household, etc.)

As a result of an amendment included in the 1987 Housing Act , the maximum income and rents in rural non-metro areas are now based on the higher of the county median income or the state-wide non-metro median income.

Appendix 1 provides the maximum income and rent levels for each metropolitan area and for the the non-metropolitan or rural portion of each of the 50 states for 1989.

The amount of the tax credit depends directly on the number of qualified low income units in the project. Only those units meeting the income and rent tests are counted in the qualified basis against which the percentage tax credit is multiplied to determine the dollar amount of tax credits for a particular project.

Projects are required to maintain the level of qualifying low income units during the entire 15-year compliance period to avoid any recapture penalties. Even though the tax credits are only provided for a 10-year period, projects are subject to recapture penalties if during the 15 years either: (a) the level of low income occupancy declines below the level for which tax credits have been received, or particularly (b) if the level of low income occupancy declines below the minimum threshold level for initial eligibility. (See fuller discussion of this subject below.)

Project owners have a choice as to the maximum income levels and the maximum rent levels that will be allowed.

DEFINITION OF ANNUAL INCOME

What constitutes annual income is based on HUD regulations at 24 CFR 813.106. Income derived from assets and investments, as well as income from government programs such as social security, unemployment compensation and welfare, and alimony and child support payments, are all included in income.

Excluded from income are earnings of children under age 18, lump sum insurance or capital gains income, scholarships, and the value of food stamps. See Appendix 10 for the exact definition of what is included or excluded from income.

THE CHOICE BETWEEN 50 PERCENT OR 60 PERCENT OF AREA MEDIAN INCOME DETERMINES MAXIMUM RENTS AND MINIMUM PERCENTAGES OF LOW INCOME UNITS

Project owners can choose whether they will be serving low income households whose incomes, based on a four-person household size, are not more than either 50 percent or 60 percent of the median family income for the local area. If they choose the 50 percent of median family income level, then a minimum of 20 percent of the units in the project must be occupied by families with incomes below this amount, adjusted by household size. The rents on these same minimum number of units must not be greater than 30 percent of the maximum incomes for the particular household size.

If owners choose the 60 percent of median family income level, then a minimum of 40 percent of the units must be occupied by families with incomes below this amount, based on a a four-person household and adjusted accordingly for different household sizes. A special exception is provided for New York City because of high costs and relatively low income levels there: only 25 percent of units need be occupied by tenants below 60 percent of the area median income for a project to be eligible for the tax credit.

These same low income occupancy requirements are also imposed for eligibility for tax-exempt bond financing for multi-family rental housing, where owners have the same choice of "20 at 50" or "40 at 60." There are <u>no</u> maximum rents with tax exempt financing, however.

Project owners must make their choice as to the 50 or 60 percent income levels by the date that the project is placed in service. They have 12 months after this date to meet the minimum required percentage of low income units (20 percent or 40 percent), and must also meet this percentage at the end of the first year for which the tax credit is claimed. Once the choice is made, it is irrevocable.

> ***Since serving the 50 percent of median income level is more difficult and requires lower rents than serving the 60 percent of median income level, the act allows a lower minimum number of units for low income occupancy at the 50 percent of income level. As long as owners intend to qualify 40 percent or more of the units in a project as low income, it is to their advantage to select the 60 percent of median income level, since the amount of the credit for each qualifying unit is the same if the 50 percent or the 60 percent of median income level is selected. This may conflict with the goals of a local community, which might prefer that these projects have lower rents and serve the more needy households below 50 percent of median income.***

In multi-building projects with two or more contiguous buildings, developers can meet the 20 or 40 percent minimum low income occupancy requirement on a combined building basis rather than on a building-by- building basis. There would not be any minimum low income occupancy requirement for any particular building, as long as the other buildings included for purposes of meeting the low income occupancy requirement are placed in service not later than 12 months after the placed-in-service date of the particular building. This provision allows owners to concentrate low income occupancy in certain buildings of a multi-building project.

The 20 percent and 40 percent test for minimum project eligibility is based on the number of units that qualify as low income. However, for purposes of calculating the amount of the tax credit received for qualifying units, the act specifies that the <u>lesser</u> of the percentage of <u>floor space</u> or the percentage of <u>units</u> meeting the low income unit requirements be used.

HOUSEHOLD SIZE ADJUSTMENTS IN MAXIMUM INCOME AND MAXIMUM RENT LEVELS

The adjustments in maximum income for various household sizes is based on the adjustments used under HUD's section 8 program. <u>Table 2</u> depicts the percentages used to determine HUD's maximum income levels for one- to eight-person households. HUD makes adjustments in maximum income levels for various household sizes at both the 50 percent and 80 percent of median income levels. The tax credit program requires household size adjustments at 50 percent and 60 percent of area median income levels. The household size adjustments used by HUD at 50 percent of area median income are the basis for the household size adjustments in the tax credit program at both the 50 and 60 percent of median income levels.

Table 3 shows how the percentage factors are used to determine the maximum income and maximum rent levels at various household sizes at the $34,000 median income level, which is the national median income for fiscal year 1989.

SPECIAL ADJUSTMENTS IN MAXIMUM INCOME AND MAXIMUM RENT LEVELS IN CERTAIN LOCAL AREAS

The official Congressional explanation accompanying the 1986 Tax Reform Act permits the maximum income levels to deviate from the area median income data to reflect current HUD policy or future Treasury policy on income limits, chiefly with respect to areas with relatively high housing costs and low incomes.

The explanation recognizes that HUD's section 8 income limits at the 50 percent of median income level ("very low income" under HUD's definition) currently contain special adjustments in a number of geographic areas. These are areas which, according to HUD, have unusually high or low housing costs relative to the income levels in the area.

According to HUD, the Section 8 very low income limits for 1989 have been reduced in 62 rural counties and 3 metropolitan areas with unusually low housing costs. The income limits have been increased for 29 metropolitan areas and 82 rural counties where housing costs are unusually high in relation to income levels in the area. The income limit for four person households in these areas is the amount where 35 percent of this limit is equal to 85 percent of the typical rent for a two-bedroom unit (i.e., 85 percent of the two-bedroom Fair Market Rent).

In addition, as a result of the 1987 Housing Act which based the income limits under the Sec. 8 program in non-metropolitan counties on the higher of the county or the state-wide non-metropolitan median income, very low income limits increased in 1,475 of the 2,416 non-metropolitan counties in the U.S., and in 21 metropolitan areas as well. At its own discretion, HUD applied the same standard in metroplitan areas where the median income was below the state-wide non-metropolitan median income level.

The Congressional explanation provides authority for the Treasury Secretary to adjust income limits "for areas with unusually low family income or high housing costs relative to family income," consistent with HUD determinations under Section 8 for very low income families at the 50 percent of median income level. This language reflects the policy behind HUD's current median income adjustments.

IRS has officially stated in Notice 89-24 that the HUD Section 8 income limits for very low income households are the basis for the tax credit income limits at 50 percent of median income at various household sizes. The tax credit income limits at 60 percent of area median income are equal to 1.2 times the comparable income limits at 50 percent of area median income. The maximum income limits and maximum rents at 60 percent of median income level for all U.S. metropolitan areas and for the non-metropolitan balance of each state for 1989 can be found in Appendix 1.

TABLE 2

PERCENTAGE FACTORS TO DETERMINE
MAXIMUM INCOME LEVELS FOR VARIOUS HOUSEHOLD SIZES

Size of Household	Percent of Area Median Income at: 50 percent of Median Income Standard	60 percent of Median Income Standard
One Person	35%	42%
Two Persons	40	48
Three Persons	45	54
Four Persons	50	60
Five Persons	54	64.8
Six Persons	58	69.6
Seven Persons	62	74.4
Eight Persons	66	79.2

TABLE 3

CALCULATION OF MAXIMUM INCOME AND GROSS RENT LEVELS
FOR QUALIFYING LOW INCOME UNITS AT VARIOUS HOUSEHOLD SIZES
FOR THE 1989 NATIONAL MEDIAN INCOME LEVEL OF $34,000

	50 Percent of Median Income			60 Percent of Median Income		
Size of Household	Percentage Factor	Maximum Income Level 1/	Maximum Gross Rent Level 2/	Percentage Factor	Maximum Income Level 1/	Maximum Gross Rent Level 2/
One Person	35%	$11,900	$298	42%	$14,280	$357
Two Persons	40	13,600	304	48	16,320	408
Three Persons	45	15,300	382	54	18,360	459
Four Persons	50	17,000	425	60	20,400	510
Five Persons	54	18,360	459	64.8	22,030	551
Six Persons	58	19,720	493	69.6	23,660	592
Seven Persons	62	21,080	527	74.4	25,300	632
Eight Persons	66	22,440	561	79.2	26,930	673

1/ Percentage factor multiplied by $34,000

2/ Calculated at 30% of maximum income amount, divided by 12 to obtain monthly maximum gross rent. Or, multiply the maximum income amount by .025.

DEDUCT TENANT-PAID UTILITIES TO DETERMINE ACTUAL MAXIMUM RENTS

The gross rent for a qualifying low income unit must not exceed 30 percent of the maximum income level for the particular size of household. Gross rent includes the cost of all utilities excluding telephone. If any utilities are paid by the tenant, then the maximum allowable rent is reduced according to proper utility allowances as provided in IRS regulations.

In a HUD-regulated building where HUD has established specific utility allowances for the building, these allowances are to be used to determine the amount to be subtracted from maximum rent for each type of utility that is paid by the tenant. In any other building where there is one or more tenants benefitting from HUD rental assistance, the schedule of utility allowances of the Public Housing Authority (PHA) for the Sec. 8 Existing Housing Program should be used .

In a building receiving any form of rental assistance from the Farmers Home Administration (FmHA), the FmHA utility allowances should be used, even if there is some form of HUD assistance in the building.

Where there is no HUD or FmHA assistance in a building, the PHA's Sec. 8 Existing utility allowance schedule should be used. In this situation, however, a tenant, building owner or state housing authority can petition a local utility company to provide an estimated cost for that utility for each unit of similar size and construction in the geographic area. The estimate of the local utility will govern. This process can be initiated at any time during the 15 year compliance period.

Under IRS Notice 89-6, an estimate from a local utility company cannot be used if there is any HUD or FmHA assistance in the building. Any utility allowance from HUD, FmHA, a PHA, or a utility company should be updated whenever rents in the building are revised. Owners have 90 days to institute any new utility allowance schedule. (See IRS Notice 89-6 in Appendix 15.)

RENT SUBSIDY PAYMENTS TO OWNERS UNDER SECTION 8 OR COMPARABLE PROGRAMS ARE NOT COUNTED TOWARD MAXIMUM RENTS

Subsidy payments to an owner under the various HUD Section 8 programs or any other comparable program are excluded and not to be considered in determining gross rent. Only the tenant's rent payment is considered in determining whether the rent exceeds the maximum rent (less an allowance for tenant-paid utilities) for the particular household size in the metropolitan area or county. This means that a project with Section 8 or a comparable program can receive considerably more rental income than the maximum rent levels specified under this program.

> *The 1988 tax code amendments provided that rent subsidy payments received by owners under programs comparable to section 8 that were non-federal --- state or local government programs or assistance from charitable or philanthropic sources --- would also be excluded in determining whether the tenant's rent payment exceeds the maximum permitted rents. However, IRS has not yet provided any guidance as to what a "section 8 comparable" program would be. Some of the issues to be decided are: periodic vs. one-time subsidies; fixed tenant rent payments vs. payments that are a percentage of each tenant's income; payments directly to owners vs. payments to tenants for transmission to owners; etc.*

Section 8 assistance can make a project work when there is a gap between the maximum qualifying rents and the rental income stream needed to cover costs after the benefits of the tax credits are factored in. However, it could lead to an unjustified windfall if the combined benefits of Section 8 assistance and the tax credits are more than needed to achieve a feasible tax credit project.

According to a congressional committee staff member in 1986, HUD was expected to take the tax credit program into account and adjust its payment amounts and program guidelines to eliminate any unjustified windfalls for property owners using tax credits along with Section 8 and similar programs. This would also enable HUD to stretch its limited appropriations to aid more units. In addition, according to committee staff, credit allocation agencies should take section 8 payments into account and allocate only the amount of tax credits needed to make a project workable.

TENANT'S RENT CAN EXCEED TAX CREDIT MAXIMUM IF MANDATED BY HUD OR FMHA

An increase in the rent paid by a section 8 or FmHA Sec. 515 tenant to an amount in excess of the maximum tax credit rent level will not disqualify the unit for tax credits if the rent increase is mandated under the provisions of the section 8 or Sec. 515 programs. Such a rent increase could happen if a tenant's income increases significantly, since HUD and FmHA are required by statute to charge tenant rents equal to 30 percent of the tenant's adjusted monthly income. The increase in the tenant's rent payment must be offset by a decrease in the HUD or FmHA subsidy payment to the owner, as is currently done under these two programs.

NO GUIDANCE ON UNIT SIZES FOR DIFFERENT HOUSEHOLD SIZES

The tax credit legislation spells out clear guidelines for maximum rent levels based on family or household size. However, it is silent on how owners determine particular unit sizes (usually the number of bedrooms) for a particular household size (number of persons per household). State and local credit allocation agencies may develop such guidelines as a condition for awarding tax credits, or as a condition for receiving tax-exempt financing or other governmental subsidies or grants. If a project involves Section 8 assistance, HUD guidelines on numbers of allowable bedrooms for a given household size would be applicable.

Barring all of the above, owners would be free to determine the size of unit for a particular family size (limited only by local code regulations on maximum numbers of occupants), as long as the rent level was below the maximum for the particular size of household for which tax credits are being claimed.

For example, an owner may plan to qualify a two-bedroom unit for tax credits based upon the qualifying rent level for a four-person household. The owner might then prohibit a three-person family from renting a two-bedroom unit because this would fail to qualify for a tax credit. The three-person family would either be required to rent a one-bedroom unit or be excluded from the project entirely.

HOUSING CAN BE FOR SPECIAL GROUPS

Eligible units must be available for use by the general public, and cannot be restricted to members of a particular organization such as a social organization or to employees of a particular employer.

Owners can give preferences in renting units and can limit occupancy to special groups or types of persons such as the elderly, or handicapped or homeless persons. However, any type of preference that violates HUD's non-discrimination provisions under fair housing and civil rights statutes and regulations would make a project ineligible for tax credits.

SIGNIFICANT SERVICES THAT ARE OPTIONAL OR INEXPENSIVE CAN BE PROVIDED

Providing services to tenants, whether or not such services are considered significant, will not make projects ineligible for tax credits. However, any charges for services where payment is mandatory as a condition of occupancy and not optional for the tenant must be included in gross rent in determining whether projects qualify under the maximum rent limitations.

> *Therefore, retirement homes which provide meals and medical care on an optional pay-for-use basis would be eligible for tax credits. Elderly housing with one mandatory meal a day and/or a daily nursing visit might also qualify for tax credits --- if the monthly charge for rent and these services combined is below the maximum rent, or if a Sec. 8 subsidy reduces the tenant payment to less than the maximum rent.*

Continual nursing, medical or psychiatric care is presumed to be a mandatory service. Thus hospitals, nursing homes, sanitariums and lifecare facilities will be ineligible for tax credits because their charges will exceed the maximum rents for the program.

IRS has established one exception to the rule that costs for mandatory services be counted as part of tenant rent --- charges under the Mandatory Meals Program in HUD-assisted housing for handicapped or elderly persons are not to be included in gross rent when determining eligibility for tax credits.

GROUP HOMES MAY QUALIFY FOR THE TAX CREDIT

Group homes for the mentally retarded or physically handicapped apparently can qualify for the low income housing tax credit. In a group home, a small number of unrelated individuals reside in a property (typically a single family dwelling) with some degree of supervision but a significant amount of independence. Each unrelated individual can be considered as a one person household for purposes of maximum income and maximum rent determinations because there is a separate landlord-tenant relationship with each individual. The group home residents should not be considered to be a single joint household.

Group homes will not be considered to be nursing homes or lifecare facilities, which are ineligible for tax credits, if the residents do not require continual medical or nursing care.

Periodic payments for housing and related services for these individuals, made by a governmental entity directly to the property owner through a program such as the Medicaid program, probably will be considered as comparable to section 8 rent subsidy payments and thus would not be counted in determining compliance with the maximum rent limitations. Payments made directly by the individual resident to the property owner would have to be within the maximum monthly rent for a one-person household in the local area. This would permit significant services to be provided without disqualifying the property from the tax credit program.

OTHER ELIGIBILITY PROVISIONS: SUITABLE FOR OCCUPANCY; SINGLE ROOM OCCUPANCY; MULTI-BUILDING PROJECTS; SINGLE-FAMILY AND CONDO UNITS; MIXED USE PROJECTS; STUDENT OCCUPANCY; ETC.

Units must be suitable for occupancy to be counted towards both the minimum eligibility requirement and as part of the qualified basis for determining the amount of the tax credit. Substandard conditions must be removed from these units.

Single room occupancy (SRO) housing is eligible for the tax credit program, as long as the housing is not used on a transient basis. Transient housing, which is not eligible for tax credits, is housing with an initial lease term of less than six months. Single room occupancy housing permits the sharing of bathrooms and cooking facilities, and shared eating facilities or a common dining area.

Multi-Building projects. A project may consist of a number of buildings with similarly constructed units that are on the same or adjacent tracts of land, are owned by the same person for tax purposes, and are financed under a common plan. A scattered site development can only get credits by treating each site as a separate project.

A building with four units or less with one unit occupied by an owner or a related person is not eligible. Single family rental properties qualify, however. Under a recent IRS ruling, a single unit in a condominium building may be submitted as a tax credit project by the owner of that unit.

A mixed use project with commercial space in the same building is eligible. The non-housing costs, which are excluded in calculating the credit amount, are to be determined based on the proportionate benefits to be derived from the various types of uses.

Dormitories and trailer parks are also ineligible for the program. Factory-built housing permanently fixed to real property is clearly eligible.

Units are not eligible for the credit if they are occupied entirely by students who are not entitled to file a joint income tax return.

Properties taking depreciation under previous income tax laws, and those projects receiving special treatment for passive losses under the 1986 act's transition rules are not eligible for the tax credit.

CALCULATING THE AMOUNT OF THE TAX CREDIT

In the technical terms used in the statute, the amount of the tax credit is determined by applying the annual tax credit percentage against the "qualified basis" of the property. The two key phrases in the statute that are important in calculating the amount of the credit are "eligible basis" and "qualified basis."

The "eligible basis" is the eligible cost elements such as new construction expenditures, rehabilitation expenditures, and building acquisition expenditures. Certain deductions from these cost elements must be made, including the cost or value of the land underlying the project and the value of any federal grants.

The "qualified basis" is the portion or percentage of the eligible basis that qualifies for the tax credit. The "applicable fraction" is determined and then multiplied against the "eligible basis" to obtain the "qualified basis."

The "applicable fraction" is the lower of the "unit fraction" or the "floor space fraction." The unit fraction is the percentage of the units in the building that are qualified low income units. The "floor space fraction" is the percentage of total rentable floor space contained in the qualified low income units.

> *The usual criteria of percentage of units is modified here to provide a lower fraction for the low income units, if the average unit size of the low income units is smaller than the average unit size of the non-low income units.*

The cost of facilities and extra amenities, such as swimming pools, parking facilities, and recreation equipment, can be included in the eligible basis of the project as long as there is no separate fee for the use of these facilities and they are available to all tenants on a comparable basis.

All expenditures must be incurred by the owner. An exception to this is provided for rehabilitation and new construction expenses incurred by a prior owner before the building is completed and placed in service. A new owner who completes construction and places the building in service can count the construction expenditures of a prior owner towards the 9 percent tax credit.

> *Developers should include a contingency allowance in their tax credit applications to cover unforeseen project costs that may be incurred through the end of the first year the tax credit is taken.*

The following depicts the steps in calculating the amount of the tax credit.

1. Eligible basis = cost elements that are eligible for obtaining tax credits.
2. Applicable fraction = portion or percentage of the building representing qualified low income units, based on lesser of floor space ratio or unit ratio.
3. Qualified basis = eligible basis, multiplied by applicable fraction.
4. Tax credit percentage = 4 percent (or present value of 30 percent) or 9 percent (or present value of 70 percent).
5. Amount of tax credit = tax credit percentage, multiplied by qualified basis.

Both the eligible basis and the applicable fraction are determined as of the last day of the initial tax year in which the tax credit is claimed or taken. At the option of the owner, this initial year is either the year in which the building is placed in service, or the year following the year in which the building is placed in service.

This provision gives the project owner some flexibility. If he/she is able to complete the project and quickly achieve the targeted low income occupancy, then the logical choice is to start to receive the tax credits as early as possible beginning in the year in which the project is placed in service. However, if a longer time is needed to complete construction and/or achieve the targeted low income occupancy, then the owner can choose to delay receipt of the credits. He/she will have until the end of the year following the year in which the project is placed in service to complete all spending on the project and achieve full low income occupancy, and thus earn the maximum amount of credits during the 10-year credit period.

For the first year in which the credit is claimed, only a partial year's credit can usually be taken. This is based on the percentage of units or floor space with low income occupancy and the average number of months of such occupancy during the year. For example, if half of the units or floor space in a project had low income occupancy and these units were occupied by low income tenants for an average of six months during the initial credit year, then the applicable fraction would be one-quarter for the initial year. The balance of the full year's credits not available in the initial year would be available to the owner in the eleventh year. In this example, the applicable fraction would be one-quarter in the first year, one-half in years two through ten, and one-quarter in the eleventh year.

An example of how the tax credit for a full year is calculated is shown in Table 4 using a 100-unit rehabilitation project with a cost of $38,500 per unit.

THE "APPLICABLE FEDERAL RATE" (AFR) INTEREST RATE DETERMINES THE TAX CREDIT PERCENTAGE AFTER 1987

The annual tax credit percentage for projects placed in service after 1987 is a "present value" calculation based on the "Applicable Federal Rate" or "AFR" monthly interest rate statistic issued by the Treasury Department. The AFR specified in the statute for calculating the amount of the tax credit is the average of the AFR interest rates for mid-term and for long-term Treasury securities with interest compounded annually.

The percentage rate used to discount the present value of the 70 percent tax credit and the 30 percent tax credit is the AFR, multiplied by 0.72 (or 1 minus the 28 percent maximum individual tax rate). This resulting percentage rate is used to determine the annual tax credit amount provided each year of the 10-year period.

The discounting calculation is done pursuant to the "annuity due" method for determining present value. The value of the credit is determined as of the last day of the first year of the 10-year credit period, and the credit amount for the first year is not discounted for present value.

TABLE 4

CALCULATING THE AMOUNT OF THE TAX CREDIT IN A TYPICAL REHABILITATION PROJECT

Assumptions
A. 100–unit Building with Total Development Costs of $3,850,000
B. Federal Grant of $500,000
C. 80 Percent Occupancy by Qualified Low Income Tenants
D. FHA Insured Financing (No Federal Subsidy or Tax–Exempt Financing)

	Total Building	Per Unit
1. Acquisition price for existing building	$ 2,000,000	$ 20,000
A. Less federal grant for building & land purchase	– 500,000	– 5,000
B. Less percentage of acquisition price attributed to value of the land (10%), applied to acquisition price less federal grant amount	– 150,000	– 1,500
2. Depreciable "soft" costs related to acquisition	+ 100,000	+ 1,000
I. Total "eligible basis" for acquisition credit (1+2)	1,450,000	14,500
3. Rehabilitation hard costs	1,500,000	15,000
4. Depreciable "soft" costs related to rehabilitation	250,000	2,500
II. Total "eligible basis" for rehabilitation credit (3+4)	1,750,000	17,500
III. "Applicable fraction": percentage of (a) total square feet or (b) number of units, whichever is less, occupied on the last day of initial tax credit year by qualified low income tenants	80%	80%

	Total Building	Per Unit	Per Qualified Unit
IV. Qualified basis for tax credit for acquisition: applicable fraction (III) multiplied by eligible basis (I)	$1,160,000	$11,600	14,500
V. Amount of annual tax credit for acquisition (4% of qualified basis) a/	46,400	464	580
VI. Qualified basis for tax credit for rehabilitation: applicable fraction (III) multiplied by eligible basis (II)	1,400,000	14,000	17,500
VII. Amount of annual tax credit for rehabilitation (9% of qualified basis) a/	126,000	1,260	1,575
VIII. Total annual tax credit (V + VII)	172,400	1,724	2,155

a/ Substitute 30 percent present value number for 4 percent credit, and 70 percent present value number for 9 percent credit after 1987.

TABLE 5

CALCULATING THE TAX CREDIT PERCENTAGE AMOUNT AFTER 1987; "DISCOUNTING" FOR THE PRESENT VALUE OF THE 70 PERCENT AND 30 PERCENT TAX CREDIT

Factors used:

1. Number of years = 10
2. Interest rate = average monthly Applicable Federal Rate (AFR) for mid-term and long-term Treasury securities with interest compounded annually.
3. Percentage rate for discounting = 72 percent of AFR interest rate as calculated in (2) above (i.e., one minus the 28 percent individual income tax rate; 1.0–.28 = .72); multiplied by the AFR expressed as a decimal (i.e., .085, not 8.5).
4. Present value = 70 percent or 30 percent.
5. Method of discounting present value = "annuity due" method (i.e., assumes credit is received on the first day of each yearly credit period).

The formula for calculating the tax credit percentage for 30 or 70 percent of present value is:

$$\frac{(.30) \text{ or } (.70) \times (.72 \times AFR)}{1 + (.72 \times AFR) - \dfrac{1}{(1 + [.72 \times AFR])^9}}$$

OWNERS HAVE A CHOICE IN DETERMINING THE "AFR" TAX CREDIT PERCENTAGE

The tax credit percentage, at the option of the owner, is the "AFR" percentage during either: a) the month when the housing credit agency makes a binding commitment to provide tax credits, or b) the month when the building is placed in service.

For the new construction and rehabilitation tax credits, the placed in service month is the month when the first unit in the building is completed and available for occupancy. For the tax credits for acquisition and minor rehabilitation of an occupied building, this is the month that the building is acquired.

Construction or rehabilitation work after the placed–in–service date can also earn tax credits, up to the last day of the year when the tax credit is first claimed. This can be the year the building is placed in service, or the subsequent year.

If the owner chooses to base the tax credit percentage rate as of the month of the binding commitment to provide the tax credits, the owner must make this choice in writing not later than the fifth day of the following month.

Most owners presumably will choose to fix the tax credit percentage as of the month of a binding commitment of tax credits, in order to know as early as possible the amount of tax credits they are likely to receive. However, owners who believe that interest rates are likely to increase in succeeding months may choose to base the tax credit percentage on AFR rates in the month when the building is placed in service.

Once the tax credit percentage is irrevocably fixed by this election, the percentage will also apply to any additional tax credit allocation for the project subsequently made by the housing credit agency.

IRS Notice 89–1 spells out the procedures and required content for the binding commitment agreement and the election to fix the tax credit percentage. The binding commitment must be a signed and binding contract under state law that is also binding on all successors in interest to the owner. (See Appendix 13.)

THE HISTORY OF THE FLUCTUATING "AFR" TAX CREDIT PERCENTAGE

The use of a tax credit percentage that changes monthly can create uncertainty for developers and non–profits arranging financing and seeking to guarantee project feasibility, since the AFR fluctuates significantly with changes in market interest rates.

> *For example, under the credit formula in the statute, expenditures eligible for the 70 percent present value tax credit would have been entitled to a 9.55 percent tax credit based on the AFR in September 1985, a 8.73 percent tax credit based on the AFR in September 1986, a 8.99 percent tax credit based on the AFR in August 1987, and a 9.14 percent tax credit based on the AFR in August 1988.*

The following Table 6 indicates the annual tax credit percentage amounts that would have been in effect under the present value formula in the statute in certain months of 1985, 1986, 1987, 1988, and 1989.

TABLE 6

WHAT THE 70 PERCENT AND 30 PERCENT PRESENT VALUE TAX CREDITS WOULD HAVE BEEN, JAN. 1985 – JAN. 1989

Month	Applicable Federal Rate (AFR) 1/	Rate for Discounting Present Value (.72 of AFR)	Annual Tax Credit Percentage Based on Present Value of 70 Percent	30 Percent
Jan. '85	11.70%	8.43%	9.81%	4.20%
Dec. '85	10.25	7.38	9.45	4.05
March '86	9.23	6.65	9.19	3.94
Sept. '86	7.34	5.28	8.73	3.74
Jan. '87	7.17	5.16	8.69	3.72
June '87	8.46	6.09	9.00	3.86
Mar. '88	8.39	6.04	8.99	3.85
Sept.'88	9.235	6.65	9.19	3.94
Jan. '89	9.24	6.66	9.20	3.94

1/ average of mid–term and long term AFR, with interest compounded annually

Source of AFR data is the Office of Finance and Market Analysis, Dept. of Domestic Finance, U.S. Treasury Department.

Interested persons may obtain current information on the AFR by calling their housing credit agency, or the IRS at (202) 566–4537. The data appears in the Wall Street Journal, in the periodical Tax Notes, the Prentice Hall Tax Service, and the CCH Tax Service, around the 21st day of the preceding month, and in the IRS periodical Internal Revenue Bulletin in the issue which typically comes out on the first Monday of the month.

According to staff at the Joint Committee on Taxation of the U.S. Congress, the 9 percent and 4 percent credit amounts provided for projects placed in service during calendar year 1987 were not determined by any specific present value calculation. These credit figures were "grandfathered" into the statute based on earlier specific decisions made in the tax writing committees of the Congress.

TWO–THIRDS TAX CREDIT FOR SUBSEQUENT LOW INCOME UNITS

An additional tax credit equal to two–thirds of the amount of the original credit can be provided if the number of qualified low income units in a project increases subsequent to the initial qualifying date for determining the amount of the tax credits. The initial qualifying date is the last day of the tax year in which the credit is first claimed. At the option of the owner, this can be the year in which the building is placed in service, or it can be the subsequent year.

An additional tax credit allocation can also be made at a two–thirds rate if the initial qualified basis (eligible basis multiplied by the applicable fraction of low income occupancy) is greater than the tax credit allocation received by the project. (See section below on projects receiving partial credits.)

This two–thirds tax credit is available for the entire balance of the 15–year compliance period, whereas the initial credits are provided only for the first 10 years of the compliance period. The compliance period begins when the tax credits are first claimed. In the initial year, this additional credit amount is reduced to reflect the portion of the year such units were occupied by low income tenants.

The additional tax credits could come from part of the original allocation that is unused because of an inability to qualify the number of units intended. Or the housing credit agency could allocate additional credits to the project subsequent to the year when it is placed in service, if there is an increase in qualified basis due to an increase in the number of qualified low income units in the project.

PER CAPITA LIMIT ON THE AMOUNT OF TAX CREDITS; STATE ALLOCATIONS

The most critical restriction in the tax credit program for low income housing is the limitation on the amount of tax credits that can be used each year in each state, the District of Columbia, and U.S. possessions. In each of the three years for which the tax credit program is authorized, the total amount of tax credits that can be issued in each state is $1.25 per capita. Ten percent of the amount in each state is reserved for use by non–profit housing groups. Each tax credit dollar is available for 10 years, but only the annual credit amount is counted towards the per capita limit. Thus if a project is awarded a $90,000 tax credit each year for 10 years, just $90,000 (not $900,000) is counted toward the allowable per capita figure.

MOST PROJECTS OBTAINING TAX EXEMPT FINANCING THROUGH 1989 AUTOMATICALLY RECEIVE TAX CREDITS

One important exception to this per capital limitation of $1.25 is that rental projects which utilize tax-exempt financing under the volume limitation on private activity bonds will automatically gain tax credits without a charge against the state's tax credit allocation. The amount of such tax credits is limited in each project to 4 percent or a 30 percent present value tax credit, however. Rehabilitation or new construction expenditures otherwise eligible for a 9 percent or 70 percent present value tax credit only benefit from a 4 percent or 30 percent present value tax credit if the project receives any tax-exempt financing.

However, tax-exempt financing for low income rental housing and other private purposes is governed by a separate per capita limitation in the 1986 Tax Reform Act. Total private activity bond volume in 1987 is limited to $75 per capita, or a minimum of $250 million in each state and the District of Columbia. In 1988 and 1989, the maximum bond volume is reduced to $50 per capita or a minimum of $150 million per state and D.C. In addition to low income multi-family housing, private activity bonds can also be issued for single family mortgages, industrial development, and student loans.

Under the 1988 amendments to the tax code, the automatic extension of tax credits to rental projects with tax exempt financing will end on December 31, 1989. All such projects will have to be completed and placed in service by that date to gain the credits. No form of carryover of tax credits for such projects placed in service after that date is provided.

The tax credit amounts are automatically awarded with tax-exempt financing and do not have to be approved by any state or local agency. The full eligible amount is available to the owners, notwithstanding the Congressional suggestion that the amount be limited to the minimum needed to make a project feasible.

This will apply both to the initial tax credits based on the number of qualified low income units achieved by the end of the year in which credits are first claimed, and to the additional two-thirds tax credits for additional qualified low income units achieved during the rest of the 15-year compliance period.

If 70 percent or more of a project's aggregate basis (total development costs including land) is financed with tax-exempt financing, all 100 percent of the project qualifies for the tax credit without any charge against the $1.25 per capita state limitation. If less than 70 percent of development costs is financed with tax exempt financing, then only those expenditures financed with tax-exempt financing automatically receive tax credits without any charge against the $1.25 per capita limitation. The balance of eligible expenditures could receive tax credits, however, from the state's credit allocation upon application to a state or local credit allocation agency.

For owners who obtain tax credits automatically without an allocation because their projects are at least 70 percent financed by tax exempt bonds, the owner can elect to base the tax credit percentage on the AFR rate for the month in which the bonds are issued, instead of waiting to base the tax credit percentage on the AFR rate for the month in which the building is placed in service. Here again, the owner must make this election in writing not later than the fifth of the month following the month when the tax exempt bonds are issued. (See IRS Notice 89-1, Appendix 13.)

DEVELOPERS MAY ONLY GET A PARTIAL CREDIT FOR THEIR PROJECTS

State and local agencies which allocate the housing credits can allocate less than the full statutory amount to which a project is entitled. Both the credit percentage and/or the dollar amount of qualified basis could be reduced by a credit allocating agency.

This policy is most likely to be implemented in states and jurisdictions with greater amounts of low income housing development activity in relation to population size. Faced with competing demands for limited tax credit resources from developers and non-profits, reductions in the tax credit amounts allocated to each project offers a solution with fewer political repercussions than choosing among competing applications.

The granting of partial credit amounts by the credit allocation agencies will be stimulated by the provision that the amount of tax credits awarded to a particular project is deducted from the state's allocation, even if the project never uses the full amount because of an inability to achieve the projected number of qualified low income units. For example, a particular project may be awarded tax credits based on its goal of setting aside 50 units for qualified low income occupancy. If for any reason the goal cannot be achieved (e.g., unreported income of existing occupants, rent-up problems for low income tenants at projected rent levels, etc.), and only 40 units qualify as low income units, a state or local credit allocating agency cannot reclaim the credit amounts for the non-qualifying 10 units. However, unused credits can be returned by the project owner before the end of the year in which they are awarded. Also, the owner can use the unclaimed credits at a later date at a two-thirds rate over the entire remaining length of the 15-year compliance period if the number of qualifying units increases during the compliance period.

If a housing credit agency is going to allocate to a project less than the maximum amount of credits to which the project is entitled, the project will benefit if this is done by awarding the maximum credit percentage and reducing the amount of qualified basis which will receive tax credits. This enables the owner to more easily qualify for the total tax credit allocation. In addition, the owner could receive a later allocation for additional qualified basis if the credit agency has unused tax credit allocations later in the year or in subsequent years. IRS regulations permit projects to be awarded a second allocation if the initial allocation is less than the full entitlement amount.

However, if the agency believes that reducing the amount of qualified basis would lead the owner to reduce the number of units rented to low income households at qualifying rents, then it might choose instead to reduce the credit percentage and award the full qualified basis. This is the method for providing partial credits described in the explanation of Congressional intent. Under this approach, the owner must achieve the full low income occupancy he/she originally projected in order to receive the full tax credit allocation.

THE TOTAL DOLLAR AMOUNTS OF TAX CREDITS AVAILABLE

The yearly tax credit allocations for the various states are based on the most recent population estimates, either final or provisional, of the Census Bureau issued prior to the beginning of each allocation year. These projections are traditionally as of July 1 of the same year. The latest such population data and the tax credit allocations based on $1.25 per capita are shown in Table 7, and are as of July 1, 1988. Based on that data, total tax credit allocations will be $311,716,000 for the 50 states, the District of Columbia, and U.S. possessions.

A rough estimate of the number of units that might be assisted in 1989 by the tax credits can be made for each state and the total U.S. The Model Tax Credit Allocation in Table 3 was based on a rehabilitation project with typical total development costs of $38,500 per unit, resulting in a tax credit amount of $2,155 per qualifying low income unit. Table 7 shows the number of units that each state's estimated tax credit allocation would produce based on a credit of $2,155 per unit. For the U.S. as a whole, this results in an estimated 144,600 units for 1989.

The actual figures will vary substantially on a state-by-state basis, due to differences in development costs and the local mix of new construction, rehabilitation with acquisition, acquisition only, and rehabilitation without acquisition projects using the tax credit. Also, many jurisdictions will not use their full allocations.

> ***As a subsequent analysis demonstrates, additional financial assistance is likely to be required in most areas to make a $38,500 per unit project with a $2,155 annual tax credit workable.***

These estimates do not include the volume of multi-family housing financed by tax-exempt financing which would automatically receive a 4 percent or 30 percent present value tax credit. These tax credits are exempt from the state per capita allocations, but the volume of such financing is subject to the separate per capita limitation of total tax exempt financing for private purposes.

The $312 million in yearly tax credits, if fully utilized, would result in $3.1 billion in tax credits over the 10-year period when they are available. The potential is a total of over $9 billion in tax credits for the three years for which the program was initially authorized. Tax-exempt financing might generate as much as an additional $500 million in tax credits over the same three years.

HOW THE TAX CREDIT DOLLARS ARE ALLOCATED WITHIN EACH STATE: THE HOUSING CREDIT AGENCY

The functions of allocating and administering the low income housing tax credit are delegated by the 1986 law to a new agency called the "housing credit agency." A housing credit agency is established at the state level, and at the local level for each local jurisdiction which receives a tax credit sub-allocation. Any state allocation plan is required to "give balanced consideration to the low income housing needs of the entire state."

The tax credit amounts can be allocated directly by the state to particular projects, or can be allocated to local agencies who would then select the particular projects. Some combination of state and local sharing of the tax credit authority can also be established. A state or local housing credit agency can sub-divide the credit authority by geographic area, and select the projects from each such area.

A state may delegate authority to a local housing credit agency until a specified date during each year, such as November 1, and then reclaim any unused authority as of that date for use elsewhere in the state. The credit is used when any project with a tax credit allocation is placed in service.

Housing credit agencies can allocate credits only to projects located within their geographic jurisdiction.

TABLE 7

TAX CREDIT ALLOCATIONS TO THE VARIOUS STATES FOR 1989
BASED ON JULY 1, 1988 POPULATION STATISTICS
AND HYPOTHETICAL NUMBERS OF UNITS THAT MIGHT BE ASSISTED

Region and State	July 1, 1988 Population (Interim)	Tax Credit Allocation at $1.25 per Capita	No. of Housing Units Aided at $2,155 Tax Credit per Unit [a/]
New England			
Maine	1,206,000	$1,508,000	700
New Hampshire	1,097,000	1,371,000	636
Vermont	556,000	695,000	323
Massachusetts	5,871,000	7,339,000	3,406
Rhode Island	995,000	1,244,000	577
Connecticut	3,241,000	4,051,000	1,880
Middle Atlantic			
New York	17,898,000	22,372,000	10,382
New Jersey	7,720,000	9,650,000	4,478
Pennsylvania	12,027,000	15,034,000	6,976
East North Central			
Ohio	10,872,000	13,590,000	6,306
Indiana	5,575,000	6,969,000	3,234
Illinois	11,544,000	14,430,000	6,696
Michigan	9,300,000	11,625,000	5,394
Wisconsin	4,858,000	6,072,000	2,818
West North Central			
Minnesota	4,306,000	5,382,000	2,497
Iowa	2,834,000	3,542,000	1,644
Missouri	5,139,000	6,424,000	2,981
North Dakota	663,000	829,000	385
South Dakota	715,000	894,000	415
Nebraska	1,601,000	2,001,000	929
Kansas	2,487,000	3,109,000	1,443
South Atlantic			
Delaware	660,000	825,000	383
Maryland	4,644,000	5,805,000	2,694
Dist. of Columbia	620,000	775,000	360
Virginia	5,996,000	7,495,000	3,478
West Virginia	1,884,000	2,355,000	1,093
North Carolina	6,526,000	8,158,000	3,786
South Carolina	3,493,000	4,366,000	2,026
Georgia	6,401,000	8,001,000	3,713
Florida	12,377,000	15,471,000	7,179
East South Central			
Kentucky	3,721,000	4,651,000	2,158
Tennessee	4,919,000	6,149,000	2,853
Alabama	4,127,000	5,159,000	2,394
Mississippi	2,627,000	3,284,000	1,524

Table 7 cont.

Region and State	July 1, 1988 Population (Interim)	Tax Credit Allocation at $1.25 per Capita	No. of Housing Units Aided at $2,155 Tax Credit per Unit a/
West South Central			
Arkansas	2,422,000	3,028,000	1,405
Louisiana	4,420,000	5,525,000	2,564
Oklahoma	3,263,000	4,079,000	1,893
Texas	16,780,000	20,975,000	9,733
Mountain			
Montana	804,000	1,005,000	466
Idaho	999,000	1,249,000	580
Wyoming	471,000	589,000	273
Colorado	3,290,000	4,112,000	1,908
New Mexico	1,510,000	1,888,000	876
Arizona	3,466,000	4,332,000	2,010
Utah	1,691,000	2,114,000	981
Nevada	1,060,000	1,325,000	615
Pacific			
Washington	4,619,000	5,774,000	2,679
Oregon	2,741,000	3,426,000	1,590
California	28,168,000	35,210,000	16,339
Alaska	513,000	641,000	297
Hawaii	1,093,000	1,366,000	634
U.S. Possessions b/			
Puerto Rico	3,292,000	4,115,000	1,910
Virgin Islands	106,000	132,000	61
Guam	130,000	162,000	75
American Samoa	38,000	48,000	22
TOTAL U.S. & POSSESSIONS	249,373,000	$ 311,716,000	144,649

a/ Based on a hypothetical rehabilitation project with a unit cost of $38,500 and a federal grant of $5,000 per unit. Does not assume that the number of units could be provided as low income housing without significant grant or subsidy assistance.

b/ data is for 1987.

Note: Housing units financed with tax exempt bonds that are placed in service before Jan. 1, 1990 automatically receive credits that are not counted against the above allocations.

Source of Population Data: U.S. Dept. of Commerce, Bureau of the Census, News Release CB88-205, Dec. 30, 1988.

A special allocation provision is provided in the statute for the state of Illinois. In that state, the city of Chicago gets a direct allocation equal to its proportion of the state's population in the most recent Census Bureau statistics issued prior to the beginning of the year.

Other than in Illinois, only New York State has subdivided its allocation among multiple credit agencies, including one New York City agency. In these states, it may be possible to receive a tax credit allocation for a particular project from more than one agency. In all the other states, a single state-wide housing credit agency administers the tax credit program.

Housing credit agencies need not investigate whether a project is eligible for the tax credit. They may rely on information submitted by the owner in an application for the tax credits. In addition, credit agencies do not have to monitor projects for compliance during the compliance period.

Tax credits are officially awarded to a project when an authorized official of a housing credit agency completes and signs Part I of Internal Revenue Service (IRS) Form 8609, Low Income Housing Credit Allocation Certification, and mails it to the owner of the project.

THE AMOUNT OF THE TAX CREDIT ALLOCATION; IRS FORMS FOR RECORDING AND TRACKING THE TAX CREDITS

The tax credit allocation consists of three parts: a dollar amount of credits; the tax credit percentage; and the qualified basis (i.e., the amount which is multiplied by the tax credit percentage to arrive at the amount of tax credits that can be claimed for the project).

The tax credit allocation is made on a building basis. In multi-building projects, the three part allocation is made separately for each building in the project. Each building is assigned a Building Identification Number (BIN) by the housing credit agency so that the IRS can keep track of the allocations.

The housing credit agency reports the three part tax credit allocation at the end of the year to the IRS on Part I of Form 8609, Low Income Housing Credit Allocation Certification, with the address of the building, the name and address of the owner, and the BIN. (See Appendix 17).

Form 8609 is also sent to the building owner, who is required to fill out Part II of the form and send it to the IRS along with Form 8586 as part of his/her income tax return for the first year the tax credit is claimed.

Owners who receive tax credits without an allocation because the building has received tax exempt financing are required to fill out Part I on Form 8609 and send it to the housing credit agency in order to receive a BIN. From this point, the process is the same as that for buildings which receive a tax credit allocation.

The fixed dollar amount of tax credits is the critical part of the allocation. The actual credit percentage may or may not be fixed at the time the allocation is made. The actual qualified basis will not be known until the end of the first year the tax credit is taken, since it is based on all expenditures on the project through the last day of that year and on the amount of eligible low income occupancy achieved as of that date.

The amount of the tax credit allocation can be changed or amended through the end of the allocation year, for either a project placed in service in that year or for a project with an allocation that is carried forward one or two years under the legislation enacted in 1988.

If additional tax credit dollars are needed for a project, a housing credit agency can award tax credits from a subsequent year's allocation. However, the housing credit agency must make a binding commitment to award the future credits by the end of the year in which the project is placed in service.

Tax credits can also be awarded after the end of the placed-in-service year for an increase in the number of qualified low income units in the project. These credits would be earned at the two-thirds rate for the balance of the 15 year compliance period, although the full amount of the tax credit allocation is subtracted from the state's allocation.

TWO YEAR CARRYOVER PROVIDES EXTRA TIME FOR PROJECT COMPLETION

When the tax credit program began, projects had to be completed and placed in service by the end of the year for which the tax credits were allocated. No carryover was permitted, so that projects that were not placed in service by the end of 1987 lost all of their calendar year 1987 tax credits.

A limited exception was initially provided in the 1986 act for a one year carryover for projects receiving tax credits during the last year of the three year program (1989) which were at least 10 percent finished by the end of the previous year (1988). However, this has now been changed extensively as a result of the 1988 technical corrections tax legislation.

The 1988 legislation provides a carryover of tax credits for new construction or rehabilitation projects which receive 1988 and 1989 tax credit allocations. Developers will now have additional time to complete projects and have them placed in service --- up to two years after the end of the year for which a tax credit allocation is made.

Thus, a developer receiving an allocation of 1988 tax credits has until December 31, 1990 to place the project in service and make it available for occupancy. A developer receiving a 1989 tax credit allocation has until the end of 1991 to place the project in service. This carryover provision does not apply to 1987 allocations.

In order to qualify for this two year carryover, however, the owner's basis in the project at the end of the allocation year must be at least 10 percent of the owner's reasonably expected basis at the end of the second year following the allocation year.

In other words, the project should be at least ten percent complete by the end of the allocation year for which a carryover of credits is allowed (1988 and 1989).

In meeting this ten percent completion test, the cost of land is included as part of basis (even though it is not part of basis in determining the tax credit amount). In a rehabilitation project, costs previously incurred in acquiring the building can also be counted towards the 10 percent expenditure requirement. Also, the owner must have title to the property at the end of the allocation year.

In a multi-building project, this 10 percent expenditure test applies to the project as a whole, although the carryover allocation applies separately for each building. This allows a building in a multi-building project to earn a carryover even if no funds have been expended on that building.

Under this ten percent completion test, an owner could argue that his expected basis at the end of the second year following the allocation year is less than total development costs. This could happen if the project is not completed at the end of the second year even though the first unit is completed and available for occupancy, or if the project is completed before the end of the second year and depreciation allowances are deducted from basis for a number of months.

IRS Notice 89–1 specifies the carryover procedures and the information that must be in an allocation document that is a valid carryover of tax credits for the succeeding two years (Appendix 13).

The major benefit of the "carryover" provision, which was enacted in lieu of a one year extension of the tax credit program, is to allow housing credit agencies to continue to allocate tax credits to projects that could not have been completed under the strict deadlines of the 1986 law.

This benefit is of little value in about 20 states which indicated they expected to use all or almost all of their 1988 and 1989 credit allocations under the old completion deadlines.

However, the new carryover provision also gives additional breathing room to 1988 and 1989 tax credit projects already under development around the country, since they will have an extra year or two to be completed.

In order to maximize the benefits of the new carryover provision, a significant number of state credit agencies with unused 1988 allocations substituted 1988 allocations for 1989 allocations with respect to projects which had 10 percent of project costs spent by the end of 1988. This action freed up 1989 credit allocations for use with additional projects that can be completed by the end of 1991.

A BUILDING IS PLACED IN SERVICE WHEN THE FIRST UNIT IS COMPLETED AND AVAILABLE FOR OCCUPANCY

According to IRS Notice 88–116, the placed–in–service date for a new or existing building for low income housing tax credit purposes is the date when the first unit in the building is certified as available for occupancy. Thus developers working towards a deadline of completing new construction or rehabilitation by the end of the year in order to qualify for tax credits need only complete one unit and get it certified by that time.

With respect to tax credits for the acquisition of a building (with or without rehabilitation) that is already functioning and occupied, the placed–in–service date is the date when ownership of the building transfers to the new owner.

For buildings in a multi–building project which meet the 20 or 40 percent minimum low income occupancy requirement only because of greater low income occupancy in other buildings, the placed–in–service date is the date when the last building used to comply with the low income occupancy requirement is considered placed in service. This puts back the date when the owner can begin to benefit from the tax credits for initial buildings, and extends the 15 year compliance period accordingly.

Developers acquiring an occupied building for a rehabilitation project need to obtain an allocation or a binding commitment of tax credits for the acquisition expenditures by the end of the year in which the building is acquired. They would need to obtain an allocation or binding commitment of tax credits for the rehabilitation expenditures by the end of the year in which the rehab work for the first unit is completed and certified.

Developers acquiring a vacant building for rehabilitation need to obtain a tax credit allocation or binding commitment for both acquisition and rehabilitation expenditures by the end of the year in which the rehab work for the first unit is completed and certified.

TAX CREDITS CAN BE OBTAINED FOR EXPENDITURES THROUGH THE END OF THE FIRST TAX CREDIT YEAR

For buildings that are completed and placed in service in portions where construction on additional units continues after the first unit is completed and certified for occupancy, all expenditures incurred through the end of the first tax credit year can be added to the eligible basis for determining the amount of tax credits.

Thus a developer can place a building in service and qualify for tax credits by having at least one unit finished with a certificate of occupancy by the end of the year, and get tax credits for all eligible expenditures incurred through the end of the following year, as long as the owner chooses to begin to claim the tax credits in the following year.

Combined with the new two year carryover provisions, this means that projects with 1988 allocations can qualify for tax credits if they have completed at least one unit by the end of 1990, and can earn tax credits on expenditures incurred either through the end of 1990 or the end of 1991.

PROJECTS CAN GET FUTURE YEAR TAX CREDITS — BUT PRIOR YEAR PROJECTS CANNOT GET TAX CREDITS

A housing credit agency can make an advance binding commitment to award a future year's tax credit allocation to a project which it believes will be placed in service during that future allocation year. It can make a binding commitment to award credits in a future year to a project completed in any earlier year, as long as that commitment is not made after the end of the year in which the project is placed in service. A tax credit agency cannot first decide in any particular year to award credits to a building or project placed in service during a previous year.

For example, if the program is reauthorized beyond 1989, a tax credit agency can decide during 1989 to award:
— 1990 credits to a project expected to be placed in service in 1989;
— 1991 credits to a project expected to be placed in service in 1989 or 1990.

During 1989, a tax credit agency cannot award credits to a project placed in service prior to 1989.

SPECIAL 10 PERCENT ALLOCATION TO NON-PROFIT PROJECTS IN EACH STATE

The legislation specifies that in each state, a minimum of 10 percent of the total annual tax credit allocation must be used each year for projects involving non-profit organizations. To qualify, an organization must be tax-exempt under Sections 501(c)(3) or 501(c)(4) of the Internal Revenue Code, and have the fostering of low income housing as one of its purposes. In addition, the non-profit organization must materially participate in the project. This means that the organization "must be involved on a regular, continuous, and substantial basis" in the development of the project and in the continued operation of the project for the duration of the 15-year compliance period. The non-profit does not have to have an ownership interest in the project.

A subsidiary of a qualified non-profit corporation can receive a part of the non-profit allocation if the subsidiary is wholly owned by qualified nonprofit corporations during its entire existence. The subsidiary involved in project does not have to be tax exempt as long as its parent non-profit organization is tax exempt. Either the subsidiary or the parent non-profit can meet the test of materially participating in the project.

The 10 percent allocation for non-profits can be used anywhere in the state. A state allocation plan can issue the non-profit set-aside to just one city or section of the state, but no state action can reduce the minimum 10 percent allocation. This also means that the credits are lost to the state if non-profits do not utilize their 10 percent allocation. Of course, a state may allocate more than 10 percent to non-profit organizations if it wishes.

COOPERATIVES ARE ELIGIBLE TO USE TAX CREDITS

Housing cooperatives which are owned and controlled by the members who are the residents of the project are eligible to obtain and use low income housing tax credits. Similarly, leasing cooperatives are eligible to obtain multi-family tax exempt financing as if they were rental housing.

Since credits and tax benefits normally flow to projects that are rental housing, a rental relationship should be established. This can be done by establishing a leasing cooperative, under which an entire building would be leased by the cooperative from the owning entity. Cooperatives also have used the tax credits by being designated as the managing general partner in limited partnership tax credit projects where there is no leasing arrangement.

After the end of the 15 year compliance period, the project could be converted to a full ownership cooperative without any leasing or rental arrangements. Mechanisms could be established to ensure that the units remain affordable during and after the 15 year compliance period. Limited equity cooperatives are cooperatives in which the downpayment or equity ownership payment is a restricted amount and can only increase according to a set formula, such as the rate of increase in the cost-of-living.

Whenever cooperatives use the tax credits, all tax benefits flow to the owners and investors rather than to the resident tenant cooperators.

Housing cooperatives can be eligible for the non-profit setaside of 10 percent of tax credits if they are 501(c)(3) tax-exempt organizations or subsidiaries of such organizations.

While the Internal Revenue Service in its Notice 88–91 indicated that cooperatives may not be eligible for the low income housing tax credit, its policy is that only cooperatives which provide home ownership-type tax benefits directly to individual tenant–stockholders are ineligible for the credits. Future regulations will clearly indicate that cooperatives with non-resident investor owners are eligible for the tax credit.

PART OF TENANT'S RENT CAN BE USED FOR PURCHASING THE UNIT

Lease–purchase arrangements where part of the monthly rent is held or credited for the tenant towards a downpayment on eventual purchase of the unit are permitted. The amount held must be refunded to tenants who move before they purchase the unit, and the purchase must occur after the end of the 15 year compliance period. The monthly amount set aside for this purpose must be counted towards the maximum rent for eligibility for tax credits.

SELLER FINANCING FROM NON–PROFIT SOURCES CAN BE INCLUDED IN CALCULATING TAX CREDIT AMOUNT

Non–profits projects benefit from a provision that seller financing from another non–profit organization will not reduce the amount of tax credits for which a project is eligible. Under the normal at–risk rules, any amount of seller financing that is non–recourse (i.e. where the borrower is not personally at risk) would be deducted from adjusted basis and therefore would reduce the amount of the tax credit for which a project is eligible.

Seller financing from a non–profit or quasi–governmental organization that is not greater than 60 percent of the basis of the property will be exempt from the at–risk rules and will not reduce the adjusted basis of the project if the organization is tax–exempt and has the fostering of low income housing as one of its purposes.

The seller financing must be secured by the property, except where a federal agency owns or insures a mortgage on the property and the agency prohibits seller financing from being secured by the property.

If the rate of interest on this non–profit seller financing is lower than one percent below the Applicable Federal Rate (AFR) (the prevailing interest rate on mid–term and long–term government securities), then the qualified basis for the amount so financed is to be reduced to equal the present value of the amount of the financing, using the AFR as the discounting rate. (For example, if the AFR is 7 percent, then the amount financed from a non–profit source with an interest rate below 6 percent would be discounted to a present value.) If the financing from the non–profit source is not fully repaid with interest by the end of the 15–year compliance period, then the amount of the tax credit for all 10 years attributed to the amount of this financing must be repaid to the Treasury with interest.

ANNUAL REVIEW OF TENANT ELIGIBILITY: INCOME INCREASES UP TO 40 PERCENT ABOVE CURRENT ELIGIBILITY LEVELS ARE ALLOWED

Continuous compliance with the requirements of the tax credit is necessary to avoid penalties and the recapture of prior tax credits. Tenant incomes need to be examined annually to assure continued compliance. The compliance period is 15 years, even though the tax credits are provided only for a 10-year period.

The tax credit program permits tenant incomes to increase above the updated and current maximum income limits without any disqualification or loss of compliance. Tenant incomes can increase up to 40 percent above the current updated maximum income levels for the tenant's household size without any penalty.

For example, if the maximum qualifying income or income limit in 1987 for a four-person family was $18,500, and after seven years this income limit increased to $22,000 in 1994 due to increases in area median incomes, then a tenant household could have an income up to $30,800 in 1994 (140 percent of $22,000) and the unit would still qualify under the program.

If the household size of that tenant decreased to three persons, the equivalent updated income limit in 1994 would be $19,800, and the maximum tenant income for continued compliance would be $27,720, or 140 percent of $19,800.

If a tenant's income increases to more than 140 percent of the current eligibility level, the project will still remain in compliance if the next vacant unit of equal or smaller size is rented to a low income qualified tenant at a qualifying rent.

This means that projects with 100 percent qualified low income units should never face the penalty of recapture since the project would normally rent out the next vacancy to a low income tenant at the same low income rent amount.

If in a mixed-income project, a tenant becomes over income and the next vacancy is for a unit that was previously occupied by a non-low income tenant paying a higher rent, then that vacancy will have to be rented to a low income tenant at a lower rent. The owner would be free to obtain a higher rent from the formerly low income tenant whose income now exceeds the income limits. If this higher rent is not as high as the rent paid by the former non-low income tenant, however, the project would suffer a loss of income.

SPECIAL EXCEPTION FOR "DEEP RENT SKEWING" PROJECTS ALLOWS INCREASES IN TENANT INCOMES UP TO 70 PERCENT ABOVE CURRENT ELIGIBILITY LEVELS

A special rule for "deep rent skewing" projects allows even greater increases in tenant income without disqualifying the unit as low income. Tenant incomes can increase to up to 70 percent above the current applicable maximum income for the household size of the tenant without disqualifying that unit, if (a) the project sets aside 15 percent of the required number of low income units for tenants with incomes under 40 percent of the area median income, adjusted for household size; and (b) the average rent for non-low income tenants in the project is at least 300 percent of the average rent for low income families in comparable units, with any rental assistance payments counted as part of the tenant's rent.

If a tenant's income increases above the 170 percent level, the project can remain in compliance if all vacant low income units are rented to tenants with incomes under 40 percent of median income until the required number of units is reached.

VACANT UNITS CAN CONTINUE TO QUALIFY

Vacant units that formerly were occupied by low income tenants and otherwise qualified for tax credits can continue to be counted towards both minimum eligibility and the qualifying tax credit amount, as long as reasonable attempts are made to fill the unit with a qualified tenant and no other vacant unit of comparable or smaller size is rented to non-qualifying tenants.

RECAPTURE PENALTIES FOR NON-COMPLIANCE

If any project fails to meet the minimum set-aside or eligibility requirements or the required number of qualified units for which tax credits were initially awarded, the penalty is recapture of the "accelerated portion" of the tax credits, plus interest, for all prior years. Also, the entire credit for the year of the recapture event is disallowed. The "accelerated portion" of the credit is the difference between (a) the actual amount of credits for that year, and (b) the amount of credits that would be available for that year if the total amount of credits were payable evenly over the entire 15-year compliance period. During the first 11 years, the accelerated portion is one-third of the total credit amount. It is 4/15ths in year 12, decreasing proportionately to 1/15th in year 15.

If the project fails to comply with the minimum eligibility requirement of either 20 percent or 40 percent of the units, then the recapture of the accelerated portion of the credits and disallowance of that year's entire credit applies to <u>all</u> units. If the non-compliance is a reduction in the number of qualified low income units or in the floor space fraction for low income units, but the minimum eligibility requirements are still met, then the recapture and the disallowance apply only to the units that are no longer in compliance. Non-compliance related to the loss of low-income units occurs only after a subsequent vacant unit is rented to a non-low income tenant.

If there is a reduction in the floor space fraction for low income units that is considered minimal or de minimus, there would be no recapture. A minimal reduction in the low income floor space fraction might occur if a unit was no longer considered low income because a tenant moved or his/her income increased in excess of maximum allowable levels, and another unit that newly qualified as low income had a smaller amount of floor space than the previously qualified unit.

There is no recapture penalty whatsoever if the number of qualifying low income units lost does not exceed the number of qualifying units added after the initial year of qualification (since there is no acceleration of the credits for these units).

There is no recapture if any noncompliance is corrected within a reasonable period after it is discovered or should have been discovered.

OWNERSHIP CHANGE IS A RECAPTURE EVENT

Any change in the ownership of a building or a partnership interest is considered to be a recapture event. Recapture can be avoided if the owner selling the building or the partnership interest posts a bond satisfactory to the IRS, and IRS determines that the project is expected to remain in compliance for the balance of the 15 year period.

When an ownership change occurs, the accelerated portion of credits taken in prior years and all credits earned by the initial owner or seller in the current year is subject to recapture. The purchaser or new owner can claim credits for the balance of the current year, however.

Developers should make every effort to obtain investors and complete their partner ships prior to the date when the buildings are placed in service. Changes in ownership after that date can result in recapture or the posting of a bond to avoid recapture.

LARGE PARTNERSHIPS CAN ASSUME RECAPTURE RESPONSIBILITIES

Paying IRS for recaptured tax credits, or the posting of a bond to avoid recapture, is the responsibility of each taxpaying member of the partnership. However, large partnerships containing 35 or more partners are considered to be the taxpayer and will pay recapture amounts or post a bond on behalf of the members of the partnership, unless the partnership elects on IRS Form 8609 to shift this responsibility to individual partners.

There can be corporate members in large partnerships which assume recapture responsibilities.

When these large partnerships take on the role of the taxpayer, then the sale of individual partnership interests is exempt from recapture, as long as the ownership of 50 percent or more of the original interests remains unchanged.

INTERIM STEP TOWARD POSTING BOND ADVISED BY IRS OFFICIAL

IRS has not yet issued any policies or procedures for posting bond to avoid recapture. In the interim, however, an IRS official is orally advising taxpayers who have undergone a recapture event to take steps towards posting bond if they want to claim tax credits on their tax returns. This official advises such taxpayers to set up an escrow account in an amount that is twice the potential recapture amount (or twice times one-third of all credits claimed on that return plus prior returns), and to write the District Director of the IRS informing him/her of this action.

However, the IRS generally advises taxpayers that they should not rely on the oral representations of IRS employees.

REPORTING REQUIREMENTS

At the end of the first taxable year for which the credit is claimed, taxpayers must report to the Internal Revenue Service with their annual tax returns on Form 8609 the date the building was placed in service, the qualified basis (the amount against which the tax credit percentage is applied), and the credit percentage taken. In addition, the taxpayer must certify every year that the project continues to comply with the minimum eligibility requirements for low income units, and state whether or not the qualified basis for the property has decreased. The IRS in the future may require taxpayers to provide additional information with their annual income tax returns. Penalties can be assessed if any such required information is not provided.

Housing credit agencies must file annual reports with the Treasury that provide: the total tax credit amounts issued; identification of each building that received tax credits and the qualified basis and credit percentage approved for that building; the fees charged to credit recipients; and other information that may be specified in regulations.

Housing credit agencies can charge reasonable fees to tax credit applicants and recipients to cover their costs in administering this program. They can charge a single fee for projects containing more than one building, or for multiple projects with one owner (such as scattered site single family developments).

3

OTHER KEY PROVISIONS OF THE 1986 TAX REFORM ACT THAT AFFECT THE LOW INCOME HOUSING TAX CREDIT

PASSIVE LOSSES LIMITATIONS RESTRICT THE USE OF THE TAX CREDIT

The 1986 Tax Reform Act limits the amount of low income housing tax credits that most taxpayers can use, and virtually eliminates the use of tax credits at very high income levels. The passive losses provisions apply primarily to depreciation deductions in rental real estate activity, but also apply to the low income housing tax credit (and the historic and older building rehabilitation tax credits as well).

The amount of tax credits that can be used to reduce taxes on a dollar–for–dollar basis on ordinary (i.e, active or non–rental) income is limited by the new act to $8,250 per year for taxpayers with a 33 percent effective marginal tax rate. This maximum is the credit equivalent of the $25,000 maximum deduction of losses in real estate activity that can be used to reduce ordinary taxable income. The $8,250 figure is calculated by applying the 33 percent tax rate against $25,000. For taxpayers with a 28 percent effective marginal tax rate, the maximum amount of credits that can be used in any year is $7,000 (28 percent of $25,000). Losses and credits can be taken together to offset taxes on ordinary income up to the $25,000 maximum, with each dollar of credit counted as $3.00 towards this maximum for taxpayers with a 33 percent marginal tax rate. For the transition year 1987 when the maximum tax rate is 38.5 percent, up to $9,625 in tax credits can be used to offset taxes on ordinary income.

This maximum amount is reduced as a taxpayer's adjusted gross income exceeds $200,000. There is a one–dollar reduction in the amount of tax credits that can be used for every $6.00 of adjusted gross income in excess of $200,000, if the marginal tax rate is 33 percent. No amount of tax credits can be used to offset taxes on ordinary income if adjusted gross income exceeds $250,000 a year. Adjusted gross income is all taxable income, less certain adjustments to income, which include employee business expenses, Keough contributions, and alimony payments.

The tax credits can be used without limit to reduce taxes on passive income from rental property, which includes cash flow income and capital gains on a sale.

If a taxpayer has more tax credits than he can use in any year, he can carry back unused credits to each of the three preceding years or carry forward unused credits to each of the following 15 years. However, credits cannot be carried back to reduce taxes in years prior to 1987. The same maximums apply in future years.

In the year in which an owner or investor sells his entire interest in a property, unused credits and losses from that property can be used to offset taxes. The losses can be used to offset taxes on both ordinary and passive income, but the credits can only be used to offset taxes on a gain in the sale of the property and other passive income.

However, only $3,000 in capital losses can be used to reduce taxable ordinary income in any one year. Capital losses can be used in full against any capital gains in the same year. Unused capital losses can be carried over to subsequent years, subject to the $3,000 limit in any year.

The passive losses limitations do not apply to most corporations. However, they do apply to Subchapter S corporations and those which provide personal services. Most corporations will be able to use an unlimited amount of tax credits and depreciation deductions to offset corporate income taxes on their regular business income. Because of this they are considered to be prime candidates for limited partner investors in low income housing.

NEW TAX RATES AFFECT LOW INCOME HOUSING INVESTORS

The 1986 tax reform act establishes just two permanent tax rates of 15 and 28 percent on the income of individual taxpayers. However, two provisions are gradually phased out for higher income taxpayers -- first, the 15 percent tax bracket and second, the personal exemptions -- in a manner which establishes an additional surcharge of 5 percent of income on top of the 28 percent tax rate. This produces an effective marginal tax rate of 33 percent for many higher income taxpayers. The income levels at which this 33 percent rate phases in and out depends upon the taxpayer's filing status and the number of personal exemptions. For a married couple with two children filing a joint return, the 33 percent effective tax rate applies to taxable income between about $72,000 and $193,000. These income levels will increase in future years as they are indexed for inflation.

The new law also eliminates the lower tax rate on capital gains, which applied to the gain on the sale or disposition of low income housing and other property and buildings. Instead of a maximum effective tax rate of 20 percent on capital gains, the new regular income tax rates apply, with a top tax bracket of 28 percent plus a 5 percent surcharge for many investors.

For corporations -- who are becoming a more active source of investment in low income housing -- the effective marginal income tax rate is now 34 percent, compared to 46 percent under the prior law.

> *The effective marginal income tax rates for investors -- including the income tax rates imposed at the state and local government level -- determine the value of depreciation deductions and other passive losses.*

THE VALUE AND USE OF DEPRECIATION ALLOWANCES ARE CONSIDERABLY REDUCED

The use of depreciation deductions to reduce taxes on ordinary income was the primary motivating force behind much of the investment in low income housing in prior years. Previously written off on an accelerated basis over 15 years, low income rental housing must now be depreciated over a 27.5 year period on a straight line basis, the same as other rental housing. This amounts to 3.636 percent of the property's initial adjusted basis each year.

Since it is a deduction against taxable income, a dollar of depreciation is worth more to taxpayers in the higher tax brackets. Under the new law, the typical investor will face a 33 percent marginal tax rate for federal income taxes. Adding the marginal tax rate for state or local income taxes brings the value of a dollar of depreciation to around 40 cents or more on an after-tax basis in many states.

Under the 1986 tax reform act, the use of depreciation deductions has been very substantially restricted. In summary, depreciation deductions are now largely limited to offsetting the tax liability on passive or real estate-related income. Except in the year when the property is disposed of, limited (non-active) partners are not able to deduct depreciation against ordinary income, and active partners will be substantially restricted in their use of depreciation deductions to offset taxes on ordinary income.

In the typical low income housing partnership, non-corporate limited partner investors will not be able to use the depreciation writeoffs. The passive losses provisions limit the use of depreciation as an offset against taxes on ordinary income to those individual taxpayers who actively participate in the operation of the property. By definition, limited partners do not actively participate in a property's operation.

Individuals who are limited partners can use depreciation deductions to offset current year taxes only on passive income such as cash flow or the gains on sale of rental property. However, unused depreciation deductions can be carried forward and used to offset taxes on ordinary income in the year in which the investor sells his interest in the property.

Depreciation deductions were very valuable in past years, because the accelerated amounts were substantial, and both marginal tax rates and the rate of inflation were considerably higher. If the current period of low inflation continues, then the loss in real value from having to use depreciation deductions in future years will not be as great as in past years.

For owner-investors who meet the test of active participation in a project, only passive losses of up to $25,000, which would mainly be depreciation deductions, can be offset against ordinary income to reduce taxes. Tax credits are also counted as part of the passive losses. Each dollar of tax credits is equal to $3.00 towards the $25,000 maximum when the tax credit limit is $8,250.

Active participation is defined as participation in a significant and bona fide sense, such as approving new tenants, deciding on rents, and approving major expenses. In addition, an owner must own at least 10 percent of the property.

While active participation is required to deduct current depreciation allowances against ordinary taxable income, it is not required for using up to $8,250 in low income housing tax credits to reduce taxes on ordinary income.

Furthermore, the use of depreciation deductions is restricted and cut off at higher income levels. The full $25,000 deduction for passive depreciation losses is allowed only for taxpayers with adjusted gross incomes of under $100,000. For each two dollars of income above $100,000, the maximum passive loss deduction is reduced by one dollar, so that taxpayers with adjusted incomes of $150,000 and over cannot use any passive depreciation losses to reduce taxes on ordinary income. The income range for phasing out use of the tax credits against ordinary income is $200,000 to $250,000, compared to $100,000 to $150,000 for depreciation losses.

Properties which benefit from the low income housing tax credit can apply depreciation against 100 percent of the basis of the property. This contrasts with the historic and old building rehabilitation credits, where the amount of the credit is deducted from adjusted basis before depreciation is applied. In a property using both the rehab credit and the low income housing tax credit, the amount of the rehab credit is deducted from basis before depreciation is applied.

THE ALTERNATIVE MINIMUM TAX CAN LIMIT THE USE OF THE LOW INCOME HOUSING TAX CREDIT

The alternative minimum tax (AMT) is a second method of determining tax liability that is imposed on wealthy taxpayers to limit the use of various tax shelters or preferences. It does this by adding back into the AMT taxable base various tax preference items that are not included in taxable income in the regular tax calculations, and by denying the use of certain credits and deductions that are used in the regular tax calculations to reduce tax liability.

Among the alternative minimum tax provisions in the 1986 law, tax credits for rental real estate activities cannot be used to reduce taxes, and the interest on most private activity tax-exempt bonds issued after August or September 1986 is a tax preference item subject to the tax. The low income housing tax credit is disallowed as a device to reduce tax liability under AMT.

The alternative minimum tax has a tax rate of 21 percent (formerly 20 percent), as compared to the new top tax rate of 28 percent in the regular income tax. However, before the AMT is applied, $40,000 of taxable income is exempted from the tax for joint returns, and $30,000 is exempted for individual returns.

However, this AMT exemption is phased out at a rate of 25 cents for each dollar of income over $150,000 for married couples, and over $112,500 for single persons. For married couples, the exemption at $250,000 income will be $15,000, and it is zero when minimum taxable income is $310,000 and above.

Corporations also face a similar alternative minimum tax, with a 20 percent AMT rate compared to the rate on individuals of 21 percent. A $40,000 exemption is also phased out between $150,000 and $310,000 income.

The AMT will have no effect on taxpayers investing in low income housing who use up to $8,250 in tax credits or $25,000 in passive losses to reduce taxes on ordinary income — unless the taxpayer has other tax preferences which bring the total above the $40,000 exemption. Each dollar of a tax credit is equal to $3.00 of tax preference income or deductions for taxpayers at the 33 percent marginal rate.

The alternative minimum tax can have a significant impact on upper income taxpayers using tax credits and/or depreciation deductions to reduce tax liability for significant amounts of passive income from other rental activity. Because of the $40,000 exemption, a large percentage of the income of taxpayers able to use the exemption has to be tax preference items before the AMT increases the individual taxpayer's liability.

Any credits or passive loss deductions that are not used because of the alternative minimum tax can be carried forward and used in subsequent years — if and when this is not precluded by the limitations on the uses of credits and losses under the regular tax and the alternative minimum tax provisions.

Passive losses arising from depreciation deductions for properties placed in service prior to enactment of the 1986 law do not benefit from any gradual phase-in or transition treatment under the AMT as they do under the regular transition provisions. Here again, this will only affect high income taxpayers with tax preference items that exceed the $40,000 or $30,000 AMT exemption.

LIMITS ON USE OF GENERAL BUSINESS CREDITS APPLY IN RARE INSTANCES

The low income housing tax credit is also affected by tax code provisions which limit the use of general business credits. All such credits in total can only be used to reduce taxes by a maximum of $25,000 plus 75 percent of tax liability over $25,000. Credits that are unused because of this provision can be carried back or carried forward to reduce taxes in other years. This provision is likely to have an impact on corporations and on high income taxpayers who might use the tax credits to reduce taxes on substantial amounts of passive income from rental real estate activity.

TIGHTER REQUIREMENTS FOR TAX EXEMPT FINANCING FOR LOW INCOME RENTAL HOUSING

The 1986 tax reform act made a number of important changes in the rules governing the use of tax-exempt bond financing by state and local government agencies for multi-family low income rental housing. Tax exempt financing provides below market mortgage interest rates because the interest earnings on the bonds are free of any income tax for most investors. The major change is the deeper targeting requirements, which parallel the minimum requirements for the use of the low income housing tax credit.

Under the prior law, multi-family rental housing could get tax-exempt financing if 20 percent of the units were occupied by tenants with incomes under 80 percent of the area median income, adjusted for household size. Under the new provisions, as under the tax credit program, an owner may choose whether the requirement will be 20 percent of the units occupied by tenants with incomes under 50 percent of the area median income, or 40 percent of the units occupied by tenants with incomes under 60 percent of the area median income. The income limits also will be adjusted for household size.

A special rule for New York City provides that only 25 percent (instead of 40 percent) of the units need be occupied by tenants under 60 percent of the area median income in order for a project to qualify for tax-exempt financing.

There is no requirement (as there is under the tax credit program) that the rents be a maximum of 30 percent of the maximum income for a particular household size. However, owners who voluntarily meet the rent limits under the tax credit program would automatically receive low income housing tax credits without needing an allocation from a housing credit agency.

The minimum compliance period for maintaining the required low income occupancy is 15 years. Low income occupancy must also be maintained while the loan is outstanding, but the loan can be repaid after 15 years. For the first time, the incomes of tenants now must be certified annually. Non-compliance occurs only when both: (a) a low income tenant's income exceeds 140 percent of the current income limit for new tenants for the applicable household size, and (b) the next vacant unit is rented to a non-low income tenant.

Owners can elect to set up a "deep rent skewed project" where the compliance income limit is 170 percent rather than 140 percent of the current income limit for new tenants. In such projects, 3 percent of all units must be occupied by tenants below 40 percent of the area median income if the project is serving tenants at the 50 percent of area median income level. This figure is 6 percent of all units if the project is serving tenants at the 60 percent of area median income level. Also, the rents charged for these units must not exceed both 30 percent of 40 percent of the area median income, and one-third of the average rent charged for comparable units in the project that are not occupied by low income tenants.

The total volume of multi-family rental housing financed by tax-exempt bonds is governed by a volume cap for each state ($50 per capita or a minimum of $150 million in 1988 and 1989) that also includes other private activity uses of tax exempt financing, including single family mortgage bonds.

The 1986 law for the first time subjected the interest earnings on newly issued private activity bonds to the alternative minimum tax (AMT). Bonds issued prior to the effective date of the 1986 Act are not subject to the AMT. Taxpayers with large amounts of sheltered income may have to pay some taxes on these bonds as a result of the alternative minimum tax. For this reason, the interest rates on these private activity bonds may be higher than the interest rates on other types of tax-exempt bonds.

Unlike the tax credits, any unused volume cap of private activity tax-exempt financing may be carried forward and used in one of the subsequent three years. Each state must first identify the specific uses for any bond volume that is carried forward.

OTHER TYPES OF TAX-EXEMPT BONDS CAN BE USED FOR HOUSING

The 1986 law permits state and local agencies to float bonds on behalf of 501(c)(3) non-profit organizations for rental housing purpose. These bonds would be outside the state volume limitation caps. However, such housing will not be able to use the tax credits. Non-profits do not have any tax liability that could be offset by tax credits, and a conversion to a limited partnership arrangement would contradict the requirement that the bonds be issued on behalf of a 501(c)(3) organization.

Qualified redevelopment bonds issued by local governments can be used to acquire and rehabilitate housing. Local government agencies either could continue to own the property or sell it to private owners at fair market value. These bonds would be subject to the state volume limitation caps, but would not be subject to the low income use requirements. Tax credits might be used for such projects after ownership is transferred to private owners.

HOUSING COOPERATIVES ARE NOW ELIGIBLE FOR MULTI-FAMILY TAX-EXEMPT FINANCING

Cooperatives now can be financed as a multi-family rental housing project with tax-exempt financing. The cooperative must be a limited equity cooperative, in which the resale price of any unit cannot exceed the original price, plus: cost of living adjustments; the cost of any improvements to the unit made by a previous occupant; and amortization payments which reduce the principal balance of the mortgage. However, residents of any co-op receiving tax-exempt financing cannot deduct any mortgage interest and property tax payments on their individual income tax returns.

Prior to the 1986 law, tax-exempt financing was only available to individual cooperative members to finance their individual units through single family mortgage revenue bonds. Now multi-family financing will make it easier to finance the development of new cooperatives and the rehabilitation of existing housing as cooperatives at favorable interest rates. These co-ops will have to meet the new low income targeting requirements for multi-family tax-exempt bonds.

THE HISTORIC STRUCTURES REHABILITATION TAX CREDIT, REDUCED IN SIZE, CAN BE USED WITH THE LOW INCOME HOUSING TAX CREDIT

The tax credit for the rehabilitation of historic structures is now 20 percent of certified rehabilitation expenditures, compared to a 25 percent credit under prior law. In addition, the adjusted basis of these properties will be reduced by the full amount of the 20 percent credit. The reduction in basis was one-half of the credit amount or 12.5 percent under the prior law.

If a property is eligible for tax credits under both the low income housing provisions and the historic structure provisions, the 20 percent historic tax credit is taken for the year in which the rehab work is completed. The 10-year low income housing tax credit is applied against the remaining 80 percent of eligible rehabilitation costs after deducting the 20 percent for the historic credit from basis, and against 100 percent of any acquisition costs.

The rehabilitation tax credit also applies to non-historic buildings constructed prior to 1936, where a 10 percent tax credit is provided. Residential properties are not eligible for this tax credit, however.

The historic and older building rehabilitation tax credits are covered by the same passive loss limitations as the low income housing tax credits (see below).

The historic rehabilitation tax credit only applies to rehabilitation and related expenditures. The expenditures must be at least $5,000 for the building, and be greater than the adjusted basis of the building at the time the rehabilitation work starts.

TRANSITION RULES PROVIDE LIMITED RELIEF FOR EXISTING LOW INCOME HOUSING PROJECTS

Existing low income housing projects, as well as rental housing generally, are negatively affected by the new passive losses limitations. Particularly for low income housing, both active owners and limited partner investors relied on depreciation allowances under prior tax codes to provide a reasonable return on their investments on an after-tax basis. The 1986 law now severely restricts the use of depreciation deductions to shelter other income from taxation.

A phase-in transition relief provision was included in the 1986 law to help cushion the impact of the passive losses provisions on all types of property. A decreasing percentage of disallowed passive losses can be deducted against active income over the next four years. In 1987, 65 percent of otherwise disallowed passive loss deductions can be deducted against other income. In 1988, 40 percent can be deducted. In 1989, the percentage is 20 percent, and in 1990 it is 10 percent. In 1991, the passive losses limitations are 100 percent effective without exception.

All remaining disallowed passive losses can be carried forward for use against ordinary income in the year in which the property interest is sold, when they will be subject to the regular limitations on the use of carryover losses.

SPECIAL TRANSITION RELIEF FOR LOW INCOME HOUSING PROJECTS WITH OBLIGATED INVESTOR PAY-INS

Additional special transition relief is provided for low income housing projects where investors were obligated to make additional investment payments to the project as of August 16, 1986. This special relief applies only if investors owed at least 50 percent of their original obligation after 1986 (35 percent for certain rural housing projects). There is no special relief if the obligated future investment pay-ins are less than these amounts.

The special relief provided is that all depreciation deductions and passive losses can be taken without limitation against ordinary income during the specified relief period. The new alternative minimum tax provisions also do not apply during the special relief period. The relief period extends through one additional year after the year in which the last investment payment is made, or six years after the year of the initial investment payment, whichever period is <u>shorter</u>.

This special relief is limited to projects either completed or subject to a binding contract for construction or acquisition on August 16, 1986 and placed in service by the end of 1988. Projects where investors made their initial payments prior to 1984 are excluded. Projects which utilize this special transition relief are not eligible for the low income housing tax credits.

The special relief also applies to projects placed in service after August 16, 1986, if an investor was obligated on December 31, 1986 to make more payments, and there was a contract to construct or acquire the project as of August 16, 1986.

4

WILL THE TAX CREDIT WORK? USING PRO FORMA BUDGETS TO ANALYZE THE FEASIBILITY OF DEVELOPMENT WITH THE LOW INCOME HOUSING TAX CREDIT

GENERAL EXPLANATION AND ASSUMPTIONS USED

This chapter is an effort to gauge the workability of the low income housing tax credits by examining a variety of different types and cost of housing development at various area median income levels representative of the range of income levels in metropolitan areas across the country. It examines the financial and economic aspects of carrying out development, reducing them to the bottom line to determine how much rent must be charged to cover all costs and bring about the development of housing.

This analysis of feasibility of the tax credit program examines the economics of development on the basis of individual housing units in a project, rather than analyzing hypothetical projects as a whole. This is done for ease of understanding and to allow widespread application of the findings of the analysis. This assumes that individual projects are either 100 percent for low income use, or if a mixed income or mixed use project is considered, that the non-low income units or space are feasible based on independent financial considerations without aid from any of the tax credits or other benefits associated with the low income units. In the cases where tax-exempt financing is provided, the non-low income housing units would benefit from the lower interest rates available to the entire project, and the dollar savings to these units from tax-exempt financing are estimated.

The types of individual units chosen as typical for this analysis are:

1. New construction costing $55,000 per unit;
2. Rehabilitation costing $38,500 per unit;
3. Rehabilitation costing $29,000 per unit; and
4. Acquisition with minor rehabilitation with a total cost of $20,000 per unit.

The first three unit types (new construction and rehabilitation) are analyzed in two ways: first with conventional or non-tax-exempt financing, and then with tax-exempt financing. The acquisition with minor rehabilitation is analyzed using only conventional financing, since it would be ineligible for tax-exempt financing because rehabilitation is less than 15 percent of total costs.

Each analysis, seven in all, is presented on a separate table (Tables 8 through 14). Each analysis looks at feasibility at four different levels of area median income with the qualifying rent level set at 50 percent of area median income. The entire analysis is then repeated with the qualifying rent level set at 60 percent of area median income. The four area median income levels, which represent the range of median income levels in major metropolitan areas, are $36,500, $32,000, $27,500, and $23,000.

The per unit costs assume an overall project size of between 50 and 200 units. For projects much smaller or larger than this, per unit costs can vary considerably, particularly with regard to services and fees connected with financing. The analysis is based on a two-bedroom unit in a major metropolitan area.

This analysis assumes that the housing is feasible on other grounds as well. The feasibility of any particular project depends on the market for rental housing in the local area. While rents may qualify for tax credits, they may be considerably higher than rents for comparable units in the immediate area. Weak demand or an oversupply of units could be a problem. Additionally, qualifying rents for the low income units are based on a payment of 30 percent of income at the very top of the income eligibility range. This means that almost all of the occupants will be paying considerably more than 30 percent of their income for rent and utilities. This may create significant hardships for certain occupants, and problems in rent collection for the owners. This contrasts with the section 8 and public housing programs, where rents are pegged at 30 percent of the adjusted income of each eligible tenant.

Most important, the many assumptions used in this pro forma analysis are hypothetical, based in part on generally available information and in part on the author's own experience. The particular situation regarding an actual project in a particular location can vary very substantially from the underlying assumptions here. Readers should be wary of this fact, and should substitute their own facts or assumptions in applying this analysis to their own situation.

A blank form for conducting this type of analysis is provided (Table 15) to enable the reader to do an independent investigation of the feasibility of using the tax credit program. Follow the line-by-line explanations, and substitute local information and experience where it is available.

LINE-BY-LINE EXPLANATION AND ASSUMPTIONS FOR ACCOMPANYING TABLES

Line 1. For projects other than new construction, the building represents 90 percent of acquisition costs, and the underlying land is valued at 10 percent of acquisition costs. The land is not subject to depreciation and therefore is not eligible for tax credits.

Line 2. Includes any developer's fee or profit taken in the development phase of the project.

Lines 1 and 2. All associated "soft" costs are included in either acquisition or construction costs as appropriate.

Line 4(b). The tax credit percentage for rehab or new construction costs is 9 percent if there are no federal subsidies or tax-exempt financing involved with these costs, or 4 percent if there are federal subsidies or tax-exempt financing.

Line 5. Depreciation of total development costs, less the underlying land value, is taken over 27.5 years. The yearly depreciation allowance is 3.636 percent of development costs.

Line 6. This figure is the amount of money generated for the project by the tax credits. It is the estimated net proceeds to the project of investor contributions raised through syndication (i.e, the sale to limited partners of the value of the tax credits). It assumes that the project is awarded all of the tax credits to which it is eligible. It also assumes that investors will make one lump sum contribution during the project's development phase, for which they will receive a fixed allocated amount of tax credits each year for 10 years. The amount of net proceeds is based on providing to the limited partner investors a yearly return of 12 percent after taxes of the amount of equity remaining in the project each year. Ten percent of total proceeds is then subtracted to pay for the estimated costs associated with carrying out the syndication process.

The rate of return to investors, the cost of carrying out the syndication, and the timing of investor payments can vary considerably in actual practice. Based on the assumptions used here, the tax credit contribution to development costs is equal to 5.085 times line 4(c), the total annual tax credit amount.

Line 7. A dollar of depreciation allowance is valued at 34 cents, based on the 34 percent federal income tax rate for corporations. For many individual investors, the marginal tax rate is the federal 33 percent rate (including the 5 percent surcharge which applies to a range of upper income levels) plus any applicable tax rate for state and local income taxes. It is assumed that the investors are corporations or are individuals with passive income who will be able to use the depreciation deductions. The total contribution to the project is based on selling to limited partners the value of depreciation for 15 years, providing a 12 percent return on equity after taxes, and a cost of syndication of 10 percent of the money raised. Based on this formula, the depreciation contribution is 7.58 percent of total development costs less the value of the land.

Line 9, loan amortization. Assumes a loan of 80 percent of remaining development costs, with a fixed 30-year term and uniform amortization of principal and interest. For conventional or non-tax-exempt financing, the interest rate is 10.5 percent, which provides an amortization constant of .1105. For tax-exempt financing, the interest rate is 9 percent on a net basis (factoring in the additional fees in tax-exempt financing). This results in an amortization constant of .0973.

Line 10, return on equity, before taxes. Assumes owner's equity of 20 percent of remaining development costs, after subtracting the contribution of the credits and depreciation allowance. This is general partner equity over and above limited partner investor payments for purchasing the tax benefits.

The return on invested equity is 10 percent in the initial year. This cash flow return is likely to increase with modest inflation in rents and operating costs, as amortization of development costs is a fixed expense for 30 years. Additional return on equity may come from a gain on any sale of the property.

In a non-profit development, amortization of additional mortgage borrowing would replace the return on equity. The amount of rent required to cover the extra amortization would not be much different from the rent amount required to provide a return on equity in the initial year. However, rent increases would probably be smaller in future years in a non-profit development.

Lines 11 and 13, total operating costs and tenant-paid utility costs are typical costs based on the author's experience. Operating costs are estimated to be higher for a rehabilitated property than for new construction. Here also, these costs may vary substantially based on the geographic location of a project.

Lines 14 and 15. The heart of this exercise is the difference between the economic gross rent, including tenant-paid utilities, and the qualifying rent levels required to qualify for the tax credits at four different levels of area median income. This analysis demonstrates the importance of the median income in the project area.

Typical income levels in metropolitan areas have been selected. Table 16 shows the median income data used in 1989 to determine tax credit eligibility in major metropolitan areas and the rural portions of selected states. The highest income level used is 59 percent greater than the lowest income level used.

A household size of 3.5 persons is used, since both 3– and 4–person households could occupy a two–bedroom unit. Based on HUD's adjustment factors, the maximum income level for this household size is 95 percent of either the 50 percent or the 60 percent level of area median income. These are the optional qualifying rent and income levels specified in the law that can be chosen by the project owner.

If the 50 percent of area median income is chosen as the targeted rent and income level, a project must have a minimum of 20 percent qualified low income units. If the 60 percent of income level is chosen, a minimum of 40 percent of the units must be qualified low income units.

For line 15 and subsequent lines, each column represents geographic areas with the area median income shown at the top of the column.

Line 16, is line 14 minus line 15. This is the amount by which the economic gross rents based on all costs and financing arrangements exceed the maximum qualifying rent level. This is the gap which must be closed if the project is to be feasible.

Line 17 is the amount of one–time development assistance that would be needed to close the gap in rents shown on line 16. Aid in some form of grant or loan would reduce the amount of the mortgage in line 9 so that the monthly mortgage loan payment is reduced by the amount of the gap in rents. With conventional financing at 10.5 percent and an amortization constant of .1105, the required development aid is 108.6 times the amount of the gap in line 16 (12 divided by .1105). For tax–exempt financing at 9 percent with an amortization constant of .0973, the required development aid is 123.3 times the amount of the gap (12 divided by .0973). The lower the interest rate, the more dollars that must be subtracted from the loan to produce a fixed amount of savings in monthly loan amortization.

The form of the assistance that is received to close the gap is very important. Certain types of aid will lead to the loss of some tax credits, requiring even additional aid to close the gap between the economic and qualifying rent levels. (This subject is also discussed in Chapters 2 and 5.) Outright grants or federal subsidies for new construction or rehabilitation work lead directly to the loss of some tax credits.

If aid in the form of a grant is used for new construction or rehabilitation costs eligible to a 9 percent credit, additional grant aid of over 80 percent of the initial grant amount would be needed to compensate for the loss in tax credits generated by both the initial grant and the additional grant. (This is based on the earlier assumption that each dollar of tax credit earned for 10 years has a net present value to the project of $5.08 after syndication.) Governmental below–market loans used for property acquisition will not reduce the amount of tax credits.

Under the Original Issue Discount rules in the tax code, below–market rate loans and deferred loans from state or local government funds will not result in reduced tax credits. Similar aid from non-government sources would lead to some reductions in tax credits because the project's adjusted basis would be reduced.

The most favorable forms of aid would appear to be two types:
1) a loan from a state or local government source (not pass-through federal aid) in the form of a fully deferred loan at a below-market interest rate, where the payment of all principal and all interest is deferred for a period of 15 years or more. Net appreciation in the value of the property in a feasible project should exceed the total of deferred payments, permitting refinancing to pay off the accrued debt when it comes due;
2) a grant to establish an independent interest-bearing fund administered by a trustee and established in the form of an annuity. Subsidy payments would be sent from the fund to the project each month for 15 years to cover the gap.

Line 18 is the reduction in the gap arising from the amount by which rent increases exceed operating cost increases for the project over a five-year period. This assumes that both rents and operating costs will increase by 3 percent per year due to inflation. Since loan amortization and the required return on equity are fixed dollar amounts for 30 years, rent levels are significantly higher than the variable operating costs for a project. If both rents and variable costs increase by the same percentage amount, the dollar amount of the rent increase will be significantly higher than the dollar amount of the increase in project costs after a number of years. This device, sometimes described as the "trending" of rents and operating costs, is often used in real estate feasibility analysis if a project cannot cover the bottom line of costs in its first year of operation.

Funds must be available over this five-year period to absorb operating deficits equal to the amount of projected gain from trending. For profit-motivated owners, the built-in 10 percent return on equity can be used, as it is larger than the projected gains. Owners should be willing to sacrifice part of their equity returns in the initial years to have a profitable project that can take advantage of potential "trending" in subsequent years, plus the other profit sources provided by the project.

Non-profits with additional fixed debt in lieu of equity may need reserves to cover these losses, but they can be repaid by the trending of rents in future years.

There should be few problems in increasing rents by a modest 3 percent a year for five years, except perhaps in extremely distressed cities where rent levels are not increasing and where the area median income remains fairly constant.

If rents are set at the maximum qualifying rent level, they can only increase under the tax credit program at a rate not more than the rate of increase in the median income for the area. On a national basis from 1979 through 1988, median income increased at an average rate of 5.5 percent per year.

Line 19 is line 16 minus line 18, and is the remaining gap after five years of "trending".

Line 20 is the amount of development assistance needed to close the remaining gap, calculated in the same manner as line 17.

A. The rent reduction from the use of tax credits and other tax benefits (upper left corner of second page of each table) is equal to the monthly payment needed to amortize the total of the tax credit contribution on line 6 and the depreciation contribution on line 7, using the loan terms described on line 9. Where tax-exempt financing is involved, the tax-related rent reduction also includes the difference between amortizing the total loan amount using the tax-exempt financing terms and using the conventional financing terms as shown on line 9.

TABLE 8

PRO FORMA BUDGETS ANALYZING THE FEASIBILITY OF THE TAX CREDITS

NEW CONSTRUCTION - $55,000 COST PER UNIT

CONVENTIONAL FINANCING

	Item	Amount	Per month
1.	Property acquisition costs	$ 5,000	
2.	Rehabilitation or new construction costs	50,000	
3.	Total development costs (1+2)	55,000	
4.	Annual tax credit eligible amount:		
	a. building acquisition: 4% of 0	0	
	b. rehab or new construct: 9% of $50,000	4,500	
	c. TOTAL (a+b)	4,500	
5.	Annual depreciation allowance	1,818	
6.	Tax credit contribution to development costs: net of syndication costs (5.085 x 4(c))	22,880	
7.	Depreciation contribution to development costs: net of syndication costs	3,790	
8.	Development costs to be financed (3-(6+7))	28,330	
9.	Loan amortization: 80% of line 8, or $22,660 @ 10.5%, 30 yrs.(.1105)	2,504/yr.	$ 209
10.	Equity return: 10% year on $5,670	567/yr.	47
11.	Total operating costs		200
12.	Economic net rent: cost-based (9+10+11)		456
13.	Tenant-paid utility costs		35
14.	Economic gross rent: cost-based (12+13)		491

TABLE 8 (cont.)

A. Rent reduction from use of tax credits & other tax benefits: $241 Month	Economic Gross Rent Compared to Qualifying Rent Level at							
	50% OF MEDIAN INCOME & Area Median Income of				60% OF MEDIAN INCOME & Area Median Income of			
	$36,500	$32,000	$27,500	$23,000	$36,500	$32,000	$27,500	$23,000
Economic Gross Rent: $491								
15. Qualifying tax credit rent level: 3.5 person average size household	433	380	327	273	520	456	392	328
16. Gap or excess of economic gross rent	58	111	164	218	0	35	99	163
17. Development aid needed to eliminate gap in first year	6,300	12,050	17,810	23,675	-	3,800	10,750	17,700
18. Reduction in gap after 5 years of rent and operating cost increases of 3 percent per year	31	23	15	6	N.A.	35	25	15
19. Remaining gap or excess of economic gross rent after 5 years	27	88	149	212	0	0	74	148
20. Development aid needed to eliminate remaining gap after 5 years	2,990	9,740	16,490	23,470	-	-	8,190	16,380

N.A. - Not applicable

TABLE 9

PRO FORMA BUDGETS ANALYZING THE FEASIBILITY OF THE TAX CREDITS

Rehabilitation - $38,500 Cost Per Unit

Conventional Financing

		Per month
1. Property acquisition costs	$ 21,000	
2. Rehabilitation or new construction costs	17,500	
3. Total development costs (1+2)	38,500	
4. Annual tax credit eligible amount:		
a. building acquisition: 4% of $18,900	756	
b. rehab or new construct: 9% of $17,500	1,575	
c. TOTAL (a+b)	2,331	
5. Annual depreciation allowance	1,320	
6. Tax credit contribution to development costs: net of syndication costs (5.085 x 4(c))	11,850	
7. Depreciation contribution to development costs: net of syndication costs	2,760	
8. Development costs to be financed (3-(6+7))	23,890	
9. Loan amortization: 80% of line 8, or $19,110 @ 10.5%, 30 yrs.(.1105)	2,112/yr.	$ 176
10. Equity return: 10% year on $4,780	478/yr.	40
11. Total operating costs		225
12. Economic net rent: cost-based (9+10+11)		441
13. Tenant-paid utility costs		35
14. Economic gross rent: cost-based (12+13)		476

TABLE 9 (cont.)

A. Rent reduction from use of tax credits & other tax benefits: $132 Month	Economic Gross Rent Compared to Qualifying Rent Level at							
	50% OF MEDIAN INCOME & Area Median Income of				60% OF MEDIAN INCOME & Area Median Income of			
	$36,500	$32,000	$27,500	$23,000	$36,500	$32,000	$27,500	$23,000
Economic Gross Rent: $476								
15. Qualifying tax credit rent level: 3.5 person average size household	433	380	327	273	520	456	392	328
16. Gap or excess of economic gross rent	43	96	149	203	0	20	84	148
17. Development aid needed to eliminate gap in first year	4,670	10,425	16,160	22,050	-	2,170	9,120	16,070
18. Reduction in gap after 5 years of rent and operating cost increases of 3 percent per year	28	20	11	2	N.A.	32	21	11
19. Remaining gap or excess of economic gross rent after 5 years	15	76	138	201	0	0	63	137
20. Development aid needed to eliminate remaining gap after 5 years	1,660	8,410	15,280	22,250	-	-	6,970	15,170

N.A. - not applicable

TABLE 10

PRO FORMA BUDGETS ANALYZING THE FEASIBILITY OF THE TAX CREDITS

Rehabilitation - $29,000 Cost per Unit

Conventional Financing

Item	Amount	Per month
1. Property acquisition costs	$ 15,000	
2. Rehabilitation or new construction costs	14,000	
3. Total development costs (1+2)	29,000	
4. Annual tax credit eligible amount:		
a. building acquisition: 4% of $13,500	540	
b. rehab or new construct: 9% of $14,000	1,260	
c. TOTAL (a+b)	1,800	
5. Annual depreciation allowance	1,000	
6. Tax credit contribution to development costs: net of syndication costs (5.085 x 4(c))	9,150	
7. Depreciation contribution to development costs: net of syndication costs	2,080	
8. Development costs to be financed (3-(6+7))	17,770	
9. Loan amortization: 80% of line 8, or $14,220 @ 10.5%, 30 yrs.(.1105)	1,570/yr.	$ 131
10. Equity return: 10% year on $3,550	355/yr.	30
11. Total operating costs		225
12. Economic net rent: cost-based (9+10+11)		386
13. Tenant-paid utility costs		35
14. Economic gross rent: cost-based (12+13)		421

TABLE 10 (cont.)

A. Rent reduction from use of tax credits & other tax benefits: $101 Month	Economic Gross Rent Compared to Qualifying Rent Level at							
	50% OF MEDIAN INCOME & Area Median Income of				60% OF MEDIAN INCOME & Area Median Income of			
	$36,500	$32,000	$27,500	$23,000	$36,500	$32,000	$27,500	$23,000
Economic Gross Rent: $421								
15. Qualifying tax credit rent level: 3.5 person average size household	433	380	327	273	520	456	392	328
16. Gap or excess of economic gross rent	0	41	94	148	0	0	29	93
17. Development aid needed to eliminate gap in first year	-	4,450	10,210	16,070	-	-	3,150	10,100
18. Reduction in gap after 5 years of rent and operating cost increases of 3 percent per year	N.A.	20	11	2	N.A.	N.A.	21	11
19. Remaining gap or excess of economic gross rent after 5 years	0	21	83	146	0	0	8	82
20. Development aid needed to eliminate remaining gap after 5 years	-	2,325	9,190	16,160	-	-	890	9,080

N.A. - not applicable

TABLE 11

PRO FORMA BUDGETS ANALYZING THE FEASIBILITY OF THE TAX CREDITS

Acquisition with Minor Rehabilitation - $20,000 Cost per Unit

Conventional Financing

Item	Amount	Per month
1. Property acquisition costs	$ 19,000	
2. Rehabilitation or new construction costs	1,000	
3. Total development costs (1+2)	20,000	
4. Annual tax credit eligible amount:		
a. building acquisition: 4% of $18,100	724	
b. rehab or new construct: - % of -	-	
c. TOTAL (a+b)	724	
5. Annual depreciation allowance	658	
6. Tax credit contribution to development costs: net of syndication costs (5.085 x 4(c))	3,680	
7. Depreciation contribution to development costs: net of syndication costs	1,370	
8. Development costs to be financed (3-(6+7))	14,950	
9. Loan amortization: 80% of line 8, or $11,960 @ 10.5%,30yrs.(.1105)	1,320/yr.	$ 110
10. Equity return: 10% year on $2,990	299/yr.	25
11. Total operating costs		225
12. Economic net rent: cost-based (9+10+11)		355
13. Tenant-paid utility costs		35
14. Economic gross rent: cost-based (12+13)		390

TABLE 11 (cont.)

A. Rent reduction from use of tax credits & other tax benefits: $46 Month	Economic Gross Rent Compared to Qualifying Rent Level at							
	50% OF MEDIAN INCOME & Area Median Income of				60% OF MEDIAN INCOME & Area Median Income of			
	$36,500	$32,000	$27,500	$23,000	$36,500	$32,000	$27,500	$23,000
Economic Gross Rent: $390								
15. Qualifying tax credit rent level: 3.5 person average size household	433	380	327	273	520	456	392	328
16. Gap or excess of economic gross rent	0	10	63	117	0	0	0	62
17. Development aid needed to eliminate gap in first year	-	1,090	6,840	12,710	-	-	-	6,730
18. Reduction in gap after 5 years of rent and operating cost increases of 3 percent per year	N.A.	20	11	2	N.A.	N.A.	N.A.	11
19. Remaining gap or excess of economic gross rent after 5 years	0	0	52	115	0	0	0	51
20. Development aid needed to eliminate remaining gap after 5 years	-	-	5,760	12,730	-	-	-	5,650

N.A. - not applicable

TABLE 12

PRO FORMA BUDGETS ANALYZING THE FEASIBILITY OF THE TAX CREDITS

New Construction – $55,000 Cost per Unit

Tax-Exempt Financing

Item	Amount		Per month
1. Property acquisition costs	5,000		
2. Rehabilitation or new construction costs	50,000		
3. Total development costs (1+2)	55,000		
4. Annual tax credit eligible amount:			
a. building acquisition: 4% of –	–		
b. rehab or new construct: 4% of $50,000	2,000		
c. TOTAL (a+b)	2,000		
5. Annual depreciation allowance	1,818		
6. Tax credit contribution to development costs: net of syndication costs (5.085 x 4(c))	10,170		
7. Depreciation contribution to development costs: net of syndication costs	3,790		
8. Development costs to be financed (3-(6+7))	41,040		
9. Loan amortization: 80% of line 8, or $32,830 @ 9%, 30yrs.(.0973)		3,194/yr.	$ 266
10. Equity return: 10% year on $8,210		821/yr.	68
11. Total operating costs			200
12. Economic net rent: cost-based (9+10+11)			534
13. Tenant-paid utility costs			35
14. Economic gross rent: cost-based (12+13)			569

TABLE 12 (cont.)

A. Rent reduction from use of tax credits & other tax benefits: $163 Month	Economic Gross Rent Compared to Qualifying Rent Level at: 50% OF MEDIAN INCOME & Area Median Income of				60% OF MEDIAN INCOME & Area Median Income of			
	$36,500	$32,000	$27,500	$23,000	$36,500	$32,000	$27,500	$23,000
Economic Gross Rent: $569								
15. Qualifying tax credit rent level: 3.5 person average size household	433	380	327	273	520	456	392	328
16. Gap or excess of economic gross rent	136	189	242	296	49	113	177	241
17. Development aid needed to eliminate gap in first year	16,770	23,300	29,840	36,500	6,040	13,930	21,825	29,720
18. Reduction in gap after 5 years of rent and operating cost increases of 3 percent per year	31	23	15	6	47	35	25	15
19. Remaining gap or excess of economic gross rent after 5 years	105	166	227	290	2	78	152	226
20. Development aid needed to eliminate remaining gap after 5 years	12,950	20,470	27,990	35,760	250	9,620	18,740	27,870

Note: Use of tax-exempt financing results in rent reduction of $48 per month for any non-low income units in the development. Gross rent on these units would be $684 per month instead of $732.

TABLE 13

PRO FORMA BUDGETS ANALYZING THE FEASIBILITY OF THE TAX CREDITS

Rehabilitation - $38,500 Cost per Unit

Tax-Exempt Financing

Item	Amount	Per month
1. Property acquisition costs	$ 21,000	
2. Rehabilitation or new construction costs	17,500	
3. Total development costs (1+2)	38,500	
4. Annual tax credit eligible amount:		
a. building acquisition: 4% of $18,900	756	
b. rehab or new construct: 4% of $17,500	700	
c. TOTAL (a+b)	1,456	
5. Annual depreciation allowance	1,320	
6. Tax credit contribution to development costs: net of syndication costs (5.085 x 4(c))	7,400	
7. Depreciation contribution to development costs: net of syndication costs	2,760	
8. Development costs to be financed (3-(6+7))	28,340	
9. Loan amortization: $22,670 @ 9%, 30yrs.(.0973)	2,206/yr.	$ 184
10. Equity return: 10% year on $5,670	567/yr.	47
11. Total operating costs		225
12. Economic net rent: cost-based (9+10+11)		456
13. Tenant-paid utility costs		35
14. Economic gross rent: cost-based (12+13)		491

TABLE 13 (cont.)

A. Rent reduction from use of tax credits & other tax benefits: $117 Month	Economic Gross Rent Compared to Qualifying Rent Level at							
	50% OF MEDIAN INCOME & Area Median Income of				60% OF MEDIAN INCOME & Area Median Income of			
	$36,500	$32,000	$27,500	$23,000	$36,500	$32,000	$27,500	$23,000
Economic Gross Rent: $491								
15. Qualifying tax credit rent level: 3.5 person average size household	433	380	327	273	520	456	392	328
16. Gap or excess of economic gross rent	58	111	164	218	0	35	99	163
17. Development aid needed to eliminate gap in first year	7,150	13,690	20,220	26,880	-	4,320	12,210	20,100
18. Reduction in gap after 5 years of rent and operating cost increases of 3 percent per year	28	20	11	2	N.A.	32	21	11
19. Remaining gap or excess of economic gross rent after 5 years	30	91	153	216	0	3	78	152
20. Development aid needed to eliminate remaining gap after 5 years	3,700	11,220	18,860	26,630	-	370	9,620	18,740

Note: Use of tax-exempt financing results in rent reduction of $34 per month for any non-low income units in the development. Gross rents on these units would be $574 per month instead of $608.

TABLE 14

PRO FORMA BUDGETS ANALYZING THE FEASIBILITY OF THE TAX CREDITS

Rehabilitation - $29,000 Cost per Unit

Tax-Exempt Financing

		Per month
1. Property acquisition costs	$ 15,000	
2. Rehabilitation or new construction costs	14,000	
3. Total development costs (1+2)	29,000	
4. Annual tax credit eligible amount:		
a. building acquisition: 4% of $13,500	540	
b. rehab or new construct: 4% of $14,000	560	
c. TOTAL (a+b)	1,100	
5. Annual depreciation allowance	1,000	
6. Tax credit contribution to development costs: net of syndication costs (5.085 x 4(c))	5,590	
7. Depreciation contribution to development costs: net of syndication costs	2,080	
8. Development costs to be financed (3-(6+7))	21,330	
9. Loan amortization: 80% of line 8, or $17,060 @ 9%, 30yrs.(.0973)	1,660/yr.	$ 138
10. Equity return: 10% year on $4,270	427/yr.	36
11. Total operating costs		225
12. Economic net rent: cost-based (9+10+11)		399
13. Tenant-paid utility costs		35
14. Economic gross rent: cost-based (12+13)		434

TABLE 14 (cont.)

A. Rent reduction from use of tax credits & other tax benefits: $88 Month	Economic Gross Rent Compared to Qualifying Rent Level at							
	50% OF MEDIAN INCOME & Area Median Income of				60% OF MEDIAN INCOME & Area Median Income of			
	$36,500	$32,000	$27,500	$23,000	$36,500	$32,000	$27,500	$23,000
Economic Gross Rent: $434								
15. Qualifying tax credit rent level: 3.5 person average size household	433	380	327	273	520	456	392	328
16. Gap or excess of economic gross rent	1	54	107	161	0	0	42	106
17. Development aid needed to eliminate gap in first year	123	6,660	13,190	19,850	-	-	5,180	13,070
18. Reduction in gap after 5 years of rent and operating cost increases of 3 percent per year	28	20	11	2	N.A.	N.A.	21	11
19. Remaining gap or excess of economic gross rent after 5 years	0	34	96	159	0	0	21	95
20. Development aid needed to eliminate remaining gap after 5 years	-	4,190	11,840	19,600	-	-	2,590	11,710

Note: Use of tax-exempt financing results in rent reduction of $26 per month for any non-low income units in the development. Gross rents on these units would be $496 per month instead of $522.

TABLE 15

BLANK PRO FORMA BUDGET FORM FOR ANALYZING THE FEASIBILITY OF THE TAX CREDITS

		Per Month		Per Month
1. Property acquisition costs	______		______	
2. Rehabilitation or new construction costs	______		______	
3. Total development costs (1+2)	______		______	
4. Annual tax credit eligible amount:				
a. building acquisition:____% of______	______		______	
b. rehab or new construct: ___% of ______	______		______	
c. TOTAL (a+b)	______		______	
5. Annual depreciation allowance	______		______	
6. Tax credit contribution to development costs: net of syndication costs (5.085 x 4(c))	______		______	
7. Depreciation contribution to development costs: net of syndication costs	______		______	
8. Development costs to be financed (3-(6+7))	______		______	
9. Loan amortization: ____________	______yr.	______	______yr.	______
10. Equity return: 10% year on ____________	______yr.	______	______yr.	______
11. Total operating costs		______		
12. Economic net rent: cost-based (9+10+11)		______		______
13. Tenant-paid utility costs		______		______
14. Economic gross rent: cost-based (12+13)		______		______

TABLE 15 (cont.)

A. Rent reduction from use of tax credits & other tax benefits: $ ____ Month	Economic Gross Rent Compared to Qualifying Rent Level at 50% OF MEDIAN INCOME & Area Median Income of	60% OF MEDIAN INCOME & Area Median Income of
15. Qualifying tax credit rent level: 3.5 person average size household		
16. Gap or excess of economic gross rent		
17. Development aid needed to eliminate gap in first year		
18. Reduction in gap after 5 years of rent and operating cost increases of 3 percent per year		
19. Remaining gap or excess of economic gross rent after 5 years		
20. Development aid needed to eliminate remaining gap after 5 years		

TABLE 16

ESTIMATED MEDIAN INCOMES FOR DETERMINING TAX CREDIT ELIGIBILITY IN 1989 IN SELECTED MAJOR METROPOLITAN AREAS AND RURAL AREAS IN SELECTED STATES

Metropolitan Area	FY 1989 Area Median Income for Tax Credit Eligibility1/	Rural Areas in Selected States: Rural Balance Outside Metropolitan Areas	FY 1989 Area Median Income for Tax Credit Eligibility2/
Atlanta, Ga.	$ 38,900	Alabama	$ 22,200
Baltimore, Md.	37,700	Arizona	23,600
Boston, Mass.	46,9001/	California	28,500
Chicago, Il.	41,700	Colorado	26,700
Cincinnati, Ohio	35,500	Florida	25,000
Cleveland, Ohio	36,700	Georgia	25,900
Dallas, Tex.	39,700	Illinois	30,600
Denver, Colo.	39,500	Iowa	28,000
Detroit, Mich.	39,900	Kansas	28,200
Honolulu, Ha.	39,100	Louisiana	23,400
Houston, Tex.	38,4001/	Maine	28,400
Indianapolis, Ind.	35,100	Maryland	31,300
Jacksonville, Fla.	32,000	Massachusetts	33,900
Kansas City, Mo.	37,000	Michigan	28,000
Los Angeles, Cal.	39,9001/	Minnesota	27,000
Memphis, Tenn.	29,300	Missouri	23,500
Miami, Fla.	33,1001/	New York	27,700
Milwaukee, Wis.	38,100	North Carolina	26,100
Minneapolis, Minn.	42,300	Ohio	30,400
New Orleans, La.	32,600	Oregon	28,100
New York City, N.Y.	33,800	Pennsylvania	27,800
Philadelphia, Pa.	36,500	Tennessee	22,700
Phoenix, Ariz.	33,100	Texas	25,500
Pittsburgh, Pa.	32,700	Utah	29,700
St. Louis, Mo.	37,200	Vermont	29,700
San Antonio, Tex.	30,000	Virginia	28,500
San Diego, Cal.	37,8001/	Washington	28,500
San Francisco, Cal.	49,5001/	Wisconsin	28,600
Seattle, Wash.	39,800		
Tampa, Fla.	29,600		
Washington, D.C.	51,000		

1/ Median income for these metropolitan areas is the adjusted median used by HUD for determining eligibility of very low income families for the Section 8 housing program. Figure shown is twice the HUD income level for a 4-person household, which in other cities is 50 percent of the area median income. HUD policy is to make special adjustments to reflect very high and very low housing costs relative to income in the area.

2/ Tax credit eligibility is based on the higher of (a) the median income in the individual county or metropolitan area, or (b) the state- wide rural or non-metropolitan median income, as shown here.

Source: U.S. Dept. of Housing & Urban Development, Division of Economic Market Analysis, Office of Economic Affairs

CONCLUSIONS ON FEASIBILITY: A HIGHLY QUALIFIED "YES" IN MANY BUT NOT ALL SITUATIONS

Tables 17 and 18 summarize the findings on feasibilty from the various scenarios of unit type, cost, and financing presented in the tables 8 through 14. Table 17 depicts resulting rent levels with and without tax credits and tax-exempt financing. The tax credits and other tax related benefits in the 1986 tax returns fact result in monthly rent savings ranging from $46 to $241 per month. The resulting rents with tax credits and conventional financing, the lowest cost scenario, range from $390 to $491 per month for various types of development where unit costs range from $20, 000 to $55,000.

In all the cases analyzed, conventional financing results in lower rents for the low income units than tax-exempt financing. This is because the 9 percent credit for new construction or rehabilitation work is worth more than the typical tax-exempt financing with the 4 percent credit. However, tax-exempt financing provides savings on any non-low income units (those without tax credits) in a project ranging from $26 to $48 per month. For the $29,000 per unit rehab project, tax-exempt financing costs $13 more a unit for the low income units, but saves $26 a unit for the non-low income units. Therefore, a mixed income development at this cost level should probably use tax-exempt financing.

TABLE 17

ESTIMATED RENTS FOR LOW INCOME UNITS USING TAX CREDITS WITH VARIOUS TYPES AND COSTS OF DEVELOPMENT AND TYPES OF FINANCING

		Monthly Gross Rent With:			
		Conventional Financing		Tax-Exempt Financing	
Type of Development	Development Costs Per Unit	No Tax Credits	Tax Credits	No Tax Credits	Tax Credits
New Construction	$ 55,000	$ 732	$ 491	$ 684	$ 569
Rehabilitation	38,500	608	476	574	491
Rehabilitation	29,000	522	421	496	434
Acquisition	20,000	436	390	N.A.	N.A.

N.A. - not applicable

Note: See the underlying assumptions regarding project financing and operating costs. Actual experience in any particular location may differ substantially from the underlying assumptions.

All projects in areas at the highest median income level ($36,500) were feasible without additional development assistance when rents are set at 60 percent of median income, except for new construction with tax-exempt financing. At the 50 percent of median income rent level, the projects were generally feasible with five years of trending of rents and variable costs, if additional development assistance of under $5,000 per unit could be obtained. Projects were rejected as not feasible if more than $10,000 per unit in grant aid was required to meet qualifying rents.

TABLE 18

IS THE LOW INCOME HOUSING TAX CREDITS A WORKABLE PROGRAM?
ESTIMATES OF DEVELOPMENT FEASIBILITY WITH VARIOUS DEVELOPMENT COSTS AND FINANCING
BASED ON QUALIFYING RENT LEVELS AT VARIOUS AREA MEDIAN INCOME (AMI) LEVELS

			Feasibility of Development Based on Achieving Qualifying Rent Levels for a Hypothetical 3.5 Person Household							
			50 Percent of Area Median Income				60 Percent of Area Median Income			
Type of Development Using the Tax Credits	Development Costs Per Unit	Monthly Rent Savings from Tax Benefits	$36,500 AMI $433/mo	$32,000 AMI $380/mo	$27,500 AMI $327/mo	$23,000 AMI $273/mo	$36,500 AMI $520/mo	$32,000 AMI $456/mo	$27,500 AMI $392/mo	$23,000 AMI $328/mo
Conventional Financing										
New Construction	$ 55,000	$241	5th yr. +$3,000	5th yr. +10,000	NO	NO	YES	Yes - 5th yr.	5th yr. +$8,000	NO
Rehabilitation	38,500	132	5th yr. +$2,000	5th yr. +$8,000	NO	NO	YES	Yes - 5th yr.	5th yr. +$7,000	NO
Rehabilitation	29,000	101	YES	5th yr. +$2,000	5th yr. +$9,000	NO	YES	YES	1st yr. +$3,000	5th yr. +$9,000
Acquisition	20,000	46	YES	1st yr. +$1,000	5th yr. +$6,000	NO	YES	YES	YES	5th yr. +$6,000
Tax-Exempt Financing[1/]										
New Construction	55,000	163	NO	NO	NO	NO	Yes - 5th yr.	5th yr. +$10,000	NO	NO
Rehabilitation	38,500	117	5th yr. +$4,000	NO	NO	NO	YES	Yes - 5th yr.	5th yr. +$10,000	NO
Rehabilitation	29,000	88	YES	5th yr. +$4,000	NO	NO	YES	YES	5th yr. +$2,500	NO

1/Would produce monthly cost savings for any non-low income units estimated at $48 for $55,000 unit; $34 for $38,500 unit; and $26 for $29,000 unit.

Note: See the underlying assumptions regarding project financing and operating costs. Actual experience in any particular location may differ substantially from the underlying assumptions.

Explanation of Conclusions:

YES. Immediately feasible in the initial year of operation. Economic gross rent is below qualifying rent level.
First Year plus Dollar Amount: Possible in first year with relatively small additional assistance of amount indicated.
Yes, Fifth Year: Feasible after five years based on 3 percent rent increases yearly reducing gap between economic rent and qualifying rent. No aid required. Gap is funded for 5 years through reduced rate of return on equity.
Fifth Year plus Dollar Amount: Can be feasible if additional assistance of amount indicated is provided, combined with five years of reducing gap between economic rent and qualifying rent through 3 percent yearly rent increases and reduced return on equity. Per unit aid required is less than $10,000.
NO. Not Feasible. Gap between economic rent and qualifying rent is too great to be bridged by reduced equity return, 3 percent yearly rent increases, plus additional assistance of $10,000 per unit or less.

At the $32,000 area median income level, projects with rents geared to 60 percent of the median were feasible either initially or after five years of trending without any outside aid, except for new construction with tax-exempt financing. With rents geared to the lower 50 percent of median income level, projects were feasible generally with five years of trending and additional assistance. New construction and the $38,500 rehabilitation unit with tax-exempt financing were not feasible at the 50 percent level.

At the $27,500 area median income level, projects with rents geared to 60 percent of the area median could be feasible with five years of trending plus additional assistance. The two lower cost projects at $29,000 and $20,000 a unit were feasible in the first year with $3,000 of assistance and no assistance respectively. At this median income level, projects with rents geared to 50 percent of median income were not feasible, except for the two lowest cost units. Here five years of trending plus larger amounts of assistance could result in feasible projects.

At the $23,000 level of area median income, the lowest level studied, none of the projects were feasible, except for the $20,000 and $29,000 units with rents geared to 60 percent of the area median, based on five years of trending and larger amounts of assistance.

The various types of units were feasible under the following conditions:

New construction at $55,000 per unit. With conventional financing, this was feasible at the $36,500 and $32,000 median income levels with rents at 60 percent of median without additional aid. In these areas with rents at the 50 percent level, and at the $27,500 median income level with rents at 60 percent, projects could be feasible with five years of trending and additional financial assistance. With tax-exempt financing, with rents geared to 60 percent of median, this was feasible at the $36,500 and $32,000 income levels with five years of trending, plus $10,000 in extra assistance at the $32,000 area income level. Elsewhere, not feasible with tax-exempt financing.

Rehabilitation at $38,500 per unit. With conventional financing, this unit was feasible at the three highest of the four area median income levels if rents are pegged at 60 percent of the median. At the $27,500 median level, five years of trending plus $7,500 in additional aid per unit is required. With rents geared to 50 percent of area income, projects were feasible only at the two highest median income levels, after five years of trending and additional assistance. With tax-exempt financing, the pattern is similar to that with conventional financing, except that where additional assistance is required, about $2,000 to $3,000 additional aid per unit is required over and above the aid required with conventional financing.

Rehabilitation at $29,000 per unit. With conventional financing, this was feasible without additional aid or with relatively modest additional aid at the three highest area median income levels with rents at 60 percent of the median, and at the two highest area median income levels with rents pegged at 50 percent of the median. For the first time, a project was feasible at the $23,000 area median income level. Rents must be pegged at 60 percent of the median, and five years of trending plus additional assistance of $9,000 per unit is required. The same $9,000 of assistance is required in areas with the national median of $27,500 when rents are set at 50 percent of the median income. The pattern with tax-exempt financing is similar except that the amount of additional assistance is larger.

Acquisition with minor rehabilitation at $20,000 per unit. At this lowest cost scenario, where tax-exempt financing would not be available because rehabilitation is less than 15 percent of total costs, projects were feasible in the first year when rents are set at 60 percent of the median income level. An exception is the areas with a $23,000 median income, where five years of trending plus $6,000 in aid is required. At the 50 percent of median rent level, projects were feasible with some financial assistance except at the $23,000 lowest median income level.

Very little was feasible in areas with low median incomes of $23,000 or under based on the assumptions in this study. However, a separate analysis indicates that new construction costing $39,000 a unit in lower cost areas of the country would be feasible with conventional financing, $4,000 additional aid and five years of trending, in areas with a median income of $23,000 per year. This configuration produces an economic gross rent including utilities of $328 per month. This assumes operating and utility costs of $210 a month compared to $235 a month for a new construction unit elsewhere.

* * * * * * *

Summary

Of the 56 different scenarios examined in this analysis, roughly one-third were feasible without additional financial aid, one-third were feasible if additional financial aid were available, and slightly more than one-third were not feasible. Of those feasible with financial aid, about one-half required aid under $5,000 per unit and the other half required aid of between $5,000 and $10,000 a unit.

5

STRATEGIES --> ACTIVITIES --> COORDINATION --> IMPLEMENTATION

HOW THE TAX CREDIT WORKS WITH EXISTING FEDERAL HOUSING PROGRAMS

The HUD Section 8 Programs

There are a number of different section 8 programs: the existing certificate program and the voucher program where the assistance is directed to applicants and not buildings; the rental rehabilitation program, where the assistance is directed to buildings initially but tenants can leave and take their certificates or vouchers with them; and the moderate rehabilitation program, where the assistance remains with the building.

The "project-based" section 8 program is a new program enacted by Congress in 1987 that allows public housing authorities (PHAs) administering section 8 existing housing certificates to allocate up to 15 percent of their certificates on a long-term basis to specific buildings in order to carry out rehabilitation projects. At least $1,000 per unit must be spent for rehab work, and owners can sign contracts which can provide the subsidies for up to a 15 year period in five year segments.

Under the tax credit program, section 8 assistance payments flowing from the federal government to an individual property owner are not counted toward the maximum rent in determining whether an owner receives tax credits. This allows the owner to receive total rental income considerably in excess of the qualifying rent levels and still earn tax credits.

While this allows federal tax expenditures to flow in some situations where they are not needed, it can play a valuable role in supporting rehabilitation projects that otherwise would not be feasible because the development costs result in rents that are in excess of the maximum allowable fair market rents. In most cases, the agencies allocating the credits will be able to use their discretion and only award tax credits in section 8 projects to the extent they are needed to make a project feasible.

The rental rehabilitation program also offers flexible grant dollars of up to $5,000 a unit towards development costs. Local housing departments use the funds to make grants, deferred loans, and amortized loans to property owners. As with other flexible forms of federal grant dollars, the way in which these funds are used can produce either zero tax credits, 4 percent tax credits, or 9 percent tax credits. This is discussed further in this chapter.

The other versions of the section 8 program do not offer any up-front development or financial assistance. They only provide periodic payment of a portion of a tenant's rent after the development work is completed. Therefore they would not affect the amount of tax credits allocated to a project.

Except under the moderate rehabilitation program and the new project-based section 8 program, section 8 or voucher assistance is portable after the first year, and the tenant can decide to move and take the subsidy to another property. Some developers have undertaken projects on the assumption that they can continue to collect the subsidy payments through the life of the project by working with the local PHA agencies administering the program and attracting certificate holders to voluntarily move into and remain in their projects.

The Community Development Block Grant Program

The CDBG program provides flexible HUD dollars to local communities. Housing development for lower income households is one of the prime uses of these funds. This program can work extremely well with the tax credit program, making projects feasible by bridging the gap between the economic rents and the qualifying rent levels in particular projects.

The CDBG aid can be spent in a manner that minimizes any loss in tax credit dollars due to the type of aid provided. It can be used for construction loans and bridge loans as well as for permanent financing. CDBG funds can be used to pay the costs of constructing new low income housing or to set up a fund to pay periodic rent subsidies to a project only if it is done through a neighborhood-based non-profit organization. CDBG funds can pay for land acquisition for new construction if the local government acquires the land and then transfers it to either a profit or non-profit development entity.

The Section 312 rehabilitation direct loan program

This program provides direct loans under strict underwriting criteria for the rehabilitation of housing for lower income families. For rental housing, the interest rate is one percent above the rate on 20-year Treasury securities. This should always be above the Applicable Federal Rate, and therefore earn a 9 percent tax credit. At least 80 percent of the units must be occupied by households with incomes below 80 percent of the area median income, adjusted for household size.

The Urban Development Action Grant and Housing Development Grant Programs

Both of these programs emphasize flexible financial assistance to make development feasible. They also are competitive programs which emphasize the leveraging of public to private dollars in awarding grants. Since the tax credits result in additional private capital for projects from the sale of the tax benefits, it enhances the chances of projects being selected. These programs can be excellent vehicles for needed additional assistance when the tax credits are insufficient for creating a feasible project. As with the other forms of flexible assistance, the aid should be structured to minimize any loss of tax credits.

The Flexible Subsidy Program

This program provides direct federal funding for troubled multi-family housing projects that are already receiving long term federal financial assistance under such programs as section 236 and section 221(d)(3). Direct federal funds are typically provided as a loan at a one percent rate of interest for such purposes as making needed repairs and covering operating deficits.

When this program is used as part of an effort to rehabilitate an existing troubled project, then the project would normally earn a 4 percent or 30 percent present value tax credit, since a one percent federal loan is a federal subsidy.

FHA insured multi-family rental housing mortgages

Since FHA insurance and co-insurance programs currently in effect provide long term mortgage funds at prevailing market interest rates, these interest rates would never be less than the Applicable Federal Rate (AFR). Therefore they could not reduce the tax credit percentage from 9 to 4 percent.

To make sure that co-insured loans to tax credit projects are economically sound, HUD is requiring lenders to obtain special HUD approval before they can co-insure any loans where more than 40 percent of the units have the rent limitations required by the tax credit program.

Existing distressed properties with certain government-insured mortgages get favorable treatment under the tax credit program. The prohibition that bars tax credits if a property was sold or significantly repaired during the last 10 years can be waived for these properties. (See full discussion of this in Chapter 2.)

Farmers Home Administration Section 515 low income rental housing program

The act specifically provides a 4 percent credit for any Farmers Home Sec. 515 project, since these projects benefit from direct loans that are well below prevailing Treasury AFR interest rates.

> *Fifty-year, one percent loans are provided under the section 515 program. Development costs are thus amortized with an annual amortization factor of about 2.5 percent, while a 4 percent annual credit is provided for all development costs less the value of land for a 10-year period. This means that rents need only cover operating costs during the 15-year compliance period. The tax credit program helps to assure that Sec. 515 projects will be able to successfully house very low income families in the rural areas of our nation.*

Appendix 3 illustrates how the tax credits can work with this program.

STRATEGIES TO OBTAIN THE MAXIMUM AMOUNT OF TAX CREDITS WHEN USING OTHER GOVERNMENTAL ASSISTANCE PROGRAMS

In using additional governmental financial assistance with the low income housing tax credit, it will be important to make the correct strategic decisions to maximize the amount of tax credits earned.

Two different sets of factors to be considered are:

1. The provisions in the tax credit legislation concerning the amount of credits available when federal grants, federal subsidies, and other forms of federal aid are involved;

2. The provisions of the Internal Revenue Code concerning the adjusted basis of a property for depreciation purposes when grants, below-market interest loans, or other forms of external subsidy are received. Any element which produces a change in the

amount of adjusted basis for a property affects the amount of tax credits. (The amount of the property's adjusted basis is used to determine the amount of eligible basis, and the amount of eligible basis determines the amount of qualified basis. This in turn, is multiplied by the appropriate tax credit percentage to determine the amount of tax credits.)

The tax credit legislation provides that federal grants to projects -- i.e., where federal funds are provided directly or indirectly with no obligation to repay -- must be deducted from the eligible basis of the property in calculating the amount of the tax credits.

If federal subsidies are provided -- i.e., loans of federal funds at interest rates that are below the Applicable Federal Rate (AFR), including tax-exempt financing and Sec. 515 Farmers Home Loans -- then the entire project qualifies only for a 4 percent credit, rather than the 9 percent credit for new construction or rehabilitation work on projects without federal subsidies.

> *The Applicable Federal Rate (AFR) for the corresponding loan duration would determine if a federal loan is a federal subsidy. Loans of 9 years or more would be compared to the Long-Term AFR; loans of from 3 to 9 years would be compared to the Mid-Term AFR; and loans of less than 3 years' duration would be compared to the Short-Term AFR. If the interest rate on the loan is less than the corresponding AFR, then it is considered a federal subsidy, and the 4 percent (or 30 percent present value) tax credit applies.*

The owner can choose to deduct the amount of the federal subsidy from basis and obtain a 9 percent credit on the remainder. This is advisable if the subsidy is less than 57.1 percent of rehab or new construction costs.

These limitations on the uses of grants and subsidies only apply to monies derived from federal funds. They do not apply to grants and subsidies from state or local government funds, or from private philanthropic sources. The other provisions of the tax code, however, can produce a reduction in the amount of tax credits obtained from development costs financed by non-federal assistance.

Under the tax code, a grant made to a project results in a reduction in the adjusted basis of the property equal to the amount of the grant, regardless of the source of funds. This would produce a loss in tax credits and depreciation benefits for the grant amount. A loan with a below-market interest rate, if provided by a governmental agency with non-federal funds, will not result in a reduction in basis under either the tax credit provisions or the Original Issue Discount rules of the tax code, and would not result in fewer tax credits.

If a grant or fully deferred loan were used to set up an independent fund from which periodic monthly subsidies were paid to a project, this would apparently not lead to an initial reduction in basis and a loss in tax credits in either the initial year or in subsequent years.

If the source of funds is a government agency, a loan where the payment of both principal and interest is fully deferred to the future would be exempt from the Original Issue Discount rules, and would not cause a reduction in the project's adjusted basis and the amount of tax credits earned. If the funds were federal funds, a fully deferred loan at an interest rate at or above the AFR would apparently not be treated as a federal subsidy requiring a 4 percent credit.

In a private letter ruling, the IRS determined that a city loan that was repaid only from any surplus cash that remained after a cash return was paid to the owners could be considered a loan and not a grant and earn tax credits, since any accrued interest or unpaid principal had to be repaid at the end of the 40 year loan period.

DIRECTING GRANTS AND SUBSIDIES TO COST ELEMENTS EARNING FEWEST CREDITS

The provisions of the tax credit legislation provide different treatment for various elements in property development costs. This provides opportunities to maximize the amount of tax credits when grants or below-market loans are necessary to make a project work. The cost or value of underlying land earns no tax credits; the cost of acquiring an existing building, less the value of the land, earns a tax credit at the 4 percent rate; and the costs of new construction or rehabilitation earn tax credits at a 9 percent rate.

In a new construction project, a grant that is used to purchase the land should not cause any loss in tax credits. In a rehabilitation project, a grant or a loan used exclusively towards the acquisition of the building will not affect the 9 percent credit on the rehabilitation work. A federal loan for new construction or rehabilitation with an interest rate equal to the long term Applicable Federal Rate on the date of issuance would be below long-term mortgage rates, but would not be a subsidy and therefore would not disturb the 9 percent credit for new construction or rehabilitation work.

The feasibility analysis of various types of development indicates that conventional or non-tax-exempt financing combined with the 9 percent credit is more advantageous for lower income units than the typical tax-exempt financing with a 4 percent credit, except in situations where rehabilitation expenditures are a small proportion of total development costs. Tax-exempt financing would, however, allow significantly lower rents for any non-low income units in a project.

In addition, tax-exempt financing for projects placed in service by the end of 1989 provides automatic eligibility for tax credits without the necessity for an apportionment by a housing credit agency from the state allocation of $1.25 per capita. This is an important option in states where there is strong competition for the credits and there is a possibility that a project will receive no credits or less credits than the maximum amount to which the project is eligible.

> *Taxable multi-family mortgage bonds is another alternative that could be used in combination with tax credits. Taxable bonds would use the capital raising capacities and credit ratings of state and local housing finance agencies to finance additional housing units outside of the strict limits on the amount of private purpose tax-exempt financing. While taxables will have a significantly higher interest rate, both market conditions and the lowering of income tax rates should produce a lowering of the differential between taxable and tax-exempt bond interest rates. Taxable bond issuances will allow owners to receive the full 9 percent tax credit for rehabilitation and new construction activities.*

SUGGESTED STRATEGIES FOR STATE AND LOCAL GOVERNMENT HOUSING AGENCIES

The new tax credit program provides additional opportunities and responsibilities for state and local government housing agencies. These agencies can be divided into three types: housing credit agencies with the delegated responsibility to award housing tax credits to particular projects; agencies offering various forms of financial assistance for lower income housing development; and agencies providing information and technical assistance to non-profit and/or profit-motivated providers of housing for lower income households.

Housing Credit Agencies. These agencies need to widely disseminate information on the process and the timing of submitting applications for housing tax credits, and on the criteria or requirements for approving or selecting among competing applications. Agencies awarding the tax credit have the inherent authority to impose their own requirements or to establish selection criteria to stimulate particular types of projects.

One very important area for policy making is the extent to which the tax credits might be reserved for projects targeted at the 50 percent of median income level rather than the 60 percent of median income level.

> ***While the 50 percent of median income level might be preferable because it will better serve the constituency on local housing agency waiting lists, it will be very difficult in most situations to achieve these lower rent levels without additional financial assistance from state or local government sources. (Additional assistance will be needed in many instances in carrying out projects at the 60 percent of median income level.)***

Housing credit agencies need to have expert underwriting skills to make sure that the full credits are not awarded to projects that are feasible and affordable to the targeted population without any tax credits, or with a lower amount of tax credits than the project is eligible for.

Housing credit agencies are allocating a relatively scarce commodity whose value is lost if it is not utilized on a timely basis. The tax credit program is a complex program that can be used in a variety of different situations. At the very same time, agencies should be exploring the potential for new construction as well as the potential of stimulating current owners to use the tax credits to make moderate repairs on their existing low rent properties without significantly increasing rents. Appendix 2 outlines such a program. Extensive efforts need to be made to explain the program to all potential users. Widely advertised information sessions using model pro forma budgets should be held to show the dollar impact of the credits.

With the various timing constraints and the continual lapsing of the value of unused credits, a regularly scheduled, highly publicized competition with deadlines for applications would appear advisable.

It is important that the credit agencies establish staff units with competent personnel able to promote and explain the program, negotiate with developers, and evaluate incoming proposals. The legislation allows housing credit agencies to establish fees for applicants and recipients of the tax credits to help cover administrative costs.

In many localities, the housing credit can only work if there is extensive additional assistance from other government aid programs, from philanthropic sources, or both.

Housing credit agencies will need to involve these other organizations and agencies to stimulate the coordinated use of the various financial resources necessary to produce lower income housing. Joint applications to direct funding agencies and housing credit agencies should be encouraged.

Housing Funding Agencies and Departments. The various state and local housing finance agencies, community development departments, and other units providing funds for lower income rental housing need to revise their programs to incorporate housing tax credits into their guidelines and funding criteria. The limited dollars made available under such programs as community development block grants, Sec. 8 moderate rehabilitation, and rental rehabilitation can now be much more effectively used with the new flexible tool provided by the housing tax credit. Properties where rehabilitation was previously not feasible because costs were too high to be covered by the moderate rehabilitation Fair Market Rents, or because of the $5,000 per unit limit on rental rehabilitation grants, may now be feasible.

Government departments with flexible funding sources such as community development block grants or state or local flexible programs will want to tailor their assistance to maximize the amount of credits a particular project can obtain. Agencies should consider using available CDBG fund balances, UDAG repayments, and other available fund balances for construction loans, and for three-to-five-year bridge loans at low interest rates when there is a significant time period before all investor pay-ins are received.

Housing finance agencies in many states have been designated as the official housing credit agency that selects the projects receiving tax credits. These agencies need to be familiar with the types of projects that can be supported by tax credits that they have not been involved with in the past. This might include acquisitions without rehabilitation, rehabilitation by present owners without a change in ownership, moderate scale rehabilitation projects, and projects where there will be no tax-exempt financing. When tax-exempt financed projects automatically receive tax credits without using the state's per capita allocation, an allocation of credits would be needed for a portion of a project where the tax-exempt financing was less than 70 percent of total development costs. (Such a project with 70 percent or more of development costs covered by tax-exempt financing receives a credit for all eligible development costs without using any of the state tax credit allocation.)

> *A project with automatic tax credits from tax-exempt financing may not reach the 70 percent threshold to qualify for 100 percent tax credits without use of the state allocation. In such situations, owner's equity might be placed in an interest-bearing account and converted to periodic subsidies instead of paying for front-end development costs. With increased borrowing of tax-exempt funds to take their place in meeting developments costs, tax-exempt financing could then increase to more than 70 percent of total development costs. The project would now qualify for automatic tax credits for 100 percent of development costs.*

Technical Assistance and Information Agencies. Governmental and private agencies charged with the responsibility of assisting the private sector and other governmental agencies to improve their capacity in housing development can play a significant role in making the tax credit program work. Because the tax credit program can be used in a wide variety of situations, an educational and marketing effort directed at the variety of potential users is needed.

State level technical assistance and information agencies can stimulate local government housing agencies to get involved with the tax credit program and to coordinate their local housing aid programs with the work of the housing credit agencies.

In addition to conducting training programs and disseminating written material (such as this publication) on the tax credit program, the technical assistance function can assist developers, non-profits, and owners of small scale rental properties to prepare applications for tax credits and other forms of financial aid that may be needed in conjunction with the credits.

Maintaining lists of interested syndicators and sources of investor capital would be a useful function as well.

These agencies can also be a vital source of information feedback to the housing credit agencies, and to the Treasury Department on the validity of its regulations.

SUGGESTIONS ON REGULATIONS AND REQUESTS FOR RULINGS CAN BE SENT TO TREASURY AND THE IRS

Staff members of the Treasury Department and the Internal Revenue Service working on the administrative aspects of the low income housing tax credit have indicated that they are interested in comments and suggestions from concerned and involved private citizens on the tax credit program. It is clear that a number of important issues will have to be addressed in future regulations.

Comments on issues of concern, as well as questions on the tax credit program, should be addressed to two offices within the Treasury Department: The Commissioner of Internal Revenue and the Assistant Secretary of the Treasury for Tax Policy. The address for both is Treasury Department, Washington, D.C. 20224.

Individual taxpayers can also request private letter rulings on particular transactions involving the credit by writing to the Internal Revenue Service, Associate Chief Counsel–Technical, 1111 Constitution Ave. N.W., Room 6545, Washington, D.C. 20224 (Attention CC:IND:D:C). Revenue Procedure 87–1 specifies the procedures to be followed and the information that must be submitted when a ruling is requested from the IRS.

6

RAISING CAPITAL IN EXCHANGE FOR TAX CREDITS THROUGH SYNDICATION OF LIMITED PARTNERSHIPS

THE POTENTIAL INVESTORS WHO MIGHT USE THE TAX CREDIT: SMALL INVESTORS, CORPORATIONS, AND INVESTORS WITH PASSIVE INCOME

In most instances, the tax credits awarded to a low income housing project will not be useful unless outside investors acquire limited partnership interests in the project. Syndication is the process of structuring the financial arrangements, drawing up the legal documents, and securing the investors for a limited partnership. Investors put up capital in exchange for a projected rate of return on their investment that is competitive with other investments based on the nature of the risks involved. The investors are called limited partners because their liability is legally limited to the amount of money they agree to invest in the project, and they generally play no active role in project management.

The provisions in the 1986 tax reform act intended to restrict the use of tax benefits in the real estate industry make it difficult for developers and non-profits to find the investors needed to "purchase" the tax credits to make the program work.

Investors in a tax credit project may be able to use some of the tax credits to offset taxes on operating income or cash flow from the project itself. However, any such income is likely to be small, and would only use a fraction of the credits available from the project.

Individual investors with 33 percent marginal federal income tax rates cannot use more than $8,250 in credits in any year to offset taxes against ordinary income. This $8,250 amount is reduced by $1 for every $6.00 that the taxpayer's adjusted gross income exceeds $200,000 per year in any of the next 10 years.

Limited partners cannot benefit from depreciation deductions to reduce their tax liability on ordinary income, except that unused depreciation can be carried forward and used to reduce tax liability in the year in which the partners sell their interest in the property.

Certain high income taxpayers will come under the alternative minimum tax and be limited in their ability to use the tax credits to reduce their taxes on large amounts of passive income.

Due to the yearly limit of $8,250 in tax credits under the passive losses rules, individual investors using the tax credits to shelter taxes on ordinary income will primarily be investing up to $55,000, and are likely to have adjusted gross incomes of less than $200,000 a year. Fifty-five thousand dollars is the maximum amount an investor would put up to receive $8,250 in tax credits for each of the next 10 years, based on earning a 15 percent annual rate of return, with principal repaid from sale proceeds in 15 years.

Other than these individual investors, there are two other categories of potential investors who can take advantage of the tax credits:

1. Corporations seeking to earn a reasonable return and to also make a social benefit investment. Regular "C" corporations are exempt from the passive losses restrictions in the tax reform law which limit the use of tax credits and depreciation deductions;

2. Individuals with significant passive income from operating profits and capital gains from rental real estate activities. Both the corporate and individual investors should be those who are under the threshold where the alternative minimum tax significantly increases tax liability and invalidates the use of passive losses.

These investors face a number of uncertainties that could significantly reduce the value of their investment:

1. An individual investor using up to $8,250 in tax credits or $25,000 in depreciation losses against ordinary income might see his or her total household income rise above $200,000 a year within 10 years, precluding the use of the credits and losses against ordinary income. Based on the annual rate of increase in median household income in the U.S. of 5.6 percent between 1979 and 1986, $200,000 annual income 10 years from now would be $116,000 today. However, an investor whose income rises to the $200,000 level can sell his/her partnership interest to another investor with income below that level to avoid loss of the investment.

2. An investor planning to use the credits and losses against his or her own passive income has to weigh the uncertainty of earning enough passive income to use the credits and losses for 10 years.

3. Congress might tighten up further on the alternative minimum tax and passive losses limitations. Investors in low income housing and other forms of rental real estate experienced a substantial reduction in the value of their previous investments as a result of the passive losses provisions in the 1986 act that were applied <u>ex post facto</u> to all existing properties.

In some instances, the tax credits might be used by owners and developers directly without bringing in new limited partner investors. Owners of small rental properties can use the tax credits directly against $8,250 in tax liability on their own ordinary income (if under $200,000) and to offset tax liability on passive income (positive cash flow) from their properties. Large developers with significant capital gains and cash flow income from other properties can probably use most of the credits directly, as long as they are not faced with a significant tax liability under the alternative minimum tax.

Non-profit organizations and small developers using regular "C" corporation construction companies to construct or rehabilitate properties might try to set up partnership arrangements with these companies, since these companies can use the credits and passive losses to offset taxes on their regular business income without restriction as long as they are not affected by the alternative minimum tax.

RESPONSE OF THE SYNDICATION AND INVESTMENT CAPITAL INDUSTRIES

Tax credits represent a potential two billion dollar-plus yearly market for the syndication industry. In the months immediately following the passage of the 1986 tax reform act, the syndication industry displayed little interest in raising equity capital for projects with low income housing tax credits.

By summer 1987 the potential of the low income housing tax credit as one of the few remaining tax shelter investments began to be recognized by the investment community. By that time, there appeared to be more investment capital in search of tax credit project investment opportunities than there are projects with tax credit potential in search of investors.

This trend has continued. As of late 1988, numerous syndication firms and capital raising sources for both profit- motivated and non-profit developers are now active with respect to the low income housing tax credit. (See list that follows.) A number of large public funds are soliciting investments in tax credit projects, and a more substantial number of private placement investment opportunities have been developed. The SEC-regulated public funds rely on a large number of small one-time investments (typically $5,000 and over), while the private placements solicit a smaller number of investors who usually will invest $30,000 to $55,000 over a number of years.

THE STRUCTURE OF TYPICAL PARTNERSHIPS

The public funds and many of the private placements are structured as two-tier partnerships. Under this arrangement, individuals invest in a fund which is then invested in a number of projects, so that each investor in effect has a small piece of a number of different projects. Each project establishes its own limited partnership, with the public fund or an affiliate typically acting as both a co-general partner and the sole limited partner. In private placements, with only one tier, individuals make direct investments as limited partners in individual low income tax credit projects.

Some of the private placements are soliciting investments from corporations, since corporations can make larger investments because they are not covered by the passive losses restrictions in the 1986 tax reform act. Corporations also can make better and more immediate use of the depreciation deductions as compared to individual limited partner investors.

Some of the syndication and investment offerings seek to make an outright purchase of a project with tax credits. The developer or previous owner would sell 100 percent of the interests in the project, and have no further role in ownership or management. More typically, the developer or property owner acts as general partner and retains a small percentage of ownership in the partnership, and is active in project management. In order to get maximum benefit from the tax credits and depreciation deductions, the percentage of ownership retained by the developer is usually only one percent. The developer typically shares in any cash flow profits beyond his/her percentage of ownership through an incentive management fee or similar device, and in a percentage of any residual gain or profit when the property is sold or refinanced.

Syndicators typically want developers to guarantee or take responsiblity to ensure that the project will fully qualify for the amount of tax credits allocated, that there will not be any recapture of tax credits in the future, and that any cost overruns in construction or deficits in project operation will be covered by the developer.

The organizations raising capital specifically for non-profit developers typically limit the possibility of profit or gain on the sale of a project. Instead, they work to assure that the project continues its low income housing use after the end of the 15-year low income occupancy compliance period.

A recent IRS private letter ruling permitted a limited partnership with non-profit organization involvement to prohibit the payment of cash flow profits to investors, and to arrange in advance to sell the project to the non-profit at the end of the 15 year compliance period at a low, predetermined price (such as the remaining mortgage balance plus taxes due on sale). Prior to this, it was generally believed that such an arrangement violated the IRS requirement that there be economic substance in tax-oriented partnership activities.

LIST OF SYNDICATORS CURRENTLY ACTIVE WITH THE TAX CREDIT

The following is a list of syndication firms who are currently (January 1989) active in securing investment capital for housing projects using the low income housing tax credit. These firms are now seeking developers with projects to invest in, and in most cases are currently seeking investors as well. These firms operate outside their immediate geographic area, and typically seek projects located anywhere in the country. (Additional syndication firms are also active with the low income housing tax credit, but they are unknown to the author at the time of writing.)

Andover Associates
81 Samoset Street
Plymouth, MA 02360
617/747-3344
Brian M. Burke

Arcand Company
1099 Southwest Columbia Street
Suite 350
Portland, Oregon 97201
503/224-4400
Bob Arcand

Associated Financial Corporation
881 Alma Real Drive
Suite 205
Pacific Palisades, CA 90272
213/459-7024
Lester Moses

Benton Mortage Company
1605 Main Street
NCNB Building, Suite 810
Sarasota, FL 33577
Frank Daniel

Boston Capital
313 Congress Street
Boston, MA 02210
617/439-0072
John P. Manning

Boston Equity Investment, Inc.
2 Faneuil Hall Marketplace
Boston, MA 02109
617/720-1766
Beth Sirull

Boston Financial Group
101 Arch Street
Boston, MA 02110
617/439-3911
William E. Haynsworth

Century Pacific
10900 Wilshire Boulevard
Murdock Plaza, Suite 510
Los Angeles, CA 90024
213/826-5995
Edward Lobrano

Community Housing Fund
1330 Sabal Palm Drive
Boca Raton, FL 33432
407/393-6857
John D. MacLachlan

DJL Enterprise, Inc.
P.O. Box 13073
Kansas City, MO 64199-3073
David L. Johnson

Federal National Mortage
Association (FNMA)
3900 Wisconsin Avenue, NW
Washington, D.C. 20016
202/752-6030
Martin D. Levinne

Feiler Enterprises, LTD.
120 Habersham Street
Savannah, GA 31499
912/232-6444

First American Holding, Inc.
27 The Plaza
Locust Valley, NY 11560
516/676-8800
Susan Valentine

First Capital Corporation
1350 Old Freeport Road
Pittsburgh, PA 15238
412/963-1320
Terry Lerman

First Continental Capital Markets
2301 Cedar Springs, #300
Dallas, TX 75201
714/871-7000
Jack Maniscalco

Frederick Investment Corporation
3900 Barrett Drive, Suite 301
P.O. Box 18447
Raleigh, NC 27619-8447
919/781-6009
Frank R. Narron

Hydeman Realty Company
13747 Montfront Drive
Suite 115
Dallas, TX 75240
Marshal Sabel

Jero Investment Corporation
723 Ocean Front Walk
Venice, CA 90291
213/392-3046
Jerry Rosenberg

MG Capital Corporation
5855 Topanga Canyon Boulevard, #300
Woodland Hills, CA 91367
818/704-5850
Michael W. McFerrin

March Company, Inc.
150 Federal Street
Boston, MA 02110
617/951-2370
Peter D. O'Connor

Martin Group, Inc.
306 Main Street
Huntingburg, IN 47542
812/683-4258
John Martin

Meridian Company
8530 Wilshire Blvd.
Suite 400
Beverly Hills, CA 90211
Scott L. Kotick

Meridian Investments, Inc.
10220 River Road, Suite 115
Potomac, Maryland 20854
301/983-5000
Timothy J. Neville

Michel Associates, LTD.
77 North Washington Street, Suite 200
Boston, MA 02114
617/523-4016
Pamela C. Adam

Mortgage Loans, Inc.
9660 East Bay Harbor Drive, Suite 204
Bay Harbor Islands, FL 33154
305/866-6250
Robert J. Wolfarth

National Corporation For Housing
Partnerships
1225 Eye Street, Northwest
Washington, D.C. 20005
202/3226-8370
Ghebre Selassie Mehreteab

Newman & Associates, Inc.
1801 California Street, Suite 3700
Denver, CO 80202-2637
303/293-8500
Scot B. Baker

Pacific Capital, Inc.
8260 Greensboro Drive, Suite 225
McLean, VA 22102
703/893-2460
Gary Eames

Raymond James & Associates, Inc.
880 Carillon Parkway
St. Petersburg, FL 37716
813/573-3800
Ronald Diner

R.E.K. Development Corporation
1194 South Florissant Road
St. Louis, MO 63121
Jeffrey Wolfson

Related Capital Corporation
625 Madison Avenue
New York, NY 10022
212/421-5333
Joseph M. Klinow

Richman Tax Credit Properties
c/o Wilder Richman Corporation
555 Madison Avenue
New York, NY 10022
212/888-7444
David Salzman

Sterling Securities
1615 Northern Boulevard
Manhasset, NY 11030
516/627-5223
Martin Soja

Summit Group
600 Stewart Street #708
Seattle, WA 98101
206/443-2320
John Hansman

Tracy Financial, Inc.
60 State Street, Suite 3320
Boston, MA 02109
Robert E. Tracy

WNC & Associates
546 South Bayfront
Balboa Island, CA 92662
714/673-7928
Will Cooper

ORGANIZATIONS RAISING CAPITAL PRIMARILY FOR NON-PROFIT HOUSING PROJECTS

A number of non-profit organizations, initially established under foundation auspices for the purpose of helping to finance low income housing under non-profit ownership, have undertaken major initiatives to carry out syndication and raise capital with the low income housing tax credit. Whether they seek to raise funds from corporate investors or private individuals, they are offering to investors rates of return competitive with rates offered by the for-profit syndication firms discussed above. The syndicators listed above also may be interested in raising equity capital for non-profit sponsors.

The Enterprise Foundation, through its subsidiary the Enterprise Social Investment Corporation (ESIC), has completed syndications where major corporations from throughout the U.S. invest as limited partners in low income housing tax credit projects. These funds are primarily supporting non-profit community-based development projects, as well as some profit-motivated projects, mostly in localities where Enterprise is active in promoting low income housing development. Local community-based development entities will be co-general partners with major responsibility for developing, managing and overseeing the projects. The corporations invest in individual projects and in multi-project funds in Cleveland and Maryland, usually in localities in which they have offices.

The Enterprise Foundation's objective is to help the very poor help themselves to obtain decent housing and self sufficiency, primarily through a national network of non-profit neighborhood groups. ESIC directly carries out syndication and provides technical assistance in raising equity capital for low income housing efforts.

Enterprise Foundation and the Enterprise Social Investment Corporation (ESIC)
American City Building, Columbia, Md. 21044
Telephone: 301/964-1230 or 964-0552
Contact: Bart Harvey (Foundation) or Mark Sissman (ESIC)

Local Initiatives Support Corporation (LISC) has established a National Equity Fund to solicit investment capital from major U.S. corporations for limited partnership investments in low income housing tax credit projects in localities where LISC is operating. This fund is a two-tiered "blind pool" partnership, and the overall partnership and not individual corporations is the investor of record in each project. The fund can help projects in any of 30 cities and locations where LISC is already active, and is now at work in 15 localities. About 2,000 units a year are now being produced with about $50 million in tax credit equity investments raised from 40 corporations. Here as well, the projects to be funded will be owned by community-based non-profit organizations, including joint venture projects with profit-motivated development entities. A LISC subsidiary is the managing general partner of the fund, and decides where the funds are invested.

Local Initiatives Support Corporation is a national foundation that provides major financial support and technical assistance for community-based housing and economic development projects.

Local Initiatives Support Corporation (LISC) - Chicago Office
118 N. Clinton, Chicago, Ill. 60606
Telephone: 312/559-9820
Contact: Patrick Johnson

Affirmative Investments, Inc. (AI Group, Inc.) is a for-profit syndicator that works with non-profit organizations and some profit motivated developers who are committed to providing long-term low income housing. It currently sponsors a national and a California "blind pool" public partnership, and has also done some private placements with tax credit projects. It concentrates on projects where there is a commitment to maintain low income affordability for at least 30 years, and typically provides an option for a non-profit sponsor to acquire the property from the partnership at the end of 15 years.

Affirmative Investments, Inc. (AI) is an SEC Registered Investment Advisor which provides services to individual and institutional investors interested in making socially motivated investments.

Affirmative Investments, Inc. (AI Group)
129 South St., Boston, Mass. 02111
Telephone: 617/350-0250
Contact: Barbara Cleary

The National Retirement Housing Trust (NRHT) is a non-profit syndicator that has established an SEC-registered public fund and private placements to raise investment capital for low income housing tax credit projects. The Shearson-Lehman-Hutton brokerage chain has been retained to solicit investors for the public fund. The funds are primarily invested in: (1) projects owned or developed by local non-profit organizations who are co-general partners responsible for operating and managing the property, and 2) the outright purchase of low income housing properties from profit-motivated owners and developers who will no longer have a role in the ownership or operation of the property. Some investments are also made in profit-motivated projects where the developer remains as a co-general partner in the partnership. Despite the name of the organization, family housing as well as senior citizen housing can be assisted under this effort.

National Retirement Housing Trust, Inc., c/o Intrust Technologies Inc.
P.O. Box 1636, Wilmington, DE 19899
Telephone: 302/571-8100
Contact: Jim Mingey

Rural Housing Services, a subsidiary of the Housing Assistance Council, is working with both non-profit and for profit housing developers in rural areas to carry out syndication of low income housing tax credit projects. Rather than directly raising investment capital, RHS will place their projects with other syndication and investment capital entities. RHS will structure the arrangements to assure that the non-profit groups remain as the operating general partners, that tenant's rights are protected, and that the project is maintained as low income housing for as long as this is feasible.

The Housing Assistance Council (HAC) is a long standing non-profit organization that provides advocacy and technical assistance on behalf of low income housing needs in rural areas of the U.S.

Rural Housing Services, Inc.
1025 Vermont Ave. N.W., Washington, D.C. 20005
Telephone: 202/842-8600
Contact: Ken Hodge

7

CONCLUSIONS ABOUT THE LOW INCOME HOUSING TAX CREDIT PROGRAM

The low income housing tax credit has now proven to be a very valuable form of financial assistance that can make low income housing possible. Like many governmental housing programs in this era of limited financial aid, it needs additional assistance to work in most instances. In some fortunate locations where costs are relatively low and incomes relatively high, projects which qualify for the tax credit have been developed without any other form of financial assistance.

The tax credits are unique. They can be used in a variety of situations -- new construction, substantial rehabilitation, moderate rehabilitation, repairs by existing owners, and acquisition with little or no repairs -- and by both the smallest property owners and the largest developers.

There are problems, however:

- Restrictions on passive losses have deterred many former large individual investors from continuing to invest in low income housing;
- The loss of tax incentives for market rate rental housing has caused many former developers of mixed-income housing to withdraw from this market;
- Investors risk financial losses if their own incomes, or if the incomes of qualified tenants in economically mixed projects, rise above maximum levels;
- Projects in most areas will need additional aid in order to work, and most of the aid needed will probably not be available;
- Rents under the program will be too high for most poor persons, who need housing with rents geared to their individual incomes, as under the section 8 and public housing programs;
- Owners have little incentive to peg rents to the lower level of 50 percent of area median income;
- The tax credit amount is rarely adequate to achieve the lower 50 percent rent level without a substantial amount of additional financial assistance.
- Projects will not be successful just because they achieve rents that qualify for the tax credits. Prevailing rent levels in many lower income neighborhoods and communities will be below the qualifying rent levels.

- o The non-profit housing development sector needs to expand and sharpen its professional skills to fully use the 10 percent set-aside and to play a larger role in providing sorely needed housing for low income people.

* * * * *

In January 1989, about two years after the low income housing tax credit program began, a task force of experts appointed by U.S. Senators George Mitchell (Dem., Maine) and John Danforth (Repub., Missouri) issued a report which evaluated the first two year of the program and made recommendations for the future of the three year program which expires on December 31, 1989.

The Mitchell-Danforth Task Force on the Low Income Housing Tax Credit concluded that the tax credit has been and should continue to be an important part of the national housing policy. It estimated that about one-fifth of the available tax credits were used in 1987, and about two-thirds of the available credits were used in 1988.

In 1987, use of the tax credit was hampered by the newness of the program, the need to educate potential developers and investors about the complexities of the program, the extremely short time for completing projects in order to earn the tax credit, the lack of regulatory guidance from Treasury and the IRS.

1988 was more successful because of the enactment of the carryover provision in the 1988 tax code amendments, and the additional time that was available for educating developers, investors, and government agencies and for completing projects. However, the tax credits were still underutilized in many areas, and in other areas were used in projects that did not meet high priority needs, because of the lack of the additional project subsidies needed in most areas to make low income rental housing feasible.

The task force concluded that the case for extending the tax credit program is clear. It also pointed out that improvements are needed in the program to increase its effectiveness and efficiency. These include restrictions to make sure that the credits are awarded where they are needed and to help assure longer term use as low income housing beyond 15 years, and liberalizations to increase the amount of credits that can be awarded to projects, to make more types of projects eligible for the credits, and to permit more higher income people to invest more money in tax credit projects.

The task force also concluded that the tax credit should be made a permanent part of the tax code, that it be structured in order to ensure that the full allocation of credits is used, that needed federal subsidies should be used without penalties, that the program be responsive to the development process, and that it be usable in all types of markets. The legislative recommendations set forth in the task force report are summarized below.

RECOMMENDED LEGISLATIVE CHANGES IN THE LOW INCOME HOUSING TAX CREDIT AS PROPOSED BY THE MITCHELL-DANFORTH TASK FORCE

1. The tax credit percentage for new construction or substantial rehabilitation should be as large as a 100 percent "present value" tax credit — about 13 percent a year — if needed to serve families below 50 percent of area income, to provide housing in distressed communities, to enable the program to work in high cost areas, or to achieve other goals set forth in an annual state housing plan adopted by the state credit agency

and approved by the Governor. The total dollar allocation of tax credits to each state should remain at $1.25 per capita, however.

2. The tax credit for new construction or substantial rehabilitation when there are federal subsidies in the project should be at the full rate of 9 percent a year (or a 70 percent present value credit). Federal subsidies should no longer reduce the credit to a 4 percent or 30 percent present value tax credit.

3. Projects should no longer be eligible for a tax credit for acquisition unless there also are rehabilitation expenditures of at least $2,000 per unit.

4. Owners should be prohibited from converting tax credit projects to other than low income housing use during the initial 15 year compliance period. The compliance period for low income occupancy at restricted rent levels should also be extended for an additional 15 years. Owners could opt out of this additional 15 years if there were no buyers during the subsequent year willing to purchase the property for continued low income use for an amount equal to the original gross equity investment in the project plus the remaining debt on the property. These provisions would not apply to projects which received tax credits under the initial 1987–1989 three year program.

5. Housing credit agencies should be required to evaluate each project seeking a tax credit allocation in order to determine the amount of tax credits each project needs. The agencies would determine the tax credit amount on the basis of accepted industry standards, local conditions, and project needs. These agencies should also be required to hold public hearings and adopt plans which set forth how they would allocate the tax credits, how they would analyze projects, the types of financial information applicants would provide, and the standards the agencies would use to determine the amount of tax credits each project needs.

6. States should be allowed to carry forward unallocated tax credits for use in the subsequent year. Credits remaining unused after that additional year would be reallocated to other states through a national pool.

7. Additional exceptions to the "10 year rule" would be provided. This rule denies tax credit eligibility for building acquisition if there was a change of ownership or placement in service in the last ten years. Projects could receive an acquisition tax credit regardless of this rule if tax credits were needed to prevent default on a mortgage or conversion of the project to market rent levels, or to remove threats to health or safety . The rule also would not apply to properties that previously were owner–occupied and not used for rental housing.

8. The automatic extension of tax credits to projects which receive tax–exempt financing under the private activity bond cap should be restored. Such projects should have the same carryover privileges as projects which receive allocations from state credit agencies.

9. The passive losses restrictions should be loosened to allow use of the tax credit against the first $20,000 of tax liability on ordinary income, plus 20 percent of such tax liability in excess of $20,000. The ban on use of tax credits by individuals with incomes over $250,000 a year should also be repealed.

10. The recapture of the accelerated portion of tax credits already taken should be eliminated for sales of individual partnership interests if such sales were not more than 49 percent of the total interests in the partnership in any year.

11. Maximum rent levels should be established according to bedroom size rather than family size. The maximum rent would be based on the income limits for the typical household size in each bedroom size. The schedule would be based on about 1.5 persons per bedroom (e.g., the maximum rent for a one bedroom unit would be based on halfway between the one person and two person income limit; the maximum rent for a two bedroom unit would be based on the three person income limit; etc.) Efficiencies and SRO units would be based on the one person income limit. In order to qualify for the tax credit, each unit would have to be occupied by a household with at least one person for each bedroom.

12. The sale of a tax credit project to a non-profit organization at the end of the initial 15 year compliance period should be encouraged. Tax liability on the gain upon such a sale would be limited to the amount of the sales price which exceeds the remaining mortgage balance.

13. Tax credits should be allowed in projects which provide significant services other than medical services.

14. Transient units with leases of less than six months should qualify for the tax credit if they are single room occupancy (SRO) units.

15. Rental units in owner-occupied buildings with two to four units should qualify for the tax credit.

16. Tax credits should be allocated to projects rather than buildings. Scattered site properties could be treated as one project if there is common financing and management.

17. The conditions under which seller financing can be used by non-profit organizations without reducing the amount of tax credits should be eased. The requirement that debt from a non-profit has to be repaid withing 15 years should be removed, and the basis for earning tax credits should not be reduced because of loans on the property with below market rates of interest.

18. Maximum rents would not decline below their level in the initial year, in situations where median income in an area declines rather than increases.

19. The low income housing tax credit should be made a permanent part of the tax code, in lieu of an extension for any fixed number of years.

* * * * * * * *

The task force report was submitted to Senators Mitchell and Danforth on January 19, 1989. On receiving the report, the senators indicated that they strongly supported the continuation of the tax credit program and the overall thrust of the recommendations. However, they indicated that they would review the report, see that it is circulated broadly in the low income housing community, and then use the report and the comments they receive on it as the basis for drafting specific legislation.

Senators Mitchell and Danforth concluded that they would be introducing legislation extending and modifying the low income housing tax credit sometime in February or March of 1989.

Similar legislation is expected to be introduced in the House of Representatives by Cong. Charles Rangel (Dem., N.Y.), the chairman of the House Ways and Means subcommittee with jurisidiction over the low income housing tax credit program.

* * * * * * * *

The low income housing crisis facing this nation seems to deepen daily with further reports of homelessness and unacceptable housing conditions. The past 8 years saw a 70 percent cutback in budget authority for federal support of low income housing --- probably the largest cutback in a major federal domestic program category in the history of the U.S. --- and the enactment of a major new tax incentive for low income housing while almost all other tax shelters were severely restricted.

Congress seems poised for a substantial debate on a new national housing policy. A new President and a new HUD Secretary have expressed real concerns for the housing problems of low income persons, while the budget deficit and an unwillingness to face the need for tax increases militates against any signficant new federal initiative in low income housing.

Amidst these obvious contradictions, the low income housing industry and concerned citizens everywhere need to deepen their commitment and their efforts to make the best possible use of the human, material, and financial resources that we individually and collectively possess in order to provide decent housing for those among us who so desperately need it.

Appendix 1

MAXIMUM INCOME AND MAXIMUM RENTS TO QUALIFY UNITS AS LOW INCOME UNDER THE TAX CREDIT PROGRAM
FOR METROPOLITAN AREAS AND NON-METROPOLITAN STATE BALANCES IN THE U.S.
BASED ON QUALIFYING INCOME OF 60 PERCENT OF AREA MEDIAN INCOME FOR FISCAL YEAR 1989

Metropolitan Area or Non-Metro Balance	Effective Median Income 1989	Size of Household: 1 person		2 persons		3 persons		4 persons		5 persons		6 persons		7 persons		8 persons	
		Max Income	Max Rent	Max Income	Max Rent	Max Income	Max Rent	Max Income	Max Rent	Max Income	Max Rent	Max Income	Max Rent	Max Income	Max Rent	Max Income	Max Rent
Alabama																	
Anniston	24,900	10,458	261	11,952	299	13,446	336	14,940	374	16,135	403	17,330	433	18,526	463	19,721	493
Birmingham	29,700	12,474	312	14,256	356	16,038	401	17,820	446	19,246	481	20,671	517	22,097	552	23,522	588
Decatur	28,600	12,012	300	13,728	343	15,444	386	17,160	429	18,533	463	19,906	498	21,278	532	22,651	566
Dothan	24,100	10,122	253	11,568	289	13,014	325	14,460	362	15,617	390	16,774	419	17,930	448	19,087	477
Florence	24,700	10,374	259	11,856	296	13,338	333	14,820	371	16,006	400	17,191	430	18,377	459	19,562	489
Gadsden	23,700	9,954	249	11,376	284	12,798	320	14,220	356	15,358	384	16,495	412	17,633	441	18,770	469
Huntsville	35,100	14,742	369	16,848	421	18,954	474	21,060	527	22,745	569	24,430	611	26,114	653	27,799	695
Mobile	28,300	11,886	297	13,584	340	15,282	382	16,980	425	18,338	458	19,697	492	21,055	526	22,414	560
Montgomery	29,900	12,558	314	14,352	359	16,146	404	17,940	449	19,375	484	20,810	520	22,246	556	23,681	592
Tuscaloosa	27,200	11,424	286	13,056	326	14,688	367	16,320	408	17,626	441	18,931	473	20,237	506	21,542	539
Non-Metro Bal.	22,200	9,324	233	10,656	266	11,988	300	13,320	333	14,386	360	15,451	386	16,517	413	17,582	440
Alaska																	
Anchorage	49,900	20,958	524	23,952	599	26,946	674	29,940	749	32,335	808	34,730	868	37,126	928	39,521	988
Non-Metro Bal.	43,100	18,102	453	20,688	517	23,274	582	25,860	647	27,929	698	29,998	750	32,066	802	34,135	853
Arizona																	
Phoenix	33,100	13,902	348	15,888	397	17,874	447	19,860	497	21,449	536	23,038	576	24,626	616	26,215	655
Tucson	30,900	12,978	324	14,832	371	16,686	417	18,540	464	20,023	501	21,506	538	22,990	575	24,473	612
Non-Metro Bal.	23,600	9,912	248	11,328	283	12,744	319	14,160	354	15,293	382	16,426	411	17,558	439	18,691	467
Arkansas																	
Fayetteville	25,200	10,584	265	12,096	302	13,608	340	15,120	378	16,330	408	17,539	438	18,749	469	19,958	499
Fort Smith	25,600	10,752	269	12,288	307	13,824	346	15,360	384	16,589	415	17,818	445	19,046	476	20,275	507
Little Rock	30,000	12,600	315	14,400	360	16,200	405	18,000	450	19,440	486	20,880	522	22,320	558	23,760	594
Pine Bluff	25,000	10,500	263	12,000	300	13,500	338	15,000	375	16,200	405	17,400	435	18,600	465	19,800	495
Non-Metro Bal.	21,500	9,030	226	10,320	258	11,610	290	12,900	323	13,932	348	14,964	374	15,996	400	17,028	426
California																	
Anaheim	46,900	19,698	492	22,512	563	25,326	633	28,140	704	30,391	760	32,642	816	34,894	872	37,145	929
Bakersfield	31,500	13,230	331	15,120	378	17,010	425	18,900	473	20,412	510	21,924	548	23,436	586	24,948	624
Chico	28,500	11,970	299	13,680	342	15,390	385	17,100	428	18,468	462	19,836	496	21,204	530	22,572	564
Fresno	30,600	12,852	321	14,688	367	16,524	413	18,360	459	19,829	496	21,298	532	22,766	569	24,235	606
Los Angeles	39,900	16,758	419	19,152	479	21,546	539	23,940	599	25,855	646	27,770	694	29,686	742	31,601	790
Merced	28,500	11,970	299	13,680	342	15,390	385	17,100	428	18,468	462	19,836	496	21,204	530	22,572	564
Modesto	31,800	13,356	334	15,264	382	17,172	429	19,080	477	20,606	515	22,133	553	23,659	591	25,186	630
Oakland	45,000	18,900	473	21,600	540	24,300	608	27,000	675	29,160	729	31,320	783	33,480	837	35,640	891
Oxnard	43,600	18,312	458	20,928	523	23,544	589	26,160	654	28,253	706	30,346	759	32,438	811	34,531	863
Redding	28,800	12,096	302	13,824	346	15,552	389	17,280	432	18,662	467	20,045	501	21,427	536	22,810	570
Riverside	32,200	13,524	338	15,456	386	17,388	435	19,320	483	20,866	522	22,411	560	23,957	599	25,502	638
Sacramento	36,100	15,162	379	17,328	433	19,494	487	21,660	542	23,393	585	25,126	628	26,858	671	28,591	715
Salinas	34,700	14,574	364	16,656	416	18,738	468	20,820	521	22,486	562	24,151	604	25,817	645	27,482	687
San Diego	37,800	15,876	397	18,144	454	20,412	510	22,680	567	24,494	612	26,309	658	28,123	703	29,938	748
San Francisco	49,500	20,790	520	23,760	594	26,730	668	29,700	743	32,076	802	34,452	861	36,828	921	39,204	980

Appendix 1 Continued

Metropolitan Area or Non-Metro Balance	Effective Median Income 1989	Size of Household: 1 person Max Income	1 person Max Rent	2 persons Max Income	2 persons Max Rent	3 persons Max Income	3 persons Max Rent	4 persons Max Income	4 persons Max Rent	5 persons Max Income	5 persons Max Rent	6 persons Max Income	6 persons Max Rent	7 persons Max Income	7 persons Max Rent	8 persons Max Income	8 persons Max Rent
California																	
San Jose	51,100	21,462	537	24,528	613	27,594	690	30,660	767	33,113	828	35,566	889	38,018	950	40,471	1012
Santa Barbara	44,900	18,858	471	21,552	539	24,246	606	26,940	674	29,095	727	31,250	781	33,406	835	35,561	889
Santa Cruz	44,100	18,522	463	21,168	529	23,814	595	26,460	662	28,577	714	30,694	767	32,810	820	34,927	873
Santa Rosa	39,200	16,464	412	18,816	470	21,168	529	23,520	588	25,402	635	27,283	682	29,165	729	31,046	776
Stockton	32,100	13,482	337	15,408	385	17,334	433	19,260	482	20,801	520	22,342	559	23,882	597	25,423	636
Vallejo	38,800	16,296	407	18,624	466	20,952	524	23,280	582	25,142	629	27,005	675	28,867	722	30,730	768
Visalia	28,500	11,970	299	13,680	342	15,390	385	17,100	428	18,468	462	19,836	496	21,204	530	22,572	564
Yuba City	28,500	11,970	299	13,680	342	15,390	385	17,100	428	18,468	462	19,836	496	21,204	530	22,572	564
Non-Metro Bal.	28,500	11,970	299	13,680	342	15,390	385	17,100	428	18,468	462	19,836	496	21,204	530	22,572	564
Colorado																	
Boulder	41,700	17,514	438	20,016	500	22,518	563	25,020	626	27,022	676	29,023	726	31,025	776	33,026	826
Colorado Springs	31,900	13,398	335	15,312	383	17,226	431	19,140	479	20,671	517	22,202	555	23,734	593	25,265	632
Denver	39,500	16,590	415	18,960	474	21,330	533	23,700	593	25,596	640	27,492	687	29,388	735	31,284	782
Fort Collins	34,300	14,406	360	16,464	412	18,522	463	20,580	515	22,226	556	23,873	597	25,519	638	27,166	679
Greeley	29,700	12,474	312	14,256	356	16,038	401	17,820	446	19,246	481	20,671	517	22,097	552	23,522	588
Pueblo	26,700	11,214	280	12,816	320	14,418	360	16,020	401	17,302	433	18,583	465	19,865	497	21,146	529
Non-Metro Bal.	26,700	11,214	280	12,816	320	14,418	360	16,020	401	17,302	433	18,583	465	19,865	497	21,146	529
Connecticut																	
Bridgeport	46,200	19,404	485	22,176	554	24,948	624	27,720	693	29,938	748	32,155	804	34,373	859	36,590	915
Bristol	43,200	18,144	454	20,736	518	23,328	583	25,920	648	27,994	700	30,067	752	32,141	804	34,214	855
Danbury	54,700	22,974	574	26,256	656	29,538	738	32,820	821	35,446	886	38,071	952	40,697	1017	43,322	1083
Hartford	45,500	19,110	478	21,840	546	24,570	614	27,300	683	29,484	737	31,668	792	33,852	846	36,036	901
Middletown	43,600	18,312	458	20,928	523	23,544	589	26,160	654	28,253	706	30,346	759	32,438	811	34,531	863
New Britain	41,500	17,430	436	19,920	498	22,410	560	24,900	623	26,892	672	28,884	722	30,876	772	32,868	822
New Haven	41,200	17,304	433	19,776	494	22,248	556	24,720	618	26,698	667	28,675	717	30,653	766	32,630	816
New London	40,100	16,842	421	19,248	481	21,654	541	24,060	602	25,985	650	27,910	698	29,834	746	31,759	794
Norwalk	63,100	26,502	663	30,288	757	34,074	852	37,860	947	40,889	1022	43,918	1098	46,946	1174	49,975	1249
Stamford	64,800	27,216	680	31,104	778	34,992	875	38,880	972	41,990	1050	45,101	1128	48,211	1205	51,322	1283
Waterbury	39,100	16,422	411	18,768	469	21,114	528	23,460	587	25,337	633	27,214	680	29,090	727	30,967	774
Non-Metro Bal.	38,600	16,212	405	18,528	463	20,844	521	23,160	579	25,013	625	26,866	672	28,718	718	30,571	764
Delaware																	
Wilmington	38,400	16,128	403	18,432	461	20,736	518	23,040	576	24,883	622	26,726	668	28,570	714	30,413	760
Non-Metro Bal.	28,900	12,138	303	13,872	347	15,606	390	17,340	434	18,727	468	20,114	503	21,502	538	22,889	572
District of Columbia																	
Washington	51,000	21,420	536	24,480	612	27,540	689	30,600	765	33,048	826	35,496	887	37,944	949	40,392	1010
Florida																	
Bradenton	28,600	12,012	300	13,728	343	15,444	386	17,160	429	18,533	463	19,906	498	21,278	532	22,651	566
Daytona Beach	27,600	11,592	290	13,248	331	14,904	373	16,560	414	17,885	447	19,210	480	20,534	513	21,859	546
Fort Lauderdale	36,400	15,288	382	17,472	437	19,656	491	21,840	546	23,587	590	25,334	633	27,082	677	28,829	721
Fort Myers	30,300	12,726	318	14,544	364	16,362	409	18,180	455	19,634	491	21,089	527	22,543	564	23,998	600
Fort Pierce	29,500	12,390	310	14,160	354	15,930	398	17,700	443	19,116	478	20,532	513	21,948	549	23,364	584
Fort Walton Beach	29,700	12,474	312	14,256	356	16,038	401	17,820	446	19,246	481	20,671	517	22,097	552	23,522	588
Gainesville	29,900	12,558	314	14,352	359	16,146	404	17,940	449	19,375	484	20,810	520	22,246	556	23,681	592

Appendix 1 Continued

Metropolitan Area or Non-Metro Balance	Effective Median Income 1989	Size of Household: 1 person Max Income	1 person Max Rent	2 persons Max Income	2 persons Max Rent	3 persons Max Income	3 persons Max Rent	4 persons Max Income	4 persons Max Rent	5 persons Max Income	5 persons Max Rent	6 persons Max Income	6 persons Max Rent	7 persons Max Income	7 persons Max Rent	8 persons Max Income	8 persons Max Rent
Florida																	
Jacksonville	32,000	13,440	336	15,360	384	17,280	432	19,200	480	20,736	518	22,272	557	23,808	595	25,344	634
Lakeland	26,500	11,130	278	12,720	318	14,310	358	15,900	398	17,172	429	18,444	461	19,716	493	20,988	525
Melbourne	34,000	14,280	357	16,320	408	18,360	459	20,400	510	22,032	551	23,664	592	25,296	632	26,928	673
Miami	33,100	13,902	348	15,888	397	17,874	447	19,860	497	21,449	536	23,038	576	24,626	616	26,215	655
Naples	34,800	14,616	365	16,704	418	18,792	470	20,880	522	22,550	564	24,221	606	25,891	647	27,562	689
Ocala	25,000	10,500	263	12,000	300	13,500	338	15,000	375	16,200	405	17,400	435	18,600	465	19,800	495
Orlando	34,200	14,364	359	16,416	410	18,468	462	20,520	513	22,162	554	23,803	595	25,445	636	27,086	677
Panama City	26,500	11,130	278	12,720	318	14,310	358	15,900	398	17,172	429	18,444	461	19,716	493	20,988	525
Pensacola	28,900	12,138	303	13,872	347	15,606	390	17,340	434	18,727	468	20,114	503	21,502	538	22,889	572
Sarasota	31,800	13,356	334	15,264	382	17,172	429	19,080	477	20,606	515	22,133	553	23,659	591	25,186	630
Tallahassee	29,900	12,558	314	14,352	359	16,146	404	17,940	449	19,375	484	20,810	520	22,246	556	23,681	592
Tampa	29,600	12,432	311	14,208	355	15,984	400	17,760	444	19,181	480	20,602	515	22,022	551	23,443	586
West Palm Beach	37,600	15,792	395	18,048	451	20,304	508	22,560	564	24,365	609	26,170	654	27,974	699	29,779	744
Non-Metro Bal.	25,000	10,500	263	12,000	300	13,500	338	15,000	375	16,200	405	17,400	435	18,600	465	19,800	495
Georgia																	
Albany	32,000	13,440	336	15,360	384	17,280	432	19,200	480	20,736	518	22,272	557	23,808	595	25,344	634
Athens	29,300	12,306	308	14,064	352	15,822	396	17,580	440	18,986	475	20,393	510	21,799	545	23,206	580
Atlanta	38,900	16,338	408	18,672	467	21,006	525	23,340	584	25,207	630	27,074	677	28,942	724	30,809	770
Augusta	32,700	13,734	343	15,696	392	17,658	441	19,620	491	21,190	530	22,759	569	24,329	608	25,898	647
Columbus	26,600	11,172	279	12,768	319	14,364	359	15,960	399	17,237	431	18,514	463	19,790	495	21,067	527
Macon	33,600	14,112	353	16,128	403	18,144	454	20,160	504	21,773	544	23,386	585	24,998	625	26,611	665
Savannah	30,300	12,726	318	14,544	364	16,362	409	18,180	455	19,634	491	21,089	527	22,543	564	23,998	600
Non-Metro Bal.	25,900	10,878	272	12,432	311	13,986	350	15,540	389	16,783	420	18,026	451	19,270	482	20,513	513
Hawaii																	
Honolulu	39,100	16,422	411	18,768	469	21,114	528	23,460	587	25,337	633	27,214	680	29,090	727	30,967	774
Non-Metro Bal.	33,500	14,070	352	16,080	402	18,090	452	20,100	503	21,708	543	23,316	583	24,924	623	26,532	663
Idaho																	
Boise City	32,700	13,734	343	15,696	392	17,658	441	19,620	491	21,190	530	22,759	569	24,329	608	25,898	647
Non-Metro Bal.	25,900	10,878	272	12,432	311	13,986	350	15,540	389	16,783	420	18,026	451	19,270	482	20,513	513
Illinois																	
Aurora	40,700	17,094	427	19,536	488	21,978	549	24,420	611	26,374	659	28,327	708	30,281	757	32,234	806
Bloomington	37,700	15,834	396	18,096	452	20,358	509	22,620	566	24,430	611	26,239	656	28,049	701	29,858	746
Champaign	35,400	14,868	372	16,992	425	19,116	478	21,240	531	22,939	573	24,638	616	26,338	658	28,037	701
Chicago	41,700	17,514	438	20,016	500	22,518	563	25,020	626	27,022	676	29,023	726	31,025	776	33,026	826
Decatur	37,000	15,540	389	17,760	444	19,980	500	22,200	555	23,976	599	25,752	644	27,528	688	29,304	733
Joliet	41,200	17,304	433	19,776	494	22,248	556	24,720	618	26,698	667	28,675	717	30,653	766	32,630	816
Kankakee	30,600	12,852	321	14,688	367	16,524	413	18,360	459	19,829	496	21,298	532	22,766	569	24,235	606
Lake County	49,000	20,580	515	23,520	588	26,460	662	29,400	735	31,752	794	34,104	853	36,456	911	38,808	970
Peoria	36,000	15,120	378	17,280	432	19,440	486	21,600	540	23,328	583	25,056	626	26,784	670	28,512	713
Rockford	36,100	15,162	379	17,328	433	19,494	487	21,660	542	23,393	585	25,126	628	26,858	671	28,591	715
Springfield	33,700	14,154	354	16,176	404	18,198	455	20,220	506	21,838	546	23,455	586	25,073	627	26,690	667
Non-Metro Bal.	30,600	12,852	321	14,688	367	16,524	413	18,360	459	19,829	496	21,298	532	22,766	569	24,235	606

Appendix 1 Continued

Metropolitan Area or Non-Metro Balance	Effective Median Income 1989	Size of Household: 1 person		2 persons		3 persons		4 persons		5 persons		6 persons		7 persons		8 persons	
		Max Income	Max Rent	Max Income	Max Rent	Max Income	Max Rent	Max Income	Max Rent	Max Income	Max Rent	Max Income	Max Rent	Max Income	Max Rent	Max Income	Max Rent
Indiana																	
Anderson	34,600	14,532	363	16,608	415	18,684	467	20,760	519	22,421	561	24,082	602	25,742	644	27,403	685
Bloomington	30,500	12,810	320	14,640	366	16,470	412	18,300	458	19,764	494	21,228	531	22,692	567	24,156	604
Elkhart	34,500	14,490	362	16,560	414	18,630	466	20,700	518	22,356	559	24,012	600	25,668	642	27,324	683
Evansville	33,700	14,154	354	16,176	404	18,198	455	20,220	506	21,838	546	23,455	586	25,073	627	26,690	667
Fort Wayne	34,600	14,532	363	16,608	415	18,684	467	20,760	519	22,421	561	24,082	602	25,742	644	27,403	685
Gary	35,800	15,036	376	17,184	430	19,332	483	21,480	537	23,198	580	24,917	623	26,635	666	28,354	709
Indianapolis	35,100	14,742	369	16,848	421	18,954	474	21,060	527	22,745	569	24,430	611	26,114	653	27,799	695
Kokomo	38,400	16,128	403	18,432	461	20,736	518	23,040	576	24,883	622	26,726	668	28,570	714	30,413	760
Lafayette	32,300	13,566	339	15,504	388	17,442	436	19,380	485	20,930	523	22,481	562	24,031	601	25,582	640
Muncie	30,100	12,642	316	14,448	361	16,254	406	18,060	452	19,505	488	20,950	524	22,394	560	23,839	596
South Bend	32,600	13,692	342	15,648	391	17,604	440	19,560	489	21,125	528	22,690	567	24,254	606	25,819	645
Terre Haute	31,200	13,104	328	14,976	374	16,848	421	18,720	468	20,218	505	21,715	543	23,213	580	24,710	618
Non-Metro Bal.	30,000	12,600	315	14,400	360	16,200	405	18,000	450	19,440	486	20,880	522	22,320	558	23,760	594
Iowa																	
Cedar Rapids	36,900	15,498	387	17,712	443	19,926	498	22,140	554	23,911	598	25,682	642	27,454	686	29,225	731
Davenport	34,100	14,322	358	16,368	409	18,414	460	20,460	512	22,097	552	23,734	593	25,370	634	27,007	675
Des Moines	35,400	14,868	372	16,992	425	19,116	478	21,240	531	22,939	573	24,638	616	26,338	658	28,037	701
Dubuque	32,200	13,524	338	15,456	386	17,388	435	19,320	483	20,866	522	22,411	560	23,957	599	25,502	638
Iowa City	35,800	15,036	376	17,184	430	19,332	483	21,480	537	23,198	580	24,917	623	26,635	666	28,354	709
Sioux City	29,400	12,348	309	14,112	353	15,876	397	17,640	441	19,051	476	20,462	512	21,874	547	23,285	582
Waterloo	31,300	13,146	329	15,024	376	16,902	423	18,780	470	20,282	507	21,785	545	23,287	582	24,790	620
Non-Metro Bal.	28,000	11,760	294	13,440	336	15,120	378	16,800	420	18,144	454	19,488	487	20,832	521	22,176	554
Kansas																	
Lawrence	31,800	13,356	334	15,264	382	17,172	429	19,080	477	20,606	515	22,133	553	23,659	591	25,186	630
Topeka	35,600	14,952	374	17,088	427	19,224	481	21,360	534	23,069	577	24,778	619	26,486	662	28,195	705
Wichita	38,000	15,960	399	18,240	456	20,520	513	22,800	570	24,624	616	26,448	661	28,272	707	30,096	752
Non-Metro Bal.	28,200	11,844	296	13,536	338	15,228	381	16,920	423	18,274	457	19,627	491	20,981	525	22,334	558
Kentucky																	
Lexington	30,100	12,642	316	14,448	361	16,254	406	18,060	452	19,505	488	20,950	524	22,394	560	23,839	596
Louisville	31,100	13,062	327	14,928	373	16,794	420	18,660	467	20,153	504	21,646	541	23,138	578	24,631	616
Owensboro	28,900	12,138	303	13,872	347	15,606	390	17,340	434	18,727	468	20,114	503	21,502	538	22,889	572
Non-Metro Bal.	22,300	9,366	234	10,704	268	12,042	301	13,380	335	14,450	361	15,521	388	16,591	415	17,662	442
Louisiana																	
Alexandria	26,500	11,130	278	12,720	318	14,310	358	15,900	398	17,172	429	18,444	461	19,716	493	20,988	525
Baton Rouge	31,800	13,356	334	15,264	382	17,172	429	19,080	477	20,606	515	22,133	553	23,659	591	25,186	630
Houma	29,700	12,474	312	14,256	356	16,038	401	17,820	446	19,246	481	20,671	517	22,097	552	23,522	588
Lafayette	33,800	14,196	355	16,224	406	18,252	456	20,280	507	21,902	548	23,525	588	25,147	629	26,770	669
Lake Charles	32,700	13,734	343	15,696	392	17,658	441	19,620	491	21,190	530	22,759	569	24,329	608	25,898	647
Monroe	27,000	11,340	284	12,960	324	14,580	365	16,200	405	17,496	437	18,792	470	20,088	502	21,384	535
New Orleans	32,600	13,692	342	15,648	391	17,604	440	19,560	489	21,125	528	22,690	567	24,254	606	25,819	645
Shreveport	30,400	12,768	319	14,592	365	16,416	410	18,240	456	19,699	492	21,158	529	22,618	565	24,077	602
Non-Metro Bal.	23,400	9,828	246	11,232	281	12,636	316	14,040	351	15,163	379	16,286	407	17,410	435	18,533	463

Appendix 1 Continued

Metropolitan Area or Non-Metro Balance	Effective Median Income 1989	Size of Household: 1 person Max Income	1 person Max Rent	2 persons Max Income	2 persons Max Rent	3 persons Max Income	3 persons Max Rent	4 persons Max Income	4 persons Max Rent	5 persons Max Income	5 persons Max Rent	6 persons Max Income	6 persons Max Rent	7 persons Max Income	7 persons Max Rent	8 persons Max Income	8 persons Max Rent
Maine																	
Bangor	31,100	13,062	327	14,928	373	16,794	420	18,660	467	20,153	504	21,646	541	23,138	578	24,631	616
Lewiston	28,900	12,138	303	13,872	347	15,606	390	17,340	434	18,727	468	20,114	503	21,502	538	22,889	572
Portland	36,100	15,162	379	17,328	433	19,494	487	21,660	542	23,393	585	25,126	628	26,858	671	28,591	715
Non-Metro Bal.	28,400	11,928	298	13,632	341	15,336	383	17,040	426	18,403	460	19,766	494	21,130	528	22,493	562
Maryland																	
Baltimore	37,700	15,834	396	18,096	452	20,358	509	22,620	566	24,430	611	26,239	656	28,049	701	29,858	746
Cumberland	31,300	13,146	329	15,024	376	16,902	423	18,780	470	20,282	507	21,785	545	23,287	582	24,790	620
Hagerstown	32,800	13,776	344	15,744	394	17,712	443	19,680	492	21,254	531	22,829	571	24,403	610	25,978	649
Non-Metro Bal.	31,300	13,146	329	15,024	376	16,902	423	18,780	470	20,282	507	21,785	545	23,287	582	24,790	620
Massachusetts																	
Boston	46,900	19,698	492	22,512	563	25,326	633	28,140	704	30,391	760	32,642	816	34,894	872	37,145	929
Brockton	40,800	17,136	428	19,584	490	22,032	551	24,480	612	26,438	661	28,397	710	30,355	759	32,314	808
Fall River	33,900	14,238	356	16,272	407	18,306	458	20,340	509	21,967	549	23,594	590	25,222	631	26,849	671
Fitchburg	35,800	15,036	376	17,184	430	19,332	483	21,480	537	23,198	580	24,917	623	26,635	666	28,354	709
Lawrence	42,200	17,724	443	20,256	506	22,788	570	25,320	633	27,346	684	29,371	734	31,397	785	33,422	836
Lowell	44,600	18,732	468	21,408	535	24,084	602	26,760	669	28,901	723	31,042	776	33,182	830	35,323	883
New Bedford	33,900	14,238	356	16,272	407	18,306	458	20,340	509	21,967	549	23,594	590	25,222	631	26,849	671
Pittsfield	36,400	15,288	382	17,472	437	19,656	491	21,840	546	23,587	590	25,334	633	27,082	677	28,829	721
Salem	45,800	19,236	481	21,984	550	24,732	618	27,480	687	29,678	742	31,877	797	34,075	852	36,274	907
Springfield	36,100	15,162	379	17,328	433	19,494	487	21,660	542	23,393	585	25,126	628	26,858	671	28,591	715
Worcester	37,900	15,918	398	18,192	455	20,466	512	22,740	569	24,559	614	26,378	659	28,198	705	30,017	750
Non-Metro Bal.	33,900	14,238	356	16,272	407	18,306	458	20,340	509	21,967	549	23,594	590	25,222	631	26,849	671
Michigan																	
Ann Arbor	40,600	17,052	426	19,488	487	21,924	548	24,360	609	26,309	658	28,258	706	30,206	755	32,155	804
Battle Creek	33,300	13,986	350	15,984	400	17,982	450	19,980	500	21,578	539	23,177	579	24,775	619	26,374	659
Benton Harbor	30,100	12,642	316	14,448	361	16,254	406	18,060	452	19,505	488	20,950	524	22,394	560	23,839	596
Detroit	39,900	16,758	419	19,152	479	21,546	539	23,940	599	25,855	646	27,770	694	29,686	742	31,601	790
Flint	38,500	16,170	404	18,480	462	20,790	520	23,100	578	24,948	624	26,796	670	28,644	716	30,492	762
Grand Rapids	35,700	14,994	375	17,136	428	19,278	482	21,420	536	23,134	578	24,847	621	26,561	664	28,274	707
Jackson	32,200	13,524	338	15,456	386	17,388	435	19,320	483	20,866	522	22,411	560	23,957	599	25,502	638
Kalamazoo	37,600	15,792	395	18,048	451	20,304	508	22,560	564	24,365	609	26,170	654	27,974	699	29,779	744
Lansing	37,900	15,918	398	18,192	455	20,466	512	22,740	569	24,559	614	26,378	659	28,198	705	30,017	750
Muskegon	29,100	12,222	306	13,968	349	15,714	393	17,460	437	18,857	471	20,254	506	21,650	541	23,047	576
Saginaw	36,200	15,204	380	17,376	434	19,548	489	21,720	543	23,458	586	25,195	630	26,933	673	28,670	717
Non-Metro Bal.	28,000	11,760	294	13,440	336	15,120	378	16,800	420	18,144	454	19,488	487	20,832	521	22,176	554
Minnesota																	
Duluth	27,600	11,592	290	13,248	331	14,904	373	16,560	414	17,885	447	19,210	480	20,534	513	21,859	546
Minneapolis	42,300	17,766	444	20,304	508	22,842	571	25,380	635	27,410	685	29,441	736	31,471	787	33,502	838
Rochester	40,600	17,052	426	19,488	487	21,924	548	24,360	609	26,309	658	28,258	706	30,206	755	32,155	804
St. Cloud	31,900	13,398	335	15,312	383	17,226	431	19,140	479	20,671	517	22,202	555	23,734	593	25,265	632
Non-Metro Bal.	27,000	11,340	284	12,960	324	14,580	365	16,200	405	17,496	437	18,792	470	20,088	502	21,384	535

Appendix 1 Continued

Metropolitan Area or Non-Metro Balance	Effective Median Income 1989	Size of Household: 1 person Max Income	1 person Max Rent	2 persons Max Income	2 persons Max Rent	3 persons Max Income	3 persons Max Rent	4 persons Max Income	4 persons Max Rent	5 persons Max Income	5 persons Max Rent	6 persons Max Income	6 persons Max Rent	7 persons Max Income	7 persons Max Rent	8 persons Max Income	8 persons Max Rent
Mississippi																	
Biloxi	25,800	10,836	271	12,384	310	13,932	348	15,480	387	16,718	418	17,957	449	19,195	480	20,434	511
Jackson	29,600	12,432	311	14,208	355	15,984	400	17,760	444	19,181	480	20,602	515	22,022	551	23,443	586
Pascagoula	30,400	12,768	319	14,592	365	16,416	410	18,240	456	19,699	492	21,158	529	22,618	565	24,077	602
Non-Metro Bal.	21,300	8,946	224	10,224	256	11,502	288	12,780	320	13,802	345	14,825	371	15,847	396	16,870	422
Missouri																	
Columbia	33,900	14,238	356	16,272	407	18,306	458	20,340	509	21,967	549	23,594	590	25,222	631	26,849	671
Joplin	24,700	10,374	259	11,856	296	13,338	333	14,820	371	16,006	400	17,191	430	18,377	459	19,562	489
Kansas City	37,000	15,540	389	17,760	444	19,980	500	22,200	555	23,976	599	25,752	644	27,528	688	29,304	733
St. Joseph	29,300	12,306	308	14,064	352	15,822	396	17,580	440	18,986	475	20,393	510	21,799	545	23,206	580
St. Louis	37,200	15,624	391	17,856	446	20,088	502	22,320	558	24,106	603	25,891	647	27,677	692	29,462	737
Springfield	28,400	11,928	298	13,632	341	15,336	383	17,040	426	18,403	460	19,766	494	21,130	528	22,493	562
Non-Metro Bal.	23,500	9,870	247	11,280	282	12,690	317	14,100	353	15,228	381	16,356	409	17,484	437	18,612	465
Montana																	
Billings	32,200	13,524	338	15,456	386	17,388	435	19,320	483	20,866	522	22,411	560	23,957	599	25,502	638
Great Falls	29,300	12,306	308	14,064	352	15,822	396	17,580	440	18,986	475	20,393	510	21,799	545	23,206	580
Non-Metro Bal.	27,200	11,424	286	13,056	326	14,688	367	16,320	408	17,626	441	18,931	473	20,237	506	21,542	539
Nebraska																	
Lincoln	35,700	14,994	375	17,136	428	19,278	482	21,420	536	23,134	578	24,847	621	26,561	664	28,274	707
Omaha	34,900	14,658	366	16,752	419	18,846	471	20,940	524	22,615	565	24,290	607	25,966	649	27,641	691
Non-Metro Bal.	26,100	10,962	274	12,528	313	14,094	352	15,660	392	16,913	423	18,166	454	19,418	485	20,671	517
Nevada																	
Las Vegas	34,800	14,616	365	16,704	418	18,792	470	20,880	522	22,550	564	24,221	606	25,891	647	27,562	689
Reno	42,900	18,018	450	20,592	515	23,166	579	25,740	644	27,799	695	29,858	746	31,918	798	33,977	849
Non-Metro Bal.	31,400	13,188	330	15,072	377	16,956	424	18,840	471	20,347	509	21,854	546	23,362	584	24,869	622
New Hampshire																	
Manchester	40,300	16,926	423	19,344	484	21,762	544	24,180	605	26,114	653	28,049	701	29,983	750	31,918	798
Nashua	46,200	19,404	485	22,176	554	24,948	624	27,720	693	29,938	748	32,155	804	34,373	859	36,590	915
Portsmouth	36,800	15,456	386	17,664	442	19,872	497	22,080	552	23,846	596	25,613	640	27,379	684	29,146	729
Non-Metro Bal.	34,600	14,532	363	16,608	415	18,684	467	20,760	519	22,421	561	24,082	602	25,742	644	27,403	685
New Jersey																	
Atlantic City	31,700	13,314	333	15,216	380	17,118	428	19,020	476	20,542	514	22,063	552	23,585	590	25,106	628
Bergen	44,900	18,858	471	21,552	539	24,246	606	26,940	674	29,095	727	31,250	781	33,406	835	35,561	889
Jersey City	31,600	13,272	332	15,168	379	17,064	427	18,960	474	20,477	512	21,994	550	23,510	588	25,027	626
Middlesex	45,800	19,236	481	21,984	550	24,732	618	27,480	687	29,678	742	31,877	797	34,075	852	36,274	907
Monmouth	38,400	16,128	403	18,432	461	20,736	518	23,040	576	24,883	622	26,726	668	28,570	714	30,413	760
Newark	41,300	17,346	434	19,824	496	22,302	558	24,780	620	26,762	669	28,745	719	30,727	768	32,710	818
Trenton	41,700	17,514	438	20,016	500	22,518	563	25,020	626	27,022	676	29,023	726	31,025	776	33,026	826
Vineland	30,400	12,768	319	14,592	365	16,416	410	18,240	456	19,699	492	21,158	529	22,618	565	24,077	602

Appendix 1 Continued

Metropolitan Area or Non-Metro Balance	Effective Median Income 1989	Size of Household: 1 person Max Income	1 person Max Rent	2 persons Max Income	2 persons Max Rent	3 persons Max Income	3 persons Max Rent	4 persons Max Income	4 persons Max Rent	5 persons Max Income	5 persons Max Rent	6 persons Max Income	6 persons Max Rent	7 persons Max Income	7 persons Max Rent	8 persons Max Income	8 persons Max Rent
New Mexico																	
Albuquerque	32,100	13,482	337	15,408	385	17,334	433	19,260	482	20,801	520	22,342	559	23,882	597	25,423	636
Las Cruces	24,100	10,122	253	11,568	289	13,014	325	14,460	362	15,617	390	16,774	419	17,930	448	19,087	477
Santa Fe	39,500	16,590	415	18,960	474	21,330	533	23,700	593	25,596	640	27,492	687	29,388	735	31,284	782
Non-Metro Bal.	23,900	10,038	251	11,472	287	12,906	323	14,340	359	15,487	387	16,634	416	17,782	445	18,929	473
New York																	
Albany	32,800	13,776	344	15,744	394	17,712	443	19,680	492	21,254	531	22,829	571	24,403	610	25,978	649
Binghamton	34,700	14,574	364	16,656	416	18,738	468	20,820	521	22,486	562	24,151	604	25,817	645	27,482	687
Buffalo	33,600	14,112	353	16,128	403	18,144	454	20,160	504	21,773	544	23,386	585	24,998	625	26,611	665
Elmira	28,800	12,096	302	13,824	346	15,552	389	17,280	432	18,662	467	20,045	501	21,427	536	22,810	570
Glens Falls	28,600	12,012	300	13,728	343	15,444	386	17,160	429	18,533	463	19,906	498	21,278	532	22,651	566
Nassau	46,300	19,446	486	22,224	556	25,002	625	27,780	695	30,002	750	32,225	806	34,447	861	36,670	917
New York	33,800	14,196	355	16,224	406	18,252	456	20,280	507	21,902	548	23,525	588	25,147	629	26,770	669
Niagara Falls	33,200	13,944	349	15,936	398	17,928	448	19,920	498	21,514	538	23,107	578	24,701	618	26,294	657
Orange County	35,300	14,826	371	16,944	424	19,062	477	21,180	530	22,874	572	24,569	614	26,263	657	27,958	699
Poughkeepsie	41,300	17,346	434	19,824	496	22,302	558	24,780	620	26,762	669	28,745	719	30,727	768	32,710	818
Rochester	40,100	16,842	421	19,248	481	21,654	541	24,060	602	25,985	650	27,910	698	29,834	746	31,759	794
Syracuse	34,400	14,448	361	16,512	413	18,576	464	20,640	516	22,291	557	23,942	599	25,594	640	27,245	681
Utica	28,400	11,928	298	13,632	341	15,336	383	17,040	426	18,403	460	19,766	494	21,130	528	22,493	562
Non-Metro Bal.	27,700	11,634	291	13,296	332	14,958	374	16,620	416	17,950	449	19,279	482	20,609	515	21,938	548
North Carolina																	
Asheville	28,500	11,970	299	13,680	342	15,390	385	17,100	428	18,468	462	19,836	496	21,204	530	22,572	564
Burlington	31,500	13,230	331	15,120	378	17,010	425	18,900	473	20,412	510	21,924	548	23,436	586	24,948	624
Charlotte	35,300	14,826	371	16,944	424	19,062	477	21,180	530	22,874	572	24,569	614	26,263	657	27,958	699
Fayetteville	26,500	11,130	278	12,720	318	14,310	358	15,900	398	17,172	429	18,444	461	19,716	493	20,988	525
Greensboro	33,200	13,944	349	15,936	398	17,928	448	19,920	498	21,514	538	23,107	578	24,701	618	26,294	657
Hickory	31,400	13,188	330	15,072	377	16,956	424	18,840	471	20,347	509	21,854	546	23,362	584	24,869	622
Jacksonville	26,100	10,962	274	12,528	313	14,094	352	15,660	392	16,913	423	18,166	454	19,418	485	20,671	517
Raleigh	40,300	16,926	423	19,344	484	21,762	544	24,180	605	26,114	653	28,049	701	29,983	750	31,918	798
Wilmington	30,300	12,726	318	14,544	364	16,362	409	18,180	455	19,634	491	21,089	527	22,543	564	23,998	600
Non-Metro Bal.	26,100	10,962	274	12,528	313	14,094	352	15,660	392	16,913	423	18,166	454	19,418	485	20,671	517
North Dakota																	
Bismarck	32,600	13,692	342	15,648	391	17,604	440	19,560	489	21,125	528	22,690	567	24,254	606	25,819	645
Fargo	33,500	14,070	352	16,080	402	18,090	452	20,100	503	21,708	543	23,316	583	24,924	623	26,532	663
Grand Forks	28,500	11,970	299	13,680	342	15,390	385	17,100	428	18,468	462	19,836	496	21,204	530	22,572	564
Non-Metro Bal.	27,400	11,508	288	13,152	329	14,796	370	16,440	411	17,755	444	19,070	477	20,386	510	21,701	543
Ohio																	
Akron	34,800	14,616	365	16,704	418	18,792	470	20,880	522	22,550	564	24,221	606	25,891	647	27,562	689
Canton	31,300	13,146	329	15,024	376	16,902	423	18,780	470	20,282	507	21,785	545	23,287	582	24,790	620
Cincinnati	35,500	14,910	373	17,040	426	19,170	479	21,300	533	23,004	575	24,708	618	26,412	660	28,116	703
Cleveland	36,700	15,414	385	17,616	440	19,818	495	22,020	551	23,782	595	25,543	639	27,305	683	29,066	727
Columbus	34,900	14,658	366	16,752	419	18,846	471	20,940	524	22,615	565	24,290	607	25,966	649	27,641	691
Dayton	34,000	14,280	357	16,320	408	18,360	459	20,400	510	22,032	551	23,664	592	25,296	632	26,928	673
Hamilton	34,600	14,532	363	16,608	415	18,684	467	20,760	519	22,421	561	24,082	602	25,742	644	27,403	685
Lima	32,700	13,734	343	15,696	392	17,658	441	19,620	491	21,190	530	22,759	569	24,329	608	25,898	647

Appendix 1 Continued

Metropolitan Area or Non-Metro Balance	Effective Median Income 1989	Size of Household: 1 person Max Income	1 person Max Rent	2 persons Max Income	2 persons Max Rent	3 persons Max Income	3 persons Max Rent	4 persons Max Income	4 persons Max Rent	5 persons Max Income	5 persons Max Rent	6 persons Max Income	6 persons Max Rent	7 persons Max Income	7 persons Max Rent	8 persons Max Income	8 persons Max Rent
Ohio																	
Lorain	35,300	14,826	371	16,944	424	19,062	477	21,180	530	22,874	572	24,569	614	26,263	657	27,958	699
Mansfield	31,900	13,398	335	15,312	383	17,226	431	19,140	479	20,671	517	22,202	555	23,734	593	25,265	632
Steubenville	30,500	12,810	320	14,640	366	16,470	412	18,300	458	19,764	494	21,228	531	22,692	567	24,156	604
Toledo	35,200	14,784	370	16,896	422	19,008	475	21,120	528	22,810	570	24,499	612	26,189	655	27,878	697
Youngstown	32,200	13,524	338	15,456	386	17,388	435	19,320	483	20,866	522	22,411	560	23,957	599	25,502	638
Non-Metro Bal.	30,400	12,768	319	14,592	365	16,416	410	18,240	456	19,699	492	21,158	529	22,618	565	24,077	602
Oklahoma																	
Enid	30,000	12,600	315	14,400	360	16,200	405	18,000	450	19,440	486	20,880	522	22,320	558	23,760	594
Lawton	28,800	12,096	302	13,824	346	15,552	389	17,280	432	18,662	467	20,045	501	21,427	536	22,810	570
Oklahoma City	33,200	13,944	349	15,936	398	17,928	448	19,920	498	21,514	538	23,107	578	24,701	618	26,294	657
Tulsa	33,900	14,238	356	16,272	407	18,306	458	20,340	509	21,967	549	23,594	590	25,222	631	26,849	671
Non-Metro Bal.	24,500	10,290	257	11,760	294	13,230	331	14,700	368	15,876	397	17,052	426	18,228	456	19,404	485
Oregon																	
Eugene	30,400	12,768	319	14,592	365	16,416	410	18,240	456	19,699	492	21,158	529	22,618	565	24,077	602
Medford	30,200	12,684	317	14,496	362	16,308	408	18,120	453	19,570	489	21,019	525	22,469	562	23,918	598
Portland	36,200	15,204	380	17,376	434	19,548	489	21,720	543	23,458	586	25,195	630	26,933	673	28,670	717
Salem	28,600	12,012	300	13,728	343	15,444	386	17,160	429	18,533	463	19,906	498	21,278	532	22,651	566
Non-Metro Bal.	28,100	11,802	295	13,488	337	15,174	379	16,860	422	18,209	455	19,558	489	20,906	523	22,255	556
Pennsylvania																	
Allentown	33,700	14,154	354	16,176	404	18,198	455	20,220	506	21,838	546	23,455	586	25,073	627	26,690	667
Altoona	28,000	11,760	294	13,440	336	15,120	378	16,800	420	18,144	454	19,488	487	20,832	521	22,176	554
Beaver County	29,100	12,222	306	13,968	349	15,714	393	17,460	437	18,857	471	20,254	506	21,650	541	23,047	576
Erie	33,000	13,860	347	15,840	396	17,820	446	19,800	495	21,384	535	22,968	574	24,552	614	26,136	653
Harrisburg	34,800	14,616	365	16,704	418	18,792	470	20,880	522	22,550	564	24,221	606	25,891	647	27,562	689
Johnstown	27,800	11,676	292	13,344	334	15,012	375	16,680	417	18,014	450	19,349	484	20,683	517	22,018	550
Lancaster	33,900	14,238	356	16,272	407	18,306	458	20,340	509	21,967	549	23,594	590	25,222	631	26,849	671
Philadelphia	36,500	15,330	383	17,520	438	19,710	493	21,900	548	23,652	591	25,404	635	27,156	679	28,908	723
Pittsburgh	32,700	13,734	343	15,696	392	17,658	441	19,620	491	21,190	530	22,759	569	24,329	608	25,898	647
Reading	34,900	14,658	366	16,752	419	18,846	471	20,940	524	22,615	565	24,290	607	25,966	649	27,641	691
Scranton	28,600	12,012	300	13,728	343	15,444	386	17,160	429	18,533	463	19,906	498	21,278	532	22,651	566
Sharon	29,600	12,432	311	14,208	355	15,984	400	17,760	444	19,181	480	20,602	515	22,022	551	23,443	586
State College	32,300	13,566	339	15,504	388	17,442	436	19,380	485	20,930	523	22,481	562	24,031	601	25,582	640
Williamsport	29,700	12,474	312	14,256	356	16,038	401	17,820	446	19,246	481	20,671	517	22,097	552	23,522	588
York	33,000	13,860	347	15,840	396	17,820	446	19,800	495	21,384	535	22,968	574	24,552	614	26,136	653
Non-Metro Bal.	27,800	11,676	292	13,344	334	15,012	375	16,680	417	18,014	450	19,349	484	20,683	517	22,018	550
Rhode Island																	
Pawtucket	38,000	15,960	399	18,240	456	20,520	513	22,800	570	24,624	616	26,448	661	28,272	707	30,096	752
Providence	38,000	15,960	399	18,240	456	20,520	513	22,800	570	24,624	616	26,448	661	28,272	707	30,096	752
Non-Metro Bal.	38,000	15,960	399	18,240	456	20,520	513	22,800	570	24,624	616	26,448	661	28,272	707	30,096	752

Appendix 1 Continued

Metropolitan Area or Non-Metro Balance	Effective Median Income 1989	Size of Household: 1 person Max Income	1 person Max Rent	2 persons Max Income	2 persons Max Rent	3 persons Max Income	3 persons Max Rent	4 persons Max Income	4 persons Max Rent	5 persons Max Income	5 persons Max Rent	6 persons Max Income	6 persons Max Rent	7 persons Max Income	7 persons Max Rent	8 persons Max Income	8 persons Max Rent
South Carolina																	
Anderson	29,000	12,180	305	13,920	348	15,660	392	17,400	435	18,792	470	20,184	505	21,576	539	22,968	574
Charleston	31,100	13,062	327	14,928	373	16,794	420	18,660	467	20,153	504	21,646	541	23,138	578	24,631	616
Columbia	36,600	15,372	384	17,568	439	19,764	494	21,960	549	23,717	593	25,474	637	27,230	681	28,987	725
Florence	27,600	11,592	290	13,248	331	14,904	373	16,560	414	17,885	447	19,210	480	20,534	513	21,859	546
Greenville	30,200	12,684	317	14,496	362	16,308	408	18,120	453	19,570	489	21,019	525	22,469	562	23,918	598
Non-Metro Bal.	26,300	11,046	276	12,624	316	14,202	355	15,780	395	17,042	426	18,305	458	19,567	489	20,830	521
South Dakota																	
Rapid City	27,800	11,676	292	13,344	334	15,012	375	16,680	417	18,014	450	19,349	484	20,683	517	22,018	550
Sioux Falls	31,700	13,314	333	15,216	380	17,118	428	19,020	476	20,542	514	22,063	552	23,585	590	25,106	628
Non-Metro Bal.	23,800	9,996	250	11,424	286	12,852	321	14,280	357	15,422	386	16,565	414	17,707	443	18,850	471
Tennessee																	
Chattanooga	27,300	11,466	287	13,104	328	14,742	369	16,380	410	17,690	442	19,001	475	20,311	508	21,622	541
Clarksville	24,600	10,332	258	11,808	295	13,284	332	14,760	369	15,941	399	17,122	428	18,302	458	19,483	487
Jackson	27,600	11,592	290	13,248	331	14,904	373	16,560	414	17,885	447	19,210	480	20,534	513	21,859	546
Johnson City	25,400	10,668	267	12,192	305	13,716	343	15,240	381	16,459	411	17,678	442	18,898	472	20,117	503
Knoxville	27,600	11,592	290	13,248	331	14,904	373	16,560	414	17,885	447	19,210	480	20,534	513	21,859	546
Memphis	29,300	12,306	308	14,064	352	15,822	396	17,580	440	18,986	475	20,393	510	21,799	545	23,206	580
Nashville	32,800	13,776	344	15,744	394	17,712	443	19,680	492	21,254	531	22,829	571	24,403	610	25,978	649
Non-Metro Bal.	22,700	9,534	238	10,896	272	12,258	306	13,620	341	14,710	368	15,799	395	16,889	422	17,978	449
Texas																	
Abilene	29,500	12,390	310	14,160	354	15,930	398	17,700	443	19,116	478	20,532	513	21,948	549	23,364	584
Amarillo	35,200	14,784	370	16,896	422	19,008	475	21,120	528	22,810	570	24,499	612	26,189	655	27,878	697
Austin	37,200	15,624	391	17,856	446	20,088	502	22,320	558	24,106	603	25,891	647	27,677	692	29,462	737
Beaumont	33,000	13,860	347	15,840	396	17,820	446	19,800	495	21,384	535	22,968	574	24,552	614	26,136	653
Brazoria	39,000	16,380	410	18,720	468	21,060	527	23,400	585	25,272	632	27,144	679	29,016	725	30,888	772
Brownsville	25,500	10,710	268	12,240	306	13,770	344	15,300	383	16,524	413	17,748	444	18,972	474	20,196	505
Bryan	30,000	12,600	315	14,400	360	16,200	405	18,000	450	19,440	486	20,880	522	22,320	558	23,760	594
Corpus Christi	30,600	12,852	321	14,688	367	16,524	413	18,360	459	19,829	496	21,298	532	22,766	569	24,235	606
Dallas	39,700	16,674	417	19,056	476	21,438	536	23,820	596	25,726	643	27,631	691	29,537	738	31,442	786
El Paso	25,500	10,710	268	12,240	306	13,770	344	15,300	383	16,524	413	17,748	444	18,972	474	20,196	505
Fort Worth	36,400	15,288	382	17,472	437	19,656	491	21,840	546	23,587	590	25,334	633	27,082	677	28,829	721
Galveston	35,700	14,994	375	17,136	428	19,278	482	21,420	536	23,134	578	24,847	621	26,561	664	28,274	707
Houston	38,400	16,128	403	18,432	461	20,736	518	23,040	576	24,883	622	26,726	668	28,570	714	30,413	760
Killeen	25,500	10,710	268	12,240	306	13,770	344	15,300	383	16,524	413	17,748	444	18,972	474	20,196	505
Laredo	25,500	10,710	268	12,240	306	13,770	344	15,300	383	16,524	413	17,748	444	18,972	474	20,196	505
Longview	30,300	12,726	318	14,544	364	16,362	409	18,180	455	19,634	491	21,089	527	22,543	564	23,998	600
Lubbock	30,300	12,726	318	14,544	364	16,362	409	18,180	455	19,634	491	21,089	527	22,543	564	23,998	600
MC Allen	25,500	10,710	268	12,240	306	13,770	344	15,300	383	16,524	413	17,748	444	18,972	474	20,196	505
Midland	42,200	17,724	443	20,256	506	22,788	570	25,320	633	27,346	684	29,371	734	31,397	785	33,422	836
Odessa	33,500	14,070	352	16,080	402	18,090	452	20,100	503	21,708	543	23,316	583	24,924	623	26,532	663
San Angelo	30,800	12,936	323	14,784	370	16,632	416	18,480	462	19,958	499	21,437	536	22,915	573	24,394	610
San Antonio	30,000	12,600	315	14,400	360	16,200	405	18,000	450	19,440	486	20,880	522	22,320	558	23,760	594
Sherman	30,200	12,684	317	14,496	362	16,308	408	18,120	453	19,570	489	21,019	525	22,469	562	23,918	598
Texarkana	29,200	12,264	307	14,016	350	15,768	394	17,520	438	18,922	473	20,323	508	21,725	543	23,126	578
Tyler	32,000	13,440	336	15,360	384	17,280	432	19,200	480	20,736	518	22,272	557	23,808	595	25,344	634

Appendix 1 Continued

Metropolitan Area or Non-Metro Balance	Effective Median Income 1989	Size of Household: 1 person Max Income	1 person Max Rent	2 persons Max Income	2 persons Max Rent	3 persons Max Income	3 persons Max Rent	4 persons Max Income	4 persons Max Rent	5 persons Max Income	5 persons Max Rent	6 persons Max Income	6 persons Max Rent	7 persons Max Income	7 persons Max Rent	8 persons Max Income	8 persons Max Rent
Texas																	
Victoria	34,600	14,532	363	16,608	415	18,684	467	20,760	519	22,421	561	24,082	602	25,742	644	27,403	685
Waco	28,400	11,928	298	13,632	341	15,336	383	17,040	426	18,403	460	19,766	494	21,130	528	22,493	562
Wichita Falls	30,000	12,600	315	14,400	360	16,200	405	18,000	450	19,440	486	20,880	522	22,320	558	23,760	594
Non-Metro Bal.	25,500	10,710	268	12,240	306	13,770	344	15,300	383	16,524	413	17,748	444	18,972	474	20,196	505
Utah																	
Provo	29,700	12,474	312	14,256	356	16,038	401	17,820	446	19,246	481	20,671	517	22,097	552	23,522	588
Salt Lake City	34,800	14,616	365	16,704	418	18,792	470	20,880	522	22,550	564	24,221	606	25,891	647	27,562	689
Non-Metro Bal.	29,700	12,474	312	14,256	356	16,038	401	17,820	446	19,246	481	20,671	517	22,097	552	23,522	588
Vermont																	
Burlington	38,500	16,170	404	18,480	462	20,790	520	23,100	578	24,948	624	26,796	670	28,644	716	30,492	762
Non-Metro Bal.	29,700	12,474	312	14,256	356	16,038	401	17,820	446	19,246	481	20,671	517	22,097	552	23,522	588
Virginia																	
Charlottesville	36,900	15,498	387	17,712	443	19,926	498	22,140	554	23,911	598	25,682	642	27,454	686	29,225	731
Danville	28,500	11,970	299	13,680	342	15,390	385	17,100	428	18,468	462	19,836	496	21,204	530	22,572	564
Lynchburg	31,700	13,314	333	15,216	380	17,118	428	19,020	476	20,542	514	22,063	552	23,585	590	25,106	628
Norfolk	34,200	14,364	359	16,416	410	18,468	462	20,520	513	22,162	554	23,803	595	25,445	636	27,086	677
Richmond	38,300	16,086	402	18,384	460	20,682	517	22,980	575	24,818	620	26,657	666	28,495	712	30,334	758
Roanoke	34,400	14,448	361	16,512	413	18,576	464	20,640	516	22,291	557	23,942	599	25,594	640	27,245	681
Non-Metro Bal.	28,500	11,970	299	13,680	342	15,390	385	17,100	428	18,468	462	19,836	496	21,204	530	22,572	564
Washington																	
Bellingham	33,600	14,112	353	16,128	403	18,144	454	20,160	504	21,773	544	23,386	585	24,998	625	26,611	665
Bremerton	34,600	14,532	363	16,608	415	18,684	467	20,760	519	22,421	561	24,082	602	25,742	644	27,403	685
Olympia	31,900	13,398	335	15,312	383	17,226	431	19,140	479	20,671	517	22,202	555	23,734	593	25,265	632
Richland	40,200	16,884	422	19,296	482	21,708	543	24,120	603	26,050	651	27,979	699	29,909	748	31,838	796
Seattle	39,800	16,716	418	19,104	478	21,492	537	23,880	597	25,790	645	27,701	693	29,611	740	31,522	788
Spokane	30,200	12,684	317	14,496	362	16,308	408	18,120	453	19,570	489	21,019	525	22,469	562	23,918	598
Tacoma	31,900	13,398	335	15,312	383	17,226	431	19,140	479	20,671	517	22,202	555	23,734	593	25,265	632
Vancouver	33,200	13,944	349	15,936	398	17,928	448	19,920	498	21,514	538	23,107	578	24,701	618	26,294	657
Yakima	28,500	11,970	299	13,680	342	15,390	385	17,100	428	18,468	462	19,836	496	21,204	530	22,572	564
Non-Metro Bal.	28,500	11,970	299	13,680	342	15,390	385	17,100	428	18,468	462	19,836	496	21,204	530	22,572	564
West Virginia																	
Charleston	33,300	13,986	350	15,984	400	17,982	450	19,980	500	21,578	539	23,177	579	24,775	619	26,374	659
Huntington	27,300	11,466	287	13,104	328	14,742	369	16,380	410	17,690	442	19,001	475	20,311	508	21,622	541
Parkersburg	32,800	13,776	344	15,744	394	17,712	443	19,680	492	21,254	531	22,829	571	24,403	610	25,978	649
Wheeling	27,200	11,424	286	13,056	326	14,688	367	16,320	408	17,626	441	18,931	473	20,237	506	21,542	539
Non-Metro Bal.	27,000	11,340	284	12,960	324	14,580	365	16,200	405	17,496	437	18,792	470	20,088	502	21,384	535
Wisconsin																	
Appleton	34,600	14,532	363	16,608	415	18,684	467	20,760	519	22,421	561	24,082	602	25,742	644	27,403	685
Eau Claire	30,600	12,852	321	14,688	367	16,524	413	18,360	459	19,829	496	21,298	532	22,766	569	24,235	606
Green Bay	35,900	15,078	377	17,232	431	19,386	485	21,540	539	23,263	582	24,986	625	26,710	668	28,433	711
Janesville	35,200	14,784	370	16,896	422	19,008	475	21,120	528	22,810	570	24,499	612	26,189	655	27,878	697
Kenosha	39,000	16,380	410	18,720	468	21,060	527	23,400	585	25,272	632	27,144	679	29,016	725	30,888	772

Appendix 1 Continued

Metropolitan Area or Non-Metro Balance	Effective Median Income 1989	Size of Household: 1 person		2 persons		3 persons		4 persons		5 persons		6 persons		7 persons		8 persons	
		Max Income	Max Rent	Max Income	Max Rent	Max Income	Max Rent	Max Income	Max Rent	Max Income	Max Rent	Max Income	Max Rent	Max Income	Max Rent	Max Income	Max Rent
Wisconsin																	
La Crosse	32,200	13,524	338	15,456	386	17,388	435	19,320	483	20,866	522	22,411	560	23,957	599	25,502	638
Madison	37,600	15,792	395	18,048	451	20,304	508	22,560	564	24,365	609	26,170	654	27,974	699	29,779	744
Milwaukee	38,100	16,002	400	18,288	457	20,574	514	22,860	572	24,689	617	26,518	663	28,346	709	30,175	754
Racine	36,700	15,414	385	17,616	440	19,818	495	22,020	551	23,782	595	25,543	639	27,305	683	29,066	727
Sheboygan	34,200	14,364	359	16,416	410	18,468	462	20,520	513	22,162	554	23,803	595	25,445	636	27,086	677
Wausau	31,500	13,230	331	15,120	378	17,010	425	18,900	473	20,412	510	21,924	548	23,436	586	24,948	624
Non-Metro Bal.	28,600	12,012	300	13,728	343	15,444	386	17,160	429	18,533	463	19,906	498	21,278	532	22,651	566
Wyoming																	
Casper	38,200	16,044	401	18,336	458	20,628	516	22,920	573	24,754	619	26,587	665	28,421	711	30,254	756
Cheyenne	34,800	14,616	365	16,704	418	18,792	470	20,880	522	22,550	564	24,221	606	25,891	647	27,562	689
Non-Metro Bal.	33,500	14,070	352	16,080	402	18,090	452	20,100	503	21,708	543	23,316	583	24,924	623	26,532	663
Guam																	
Pacific Islands	34,100	14,322	358	16,368	409	18,414	460	20,460	512	22,097	552	23,734	593	25,370	634	27,007	675
Puerto Rico																	
Aguadilla	25,900	10,878	272	12,432	311	13,986	350	15,540	389	16,783	420	18,026	451	19,270	482	20,513	513
Arecibo	27,400	11,508	288	13,152	329	14,796	370	16,440	411	17,755	444	19,070	477	20,386	510	21,701	543
Caguas	26,900	11,298	282	12,912	323	14,526	363	16,140	404	17,431	436	18,722	468	20,014	500	21,305	533
Mayaguez	26,900	11,298	282	12,912	323	14,526	363	16,140	404	17,431	436	18,722	468	20,014	500	21,305	533
Ponce	26,900	11,298	282	12,912	323	14,526	363	16,140	404	17,431	436	18,722	468	20,014	500	21,305	533
San Juan	26,900	11,298	282	12,912	323	14,526	363	16,140	404	17,431	436	18,722	468	20,014	500	21,305	533
All Other	26,900	11,298	282	12,912	323	14,526	363	16,140	404	17,431	436	18,722	468	20,014	500	21,305	533
Virgin Islands	35,000	14,700	368	16,800	420	18,900	473	21,000	525	22,680	567	24,360	609	26,040	651	27,720	693

EXPLANATION OF APPENDIX 1

Data are presented for metropolitan areas and for the rural portion of each state outside of metropolitan areas. Suburban areas are covered under the central city of the metropolitan area, which could be in another state (e.g., Arlington, Virginia is part of the Washington, D.C. metropolitan area, and Camden County, New Jersey is part of the Philadelphia, Pa. metropolitan area).

The maximum income and qualifying rent levels in Appendix 1 are based on the data and adjustments to data used to arrive at the current income limits of the U.S. Department of Housing and Urban Development (HUD) for very low income households in each area for fiscal year 1989.

The data in the appendix are the maximum incomes and qualifying rent levels at 60 percent of median income for the area.

To determine the maximum income and qualifying rent level at 50 percent of median area income, multiply the appropriate figure shown for the 60 percent level by 0.8333.

For the maximum income and qualifying rent level at 40 percent of median income, multiply the appropriate figure shown for the 60 percent level by 0.6667.

To determine the maximum incomes at 140 and 170 percent of area median income, multiply the appropriate figure shown for the 60 percent level by 2.333 and 2.833 respectively.

For families larger than 8 persons, an adjustment of 8 percent above the 8-person figure is made for each additional person in the household.

HUD's income limits are typically rounded to the nearest $50. The data presented here are rounded to the nearest dollar.

In recent years, the average annual rate of increase in the national median income has been 5.5 percent. The 1988 national median income is 4.94 percent higher than the 1987 median. The rate of increase for any particular area can vary considerably from the rate of increase in the national median income.

Source: U.S. Dept. of Housing and Urban Development, Division of Economic Market Analysis, Office of Economic Affairs.

APPENDIX 2

A POSSIBLE LOCAL OR STATE GOVERNMENT PROGRAM TO USE THE TAX CREDIT TO STIMULATE NEEDED REPAIRS OF EXISTING LOW RENT HOUSING WITHOUT SYNDICATION AND WITHOUT RAISING RENTS

I. Required Conditions

The low income housing tax credit can be used by local government to assist owners of small rental properties to make needed repairs on substandard housing. These owners can use the tax credits directly to reduce their own tax liability without having to syndicate or form limited partnerships. Each dollar of tax credits (as well as depreciation deductions) can directly pay for needed repairs. To avoid the need to raise rents, financial aid from local government is needed to cover repair costs that exceed the tax benefits to the owner. The participation of a local lending institution is also needed.

1. Existing properties can be located which need repairs of at least $2,000 a unit and have rents (including tenant-paid utility costs) which are below the area's maximum qualifying rents for tax credits;

2. All or most of the units in each property have tenants with household incomes that qualify for the tax credit, or are vacant;

3. The existing owner has sufficient passive income (income from rental properties) that is unsheltered and with no liability under the alternative minimum tax, so that he or she could personally use tax credits and additional depreciation deductions generated by the repairs over and above the maximum amount of passive losses an individual taxpayer can use against tax liability on ordinary types of income;

4. A local lending institution or agency is willing to make 10-year, second mortgage market rate loans for rental property repairs, with repayments based on the income stream generated from tax credits and depreciation deductions. Additional guarantees from a public agency may be needed to secure lender participation;

5. A state or local government agency is willing to make direct third mortgage loans to owners for 15 years, with both principal and interest payments fully deferred for the term of the loan. State or local funds should be used if possible. If federal funds are the source of these loan funds, then the interest rate should not be less than the long-term Applicable Federal Rate (AFR), compounded annually.

6. If pre-rehab rent levels plus tenant utility costs are significantly below the maximum qualifying rents under the tax credit program and the rent levels for repaired units in the community, the local housing agency might want to obtain the owner's written agreement to keep rents affordable (i.e., keeping rent increases from exceeding the rate of increase in area median incomes or in the cost-of-living in the local area).

II. Rationale

With a tax credit for rehabilitation expenditures of 9 percent a year for 10 years, the value of tax credits and depreciation deductions combined should, for each year of a 10 year period, be equal to 10.2 percent of rehab and related soft costs for qualifying low income units. A 10-year, fully amortized loan with an interest rate of 10 percent and an amount equal to 60 percent of total development costs can be repaid entirely from the value to the owner of the tax credits and additional depreciation deductions. The fully deferred third mortgage loan from a government agency would be about 40 percent of total costs. The housing credit agency would have to commit to the property the full amount of eligible tax credits. Rent increases would not be needed.

The owner would receive a significantly upgraded property without any direct dollar outlays. To stimulate owner participation, a developer's fee for the owner could be included in the development budget and in the basis for calculating the tax credit amount. Owners should benefit from reduced operating costs, decreased vacancy losses, the value of additional depreciation deductions, and, in most cases, appreciation in the value of the property in excess of deferred principal and interest payments.

Owners would have to be able to directly use the $1,020 in reduced taxes generated annually for each $10,000 of repair work. An owner of a property with more than 10–20 units would either have to be a high income individual, an existing partnership, or an entity owning a considerable number of rental units in order to utilize the tax credits and related depreciation deductions. (Syndication would be needed if the owner could not use all the tax credits and depreciation deductions.)

III. Steps

1. The local or state government agency should vigorously publicize the program and meet with interested property owners to explain it. Develop a simplified model pro forma budget and review all the relevant numbers.

2. Interested owners would have to survey tenant incomes and analyze their rent structure to determine the number of qualifying low income units (i.e., the "applicable fraction," based on the lesser of the unit ratio or the floor space ratio). Include vacant units which will only be rented to income eligible families. Owner should meet and consult with tenants to gain their participation and cooperation.

3. Develop repair specifications and firm construction bids or reliable estimates.

4. Get a commitment on the amount of tax credits allocated to the project by the housing credit agency.

5. Calculate total development costs including financing fees, developer's fee, appraisal costs, closing costs, and other soft costs that would be used to determine the amount of the tax credit.

6. Get a commitment on second mortgage loan terms from a lending institution. Calculate the amount of loan that could be fully repaid based on value to the owner of credits and depreciation deductions. Alternatively, seek a new blanket mortgage to refinance existing debt and cover 60 percent of total development costs, if this is necessary or more advantageous.

7. Review financing plan with owner to help assure he will be able to utilize credits and deductions over 10–year period, as well as the commitment to maintain rent levels and income limits over the 15–year compliance period.

8. Get commitment from government entity on residual third mortgage loan on deferred basis.

9. Process loan applications, conduct simultaneous closings, and begin construction.

APPENDIX 3
A SPECIAL CASE PRO FORMA BUDGET ANALYSIS: RURAL NEW CONSTRUCTION OF $39,000 COST PER UNIT WITH A FARMER'S HOME ADMINISTRATION SEC. 515 LOAN AND THE TAX CREDIT

Loan Terms: 50 Year Mortgage Term, 1% Interest Rate, Loan of 95% of Value

A. Determining Tax Credit and Depreciation Contributions to the Project

1. Property acquisition costs (land)	$ 2,000	
2. New construction costs	37,000	
3. Total development costs (1+2)	39,000	
4. Annual tax credit amount:		
a. building acquisition:	0	
b. New construction: 4% of $37,000	1,480	
c. TOTAL (a+b)	1,480	
5. Annual depreciation allowance	1,345	
6. Tax credit contribution to project (5.085 x 4(c))	7,525	
7. Depreciation contribution to project	2,800	
8. Total tax credit and depreciation contribution to project	10,325	

B. Calculating Economic Rent Levels Without Benefit of Tax Credits

		Per Month
9. Loan amortization: 95% of line 3, or $37,050 @ 1%, 50 years (.0255)	$ 945 yr.	$ 79
10. First year equity return: 10% of 5% of line 3	195 yr.	16
11. Total operating costs		175
12. Economic net rent: cost-based (9+10+11)		270
13. Tenant-paid utility costs		35
14. Economic gross rent: cost-based (12+13)		305

C. Applying Tax Credit and Depreciation Contribution ($10,325) by Establishing an Annuity-type Fund (Earning Interest at 7 percent a Year) to Make Monthly Subsidy Payments to Reduce Tenant Rent Payment Below Economic Gross Rent of $305 per month

	Economic Gross Rent Compared to Qualifying Rent Level at							
	50% OF MEDIAN INCOME Area Median Income of				60% OF MEDIAN INCOME Area Median Income of			
	$25,000	$22,000	$19,000	$16,000	$25,000	$22,000	$19,000	$16,000
15. Qualifying tax credit rent level: 3.5 person average size household	$ 297	261	226	190	356	313	271	228
16. Gap or excess of cost-based payment/per month (14-15)	8	44	74	115	0	0	34	77
17. Additional assistance needed to provide a subsidy equal to the gap in line 16 for the 15-year compliance period	None	None	None	$2,400	None	None	None	None
18. Number of years for which a monthly subsidy equal to gap in line 16 can be provided with tax credit and depreciation contribution	50+	50+	25	11	N.A.	N.A.	50+	22.5

Alternate 1: The $10,325 tax benefit contribution (line A8 above) can provide a monthly subsidy of $94 for a 15-year period. This is sufficient to cover the gap in line 16 in all cases except for housing units in areas with $16,000 median income level where the rent is set at 50 percent of area median income. Additional assistance of $2,400 per unit would have to be added to the fund to provide a $115 month subsidy for the 15-year compliance period in this case. See line 17.

Alternate 2: Provide a monthly subsidy equal to the amount of the gap in line 16 for as many years as possible with the $10,325 tax credit and depreciation contribution, up to a maximum of the 50 year mortgage term. This will assure affordable low income occupancy for the maximum possible period, as compared to the minimum 15-year compliance period required under the tax credit program. Line 18 above shows the number of years of subsidy that can be provided.

EXPLANATION OF APPENDIX 3

A SPECIAL CASE PRO FORMA BUDGET ANALYSIS: RURAL NEW CONSTRUCTION OF $39,000 COST PER UNIT WITH A FARMERS HOME ADMINISTRATION SEC. 515 LOAN AND THE TAX CREDIT

A separate pro forma budget analysis for rural housing which uses the Farmers Home Administration (FmHA) section 515 program is presented separately in this appendix because of substantial deviations from the method of using the tax credit described in Chapter 4.

The preceeding table analyzes rural new construction costing $39,000 a unit with total operating and utility costs of $210 a month. Four different area median income (AMI) levels are analyzed at both the 50 percent and 60 percent of median income rent levels. The AMI levels are $25,000; $22,000; $19,000; and $16,000.

FmHA Section 515 loans for low and moderate income housing provide 50–year mortgages at an interest rate of 1 percent a year. With such a long term mortgage and very low interest rate, it is not advantageous to use the tax credits to reduce the amount of the mortgage loan on the project as is done in Chapter 4. In this analysis, the proceeds or contribution from the tax credits and other tax benefits are placed in an interest bearing fund and used instead to make periodic monthly subsidy payments to the project to reduce the rent obligation of the tenants.

The preceeding table uses the format and line–by–line explanations through line 8 in Tables 8–14 for calculating the total benefits from both the tax credits and depreciation deductions.

The economic gross rent and the gap between that figure and the rent levels required to qualify for the tax credit are first calculated without including the contributions of the tax credits and depreciation allowance. These contributions are used to set up an annuity–type fund that will make monthly payments to the project to cover the gap between (a) the required rent level and (b) the economic gross rent or costs that must be covered.

The adequacy of the amount of tax benefit contributions to cover the gap is analyzed in two alternate ways. Alternate 1 compares the gap with the maximum monthly annuity amount that the tax credit contributions could provide for the minimum 15–year tax credit compliance period. Alternate 2 measures the number of years that a monthly annuity that is equal in size to the amount of the gap could be provided, up to a maximum of the 50–year mortgage term.

This analysis indicates that rural new construction under the FmHA 515 program is clearly feasible with the low income housing tax credit. In only one instance, the 50 percent of median income rent level in areas with a median income of $16,000, is additional assistance required to qualify for the tax credit for the 15–year period. The amount needed in this case is only $2,400 per unit. The contributions from the tax credit and depreciation deductions are able to keep rents at the tax credit qualifying levels for at least 22.5 years in the other seven scenarios studied.

1-27-89

APPENDIX 4

LOW INCOME HOUSING TAX CREDIT
CREDIT ALLOCATING AGENCY LIST
Compiled by the National Council of State Housing Agencies

Alabama Housing Finance Authority
614 Adams Avenue
Montgomery, AL 36130
Robert Strickland
(205) 261-4310

Alaska State Building Authority
624 West International Airport Road
P.O. Box 100080
Anchorage, AK 99510
Julia Tucker
(907) 786-6222

Arizona Housing Finance Review Board
1700 West Washington St. - 5th Floor
Phoenix, AZ 85001
Gloria Munoz
(602) 255-4920

Arkansas Development Finance Authority
100 Main Street, Suite 200
Technology Center
P.O. Box 8023
Little Rock, AR 72201-8023
Bernard Henry
(501) 682-5900

California Mortgage Bond and Tax Credit
Allocation Commission
915 Capitol Mall, Room 280
Sacramento, CA 95814
Carole Onorato
(916) 324-7419

Colorado Housing & Finance Authority
777 Pearl Street
Denver, Colorado 80203-3716
Grace Buckley/Jo Untiedt
(303) 861-8962

Connecticut Housing Finance Authority
40 Cold Spring Road
Rocky Hill, CT 06067
Betty Close
(203) 721-9501

Delaware State Housing Authority
18 The Green
Dover, DE 19901
Paula M. Sims
(302) 571-3720

DC Housing & Community Development
Agency
1133 North Capitol St., N.E., Rm 204
Washington, DC 20002
Dwight Reeves
(202) 535-1269

Florida Housing Finance Agency
2740 The Rhyne Building
Koger Center
Tallahassee, FL 32399-2100
Beauvais McCaddon
(904) 488-4197

Georgia Residential Finance Authority
60 Executive Parkway South
Suite 250
Atlanta, GA 30329
Birgit Nomura/Kate Little
(404) 320-4840

Hawaii Housing Authority
1002 North School Street
P.O. Box 17907
Honolulu, HI 96817
Donald L. Tarleton
(808) 848-3230

Idaho Housing Agency
760 West Myrtle
Boise, ID 83702
Gary Machacek
(208) 336-0161

Illinois-Chicago Department of Housing
318 South Michigan
Chicago, IL 60604
Norma Carter
(312) 922-7922, ext. 710

Illinois Housing Development
Authority
401 North Michigan Avenue, Suite 900
Chicago, IL 60611
Ed Solan
(312) 836-5371

Indiana Housing Finance Authority
1 North Capitol Avenue
Suite 515
Indianapolis, IN 46204
Michael R. Swanson
(317) 232-7777

Iowa Finance Authority
East Grand Office Park
200 East Grand Avenue - Suite 222
Des Moines, IO 50309
Janet Pressey
(515) 281-4058

Kansas Dept. of Commerce
400 SW 8th, 5th Floor
Topeka, KS 66603
Harland Priddle
(913) 296-3480
Fran Squyres - (913) 296-3485

Kentucky Housing Corporation
1231 Louisville Road
Frankfort, KY 40601
Bob Adams
(502) 564-7630

Louisiana Housing Finance Agency
5615 Corporate - Suite 6A
Baton Rouge, LA 70808-2515
V. Jean Butler
(504) 925-3675

Maine State Housing Authority
295 Water Street
P.O. Box 2669
Augusta, ME 04330
Lila Ware
(207) 623-2981

Maryland Community Development Administration
45 Calvert Street
Annapolis, MD 21401
Richard Hillman
(301) 974-3821

Massachusetts Executive Office of Communities and Development
100 Cambridge Street - 14th Floor
Boston, MA 02202
Brian DeLorey
(617) 727-8495

Massachusetts Housing Finance Agency
50 Milk Street
Boston, MA 02109
Brian Frawley
(617) 451-3480

Michigan State Housing Development Authority
Plaza One Building -
401 South Washington
P.O. Box 30044
Lansing, MI 48909
Ben Fedewa
(517) 335-2039

Minnesota Housing Finance Agency
400 Sibley Street, Suite 300
St. Paul, MN 55101
John Madson
(612) 296-3029

Mississippi Dept. of Community Development
301 West Pearl Street
Jackson, MS 39203-3096
Shirley George
(601) 949-2002 - 2217

Missouri Housing Development Commission
3770 Broadway
Kansas City, MO 64111
Steve Sillimon
(816) 756-3790

Montana Board of Housing
2001 11th Avenue
Helena, MT 59620
Richard Kain
(406) 444-3040

Nebraska Investment Finance Authority
Gold's Galleria, Suite 218
1033 O Street
Lincoln, NB 68508
Dennis Vellek
(402) 477-4406

Nevada Housing Division
Department of Commerce
1050 East William, Suite 435
Carson City, NV 89710
Mamie Chinn
(702) 885-4258

New Hampshire Housing Finance Authority
24 Constitution Drive
Bedford, NH 03102
Chris Miller
(603) 472-8623

New Jersey Housing & Mortgage Finance Agency
CN 18550, 3625 Quakerbridge Road
Trenton, NJ 08650-2085
Kevin Quince/Bob Joy
(609) 890-8900

New Mexico State Housing Authority
1100 St. Francis Drive, P.O. Box 20003
Joseph Montoya Building
Santa Fe, NM 87503
Kathy McCormick
(505) 827-0258

New York City Housing Development Corporation
75 Maiden Lane, 8th Floor
New York, NY 10038
Chuck Brass /Judy Blaylock
(212) 344-8080

New York City Department of Housing Preservation & Development
100 Gold Street, Room 9I9
New York, NY 10038
Merilyn Rovira
(212) 566-1626

New York State Division of Housing and Community Renewal
3840 State St., 6th Floor
Albany, NY 12207
Mike Sullivan
(518) 474-8580

New York State Housing Finance Agency
Three Park Avenue
New York, NY 10016
Gene Myers
(212) 686-9700

New York State Mortgage Loan Enforcement & Administration Corporation
11 West 42nd Street
New York, NY 10036
Marian Roslyn
(212) 790-2414

Mortgage Bond Allocation Committee
c/o North Carolina Housing Finance Agency
3300 Drake Circle, Suite 200
P.O. Box 28066
Raleigh, NC 27611
James T. Quinn
(919) 781-6115

North Dakota Housing Finance Agency
1012 East Central Avenue
P.O. Box 1535
Bismarck, ND 58502
Pat Fricke
(701) 224-3434

Ohio Housing Finance Agency
65 East State Street, Suite 208
Columbus, OH 43215
Joe Hagan
(614) 466-7970

Oklahoma Housing Finance Agency
1140 Northwest 63rd
Suite 200
Oklahoma City, OK 73116-6519
Ronnie Williams
(405) 848-1144

Oregon Housing Division
Department of Commerce
1600 State St., Suite 100
Salem, OR 97310
Larry Dowd
(503) 378-4343

Pennsylvania Housing Finance Agency
2101 North Front Street
P.O. Box 8029
Harrisburg, PA 17105-8029
Mark Moonin
(717) 780-3800

Puerto Rico Housing Finance Corp.
Call Box 71361 GPO
San Juan PR 00936-1361
Enid Rivera Sanchez
(809) 765-7577

Rhode Island Housing & Mortgage Finance Corporation
60 Eddy Street, 2nd Floor
Providence, RI 02903-1733
Jim Beachler
(401) 751-5566

South Carolina State Housing
Authority
1710 Gervais Street, Suite 300
Columbia, SC 29201
Linda Whitmeyer
(803) 734-8734

South Dakota Housing
Development Authority
221 South Central
P.O. Box 1237
Pierre, SD 57501-1237
Darlys J. Baum
(605) 773-3181

Tennessee Housing Development
Agency
700 Landmark Center
401 Church Street
Nashville, TN 37219-2202
Stan Houle/Clark Conn
(615) 741-2473

Texas Housing Agency
P.O. Box 13941
Capitol Station
Austin, TX 78711-3941
Edwina Carrington
(512) 474-2974

Utah Housing Finance Agency
177 East 100 South
Salt Lake City, UT 84111
Bill Erikson
(801) 521-6950

Vermont Housing Finance Agency
One Burlington Square
P.O. Box 408
Burlington, VT 05402-0408
Meg Pond
(802) 864-5743

Virgin Islands Housing Finance Authority
P.O. Box 12029
Kogens Gade #5-6
St. Thomas, VI 00801
Sherri George
(809) 774-4481

Virginia Housing Development Authority
13 South 13th Street
Richmond, VA 23219
H. Larkin Goshorn
(804) 782-1986

Washington State Housing
Finance Commission
710 2nd Avenue
Suite 1090/Dexter-Horton Bldg.
Seattle, WA 98104
Sallie Sweet
(206) 464-7139

West Virginia Housing
Development Fund
814 Virginia Street, East
Charleston, WV 25301
Michael L. McCullough
(304) 345-6475

Wisconsin Housing and Economic
Development Authority
1 South Pinckney - Suite 500
P.O. Box 1728
Madison, WI 53701-1728
John Habeck
(608) 266-3385

Wyoming Community Development
Authority
123 South Durbin Street, 2nd Floor
Casper, WY 82602
Tom Fischer
(307) 265-0603

For further information contact:
National Council of State Housing Agencies
444 North Capitol Street, NW
Suite 118
Washington, DC 20001
Ronne Thielen
(202) 624-7710

TEXT OF THE LOW INCOME HOUSING TAX CREDIT PROVISIONS (SECTION 42) OF THE INTERNAL REVENUE CODE, AS ADOPTED IN 1986 AND INCLUDING AMENDMENTS MADE IN 1988

IRC SECTION 42—LOW INCOME HOUSING CREDIT, EFFECTIVE DATE, AND TRANSITIONAL RULES

SEC. 252 LOW-INCOME HOUSING CREDIT.*

(A) IN GENERAL—Subpart D of part IV of subchapter A of chapter 1 (relating to business credits) is amended by adding at end thereof the following new section:

SEC. 42 LOW INCOME HOUSING CREDIT.

(a) (a) IN GENERAL—For purposes of section 38, the amount of the low-income housing credit determined under this section for any taxable year in the credit period shall be an amount equal to—

(1) the applicable percentage of

(2) The qualified basis of each qualified low-income building.

(b) (b) Applicable Percentage: 70 Percent Present Value Credit for Certain New Buildings: 30 Percent Present Value Credit for Certain Other Buildings.—For Purposes of this section—

1 (1) BUILDING PLACED IN SERVICE DURING 1987.—In the case of any qualified low-income building placed in service by the taxpayer during 1987, the term 'applicable percentage' means—

(A) 9 percent of new buildings which are not federally subsidized for the taxable year, or

(B) 4 percent for—

(i) new buildings which are federally subsidized for the taxable year, and

(ii) existing buildings.

2 (2) BUILDINGS PLACED IN SERVICE AFTER 1987.—

(A) IN GENERAL.—In the case of any qualified low-income building placed in service by the taxpayer after 1987, the term applicable percentage means the appropriate percentage prescribed by the Secretary for the earlier of—

(i) the month in which such building is placed in service, or

(ii) at the election of the taxpayer—

(I) the month in which the taxpayer and the housing credit agency enter into an agreement with respect to such building (which is binding on such agency, the taxpayer, and all successors in interest) as to the housing credit dollar amount to be allocated to such building, or

(II) the case of any building to which subsection (h)(4)(B) applies, the month in which the tax-exempt obligations are issued.

A month may be elected under clause (ii) only if the election is made not later than the 5th day after the close of such month. Such an election, once made, is irrevocable.

(B) METHOD OF PRESCRIBING PERCENTAGES.— The percentages prescribed by the Secretary for any month shall be percentages which will yield over a 10-year period amounts of credit under subsection (a) which have present value equal to—

(i) 70 percent of the qualified basis of a building described in paragraph (1)(A), and

(ii) 30 percent of the qualified basis of a building described in paragraph (1)(B).

(C) METHOD OF DISCOUNTING.—The present value under subparagraph (B) shall be determined—

(i) as of the last day of the 1st year of the 10-year period referred to in subparagraph (B).

(ii) by using a discount rate equal to 72 percent of the average of the annual Federal mid-term rate and the annual Federal long-term rate applicable under section section 1274(d)(1) to the month applicable under clause (i) or (ii) of subparagraph (A) and compounded annually, and

(iii) by assuming that the credit allowable under this section for any year is received on the last day of such year.

3 (3) CROSS REFERENCES.—

(A) For treatment of certain rehabilitation expenditures as separate new buildings, see subsection (e).

(B) for determination of applicable percentage for increases in qualified basis after the 1st year of the credit period, see subsection (f)(3).

(C) For authority of housing credit agency to limit applicable percentage an qualified basis which may be taken into account under this section with respect to any building, see subsection (h)(6).

(c) (c) QUALIFIED BASIS; QUALIFIED LOW-INCOME BUILDING.—For purposes of this section—

1 (1) QUALIFIED BASIS.—

(A) DETERMINATION.—The qualified basis of any qualified low-income building for any taxable year is an amount equal to—

(i) the applicable fraction (determined as of the close of such taxable year) of

---

*Sec. 252 of the Tax Reform Act of 1986, Public Law 99-514, October 22, 1986; as amended by the Technical and Miscellaneous Revenue Act of 1988, Public Law 100-647, November 10, 1988.

(ii) the eligible basis of such building (determined under subsection (d)(5)).

(B) APPLICABLE FRACTION.—For purposes of subparagraph (A), the term applicable fraction means the smaller of the unit fraction or the floor space fraction.

(C) UNIT FRACTION.—For purposes of subparagraph (B), the term 'unit fracton' means the fraction—

(i) the numerator of which is the number of low-income units in the building, and

(ii) the denominator of which is the number of residential rental units (whether or not occupied) in such building.

(D) FLOOR SPACE FRACTION.—For purposes of subparagraph (B), the term 'floor space fraction' means the fraction—

(i) the numerator of which is the total floor space of the low-income units in such building, and

(ii) the denominator of which is the total floor space of the residential rental units (whether or not occupied) in such building.

2 (2) QUALIFIED LOW-INCOME BUILDING.—The term 'qualified low-income building' means any building—

(A) which is part of a qualified low-income housing project at all times during the period—

(i) beginning on the 1st day in the compliance period on which such building is part of such a project, and

(ii) ending on the last day of the compliance period with respect to such building, and

(B) to which the amendments made by section 201(a) of the Tax Reform Act of 1986 apply.

(d) (d) ELIGIBLE BASIS.—For purposes of this section—

1 (1) NEW BUILDINGS.—The eligible basis of a new building is its adjusted basis.

2 (2) EXISTING BUILDINGS.—

(A) IN GENERAL.—The eligible basis of an existing building is—

(i) in the case of a building which meets the requirements of subparagraph (B), the sum of—

(I) The portion of its adjusted basis attributable to its acquisition cost, plus

(II) amounts chargeable to capital account and incurred by the taxpayer (before the close of the 1st taxable year of the credit period for such building) for property (or additions or improvements to property) of a character subject to the allowance for depreciation, and

(ii) zero in any other case.

(B) REQUIREMENTS.—A building meets the requirements of this subparagraph if—

(i) the building is acquired by purchase (as defined in section 179(d)(2)).

(ii) there is a period of at least 10 years between the date of its acquisition by the taxpayer and the later of—

(I) the date the building was last placed in service, or

(II) the date of most recent nonqualified substantial improvement of the building, and

(iii) the building was not previously placed in service by the taxpayer or by any person who was a related person with respect to the taxpayer as of the time previously placed in service.

(C) ACQUISITION COST.—For purposes of subparagraph (A), the cost of any building shall not include so much of the basis of such building as is determined by reference to the basis of other property held at any time by the person acquiring the building.

(D) SPECIAL RULES FOR SUBPARAGRAPH (B).—

(i) NONQUALIFIED SUBSTANTIAL IMPROVEMENT.—For purposes of subparagraph (B)(ii)—

(I) IN GENERAL.—The term 'nonqualified substantial improvement' means any substantial improvement if section 167(k) was elected with respect to such improvement or section 168 (as in effect on the day before the date of the enactment of the Tax Reform Act of 1986) applied to such improvement.

(II) DATE OF SUBSTANTIAL IMPROVEMENT.—The date of a substantial improvement is the last day of the 24-month period referred to in subclause (III).

(III) SUBSTANTIAL IMPROVEMENTS.—The term 'substantial improvement' means the improvements added to capital account with respect to the building during any 24-month period, but only if the sum of the amounts added to such account during such period equals or exceeds 25 percent of the adjusted basis of the building (determined without regard to paragraphs (2) and (3) of section 1016(a)) as of the 1st day of such period.

(ii) SPECIAL RULES FOR CERTAIN TRANSFERS.—For purposes of determining under subparagraph (B)(ii) when a building was last placed in service, there shall not be taken into account any placement in service—

(I) in connection with the acquisition of the building in a transaction in which the basis of the building in the hands of the person acquiring it is determined in whole or in part by reference to the adjusted basis of such building in the hands of the person from whom acquired,

(II) by a person whose basis in such building is determined under section 1014(a) (relating to property acquired from a decedent),

(III) by any governmental unit or qualified nonprofit organization (as defined in subsection (h)(5)) if the requirements of subparagraph (B)(ii) are met with respect to the placement in service by such unit or organization and all the income from such property is exempt from Federal income taxation, or

(IV) by any person who acquired such building by foreclosure (or by instrument in lieu of foreclosure) of any purchase-money security interest held by such person if the requirements of subparagraph (B)(ii) are met with respect to the placement in service by such person and such building is resold within 12 months after the date such building is placed in service by such person after such foreclosure.

(iii) RELATED PERSON, ETC.—

(I) APPLICATION OF SECTION 179.—For purposes of subparagraph (B)(i), section 179(d) shall be applied by substituting "10 percent" for "50 percent" in section 267(b) and 707(b) and in section 179(b)(7).

(II) RELATED PERSON.—For purposes of subparagraph (B)(iii), a person (hereinafter in this subclause referred to as the 'related person') is related to any person if the related persons bears a relationship to such person specified in section 267(b) or 707(b)(1), or the related person and such person are engaged in trades or businesses under common control (within the meaning of subsections (a) and (b) of section 52). For purposes of the preceding sentence, in applying section 267(b) or 707(b)(1), '10 percent' shall be substituted for '50 percent.'

3 (3) ELIGIBLE BASIS REDUCED WHERE DISPROPORTIONATE STANDARDS FOR UNITS.—

(A) IN GENERAL.—Except as provided in subparagraph (B), the eligible basis of any building shall be reduced by an amount equal to the portion of the adjusted basis of the building which is attributable to residential units in the building which are not low-income units and which are above the average quality standard of the low-income units in the building.

(B) EXCEPTIONS WHERE TAXPAYER ELECTS TO INCLUDE EXCESS COST.—

(i) IN GENERAL.—Subparagraph (A) shall not apply with respect to a residential rental unit in a building which is not a low-income unit if—

(I) the excess described in clause (ii) with respect to such unit is not greater than 15 percent of the cost described in clause (ii)(II), and

(II) the taxpayer elects to exclude from the eligible basis of such building the excess described in clause (ii) with respect to such unit.

(ii) EXCESS.—The excess described in this clause with respect to any unit is the excess of—

(I) the cost of such unit, over

(II) the amount which would be the cost of such unit if the average cost per square foot of low-income units in the building were substituted for the cost per square foot of such unit.

The Secretary may by regulation provide for the determination of the excess under this clause on a basis other than square foot costs.

4 (4) SPECIAL RULES RELATING TO DETERMINATION OF ADJUSTED BASIS.—For purposes of this subsection—

(A) IN GENERAL.—Except as provided in subparagraph (B), the adjusted basis of any building shall be determined without regard to the adjusted basis of any property which is not residential rental property.

(B) BASIS OF PROPERTY IN COMMON AREAS, ETC., INCLUDED.—The adjusted basis of any building shall be determined by taking into account the adjusted basis of property (or a character subject to the allowance for depreciation) used in common areas or provided as comparable amenities to all residential rental units in such building.

(C) NO REDUCTION FOR DEPRECIATION.—The adjusted basis of any building shall be determined without regard to paragraphs (2) and (3) of section 1016(a).

5 (5) ELIGIBLE BASIS DETERMINED WHEN BUILDING PLACED IN SERVICE.—

(A) IN GENERAL.—Except as provided in subparagraphs (B) and (C), the eligible basis of any building for the entire compliance period for such building shall be its eligible basis on the date such building is placed in service (increased in the case of an existing building which meets the requirements of paragraph (2)(B), by the amounts described in paragraph (2)(A)(i)(II)).

(B) ELIGIBLE BASIS REDUCED BY FEDERAL GRANTS.—If, during any taxable year of the compliance period, a grant is made with respect to any building or the operation thereof and any portion of such grant is funded with Federal funds (whether or not includible in gross income), the eligible basis of such building for such taxable year and all succeeding taxable years shall be reduced by the portion of such grant which is so funded.

(C) ELIGIBLE BASIS NOT TO INCLUDE EXPENDITURES WHERE 167(k) ELECTED.—The eligible basis of any building shall not include any portion of its adjusted basis which is attributable to amounts with respect to which an election is made under section 167(k).

6 (6) CREDIT ALLOWABLE FOR CERTAIN FEDERALLY-ASSISTED BUILDINGS ACQUIRED DURING 10-YEAR PERIOD DESCRIBED IN PARAGRAPH (2)(B)(II).—

(A) IN GENERAL.—On application by the taxpayer, the Secretary (after consultation with the appropriate Federal official) may waive paragraph (2)(B)(ii) with respect to any federally-assisted building if the Secretary determines that such waiver is necessary—

(i) to avert an assignment of the mortgage secured by property in the project (of which such building is a part) to the Department of Housing and Urban Development or the Farmers' Home Administration, or

(ii) to avert a claim against a Federal mortgage insurance fund (or such Department or Administration) with respect to a mortgage which is so secured.

(B) FEDERALLY-ASSISTED BUILDING.—For purposes of subparagraph (A), the term 'federally-assisted building' means any building which is substantially assisted, financed, or operated under—

(i) section 8 of the United States Housing Act of 1937,

(ii) section 221(d)(3) or 236 of the National Housing Act, or

(iii) section 515 of the Housing Act of 1949, as such Acts are in effect on the date of the enactment of the Tax Reform Act of 1986.

(C) APPROPRIATE FEDERAL OFFICIAL.—For purposes of subparagraph (A), the term 'appropriate Federal official' means—

(i) the Secretary of Housing and Urban Development in the case of any building described in subparagraph (B) by reason of clause (i) or (ii) thereof and

(ii) the Secretary of Agriculture in the case of any building described in subparagraph (B) by reason of clause (iii) thereof.

7 (7) ACQUISITION OF BUILDING BEFORE END OF PRIOR COMPLIANCE PERIOD.—

(A) IN GENERAL.—Under regulations prescribed by the Secretary, in the case of a building described in subparagraph (B) which is acquired by the taxpayer—

(i) paragraph (2)(B) shall not apply, but

(ii) the credit allowable by reason of subsection (a) to the taxpayer for any period after such acquisition shall be equal to the amount of credit which would have been allowable under subsection (a) for such period to the prior owner referred to in subparagraph (B) has such owner not disposed of the building.

(B) DESCRIPTION OF BUILDING.—A building is described in this subparagraph if—

(i) a credit was allowed by reason of subsection (a) to any prior owner of such building, and

(ii) the taxpayer acquired such building before the end of the compliance period for such building with respect to such prior owner (determined without regard to any disposition by such prior owner).

(e) (e) REHABILITATION EXPENDITURES TREATED AS SEPARATE NEW BUILDING.—

1 (1) IN GENERAL.—Rehabilitation expenditures paid or incurred by the taxpayer with respect to any building shall be treated for purposes of this section as a separate new building.

2 (2) REHABILITATION EXPENDITURES.—For purposes of paragraph (1)—

(A) IN GENERAL.—The term 'rehabilitation expenditures' means amounts chargeable to capital account and incurred for property (or additions or improvements to property) of a character subject to the allowance for depreciation in connection with the rehabilitation of a building.

(B) COST OF ACQUISITION, ETC., NOT INCLUDED.—Such term does not include the cost of acquiring and building (or interest therein) or any amount not permitted to be taken into account under paragraph (3) or (4) subsection (d).

3 (3) AVERAGE OF REHABILITATION EXPENDITURES MUST BE $2,000 OR MORE.—

(A) IN GENERAL.—Paragraph (1) shall apply to rehabilitation expenditures with respect to any building only if the qualified basis attributable to such expenditure incurred during any 24-month period, when divided by the low-income units in the building, is $2,000 or more.

(B) DATE OF DETERMINATION.—The determination under subparagraph (A) shall be made as of the close of the 1st taxable year in the credit period with respect to such expenditures.

4 (4) SPECIAL RULES.—For purposes of applying this section with respect to expenditures which are treated as a separate building by reason of this subsection—

(A) such expenditures shall be treated as placed in service at the close of the 24-month period referred to in paragraph (3)(A), and

(B) the applicable fraction under subsection (c)(1) shall be the applicable fraction for the building (without regard to paragraph (1)) with respect to which the expenditures were incurred.

Nothing in subsection (d)(2) shall prevent a credit from being allowed by reason of this subsection.

5 (5) NO DOUBLE COUNTING.—Rehabilitation expenditures may, at the election of the taxpayer, be taken into account under this subsection or subsection (d)(2)(A)(i)(II) but not under both such subsections.

(6) REGULATIONS TO APPLY SUBSECTION WITH RESPECT TO GROUP OF UNITS IN BUILDING.—The Secretary may prescribe regulations, consistent with the purposes of this subsection, treating a group of units with respect to which rehabilitation expenditures are incurred as a separate new building.

(f) (f) DEFINITION AND SPECIAL RULES RELATING TO CREDIT PERIOD.—

1 (1) CREDIT PERIOD DEFINED.—For purposes of this section, the term 'credit period' means, with respect to any building, the period of 10 taxable years beginning with—

(A) the taxable year in which the building is placed in service, or

(B) at the election of the taxpayer, the succeeding taxable year,

but only if the building is a qualified low-income building as of the close of the 1st year of such period. The election under subparagraph (B), once made, shall be irrevocable.

2 (2) SPECIAL RULE FOR 1ST YEAR OF CREDIT PERIOD.

(A) IN GENERAL.—The credit allowable under subsection (a) with respect to any building for the 1st taxable year of the credit period shall be determined by substituting for the applicable fraction under subsection (c)(1) the fraction—

(i) the numerator of which is the sum of the applicable fractions determined under subsection (c)(1) as of the close of each full month of such year during which such building was in service, and

(ii) the denominator of which is 12.

(B) DISALLOWED 1ST YEAR CREDIT ALLOWED IN 11TH YEAR.—Any reduction by reason of subparagraph (A) in the credit allowable (without regard to subparagraph (A)) for the 1st taxable year of the credit period shall be allowable under subsection (a) for the 1st taxable year following the credit period.

3 (3) DETERMINATION OF APPLICABLE PERCENTAGE WITH RESPECT TO INCREASES IN QUALIFIED BASIS AFTER 1ST YEAR OF CREDIT PERIOD.—

(A) IN GENERAL.—In the case of any building which was a qualified low-income building as of the close of the 1st year of the credit period, if—

(i) as of the close of any taxable year in the compliance period (after the 1st year of the credit period) the qualified basis of such building exceeds

(ii) the qualified basis of such building as of the close of the 1st year of the credit period,

the applicable percentage which shall apply under subsection (a) for the taxable year to such excess shall be the percentage equal to ⅔ of the applicable percentage which (after the application of subsection (h)) would but for this paragraph apply to such basis.

(B) 1ST YEAR COMPUTATION APPLIES.—A rule similar to the rule of paragraph (2)(A) shall apply to any increase in qualified basis to which subparagraph (A) applies for the 1st year of such increase.

(g) (g) QUALIFIED LOW-INCOME HOUSING PROJECT.—For purpose of this section—

1 (1) IN GENERAL.—The term 'qualified low-income housing project' means any project for residential rental property if the project meets the requirements of subparagraph (A) or (B) whichever is elected by the taxpayer.

(A) 20-50 TEST.—The project meets the requirements of this subparagraph if 20 percent or more of the residential units in such project are both rent-restricted and occupied by individuals whose income is 50 percent or less of area median gross income.

(B) 40-60 TEST.—The project meets the requirements of this subparagraph if 40 percent or more of the residential units in such project are both rent-restricted and occupied by individuals whose income is 50 percent or less of area median gross income.

2 (2) RENT-RESTRICTED UNITS.—

(A) IN GENERAL.—For purposes of paragraph (1), a residential unit is rent-restricted if the gross rent with respect to such unit does not exceed 30 percent of the income limitation under paragraph (1) applicable to individuals occupying such unit.

(B) GROSS RENT.—For purposes of subparagraph (A), gross rent—

(i) does not include any payment under section 8 of the United States Housing Act of 1937 or any comparable rental assistance program (with respect to such unit or occupants thereof), and

(ii) includes any utility allowance determined by the Secretary after taking into account such determinations under section 8 of the United States Housing Act of 1937.

(C) UNITS WHERE FEDERAL RENTAL ASSISTANCE IS REDUCED AS TENANT'S INCOME INCREASES.—If the gross rent with respect to a residential unit exceeds the limitation under subparagraph (A) by reason of the fact that the income of the occupants thereof exceeds the income limitation applicable under paragraph (1), such unit shall, nevertheless, be treated as a rent-restricted unit for purposes of paragraph (1) if—

(i) a Federal rental assistance payment described in subparagraph (B)(i) is made with respect to such unit or its occupants, and

(ii) the sum of such payment and the gross rent with respect to such unit does not exceed the sum of the amount of such payment which would be made and the gross rent which would be payable with respect to such unit if—

(I) the income of the occupants thereof did not exceed the income limitation applicable under paragraph (1), and

(II) such units were rent-restricted within the meaning of subparagraph (A).

The preceding sentence shall apply to any unit only if the result described in clause (ii) is required by Federal statute as of the date of the enactment of this subparagraph and as of the date the Federal rental assistance payment is made.

3 (3) DATE FOR MEETING REQUIREMENTS.—

(A) IN GENERAL.—Except as otherwise provided in this paragraph, a building shall be created as a qualified low-income building only if the project (of which such building is a part) meets the requirements of paragraph (1) not later than the close of the 12-month period beginning on the date the building is placed in service.

(B) BUILDINGS WHICH RELY ON LATER BUILDINGS FOR QUALIFICATION.—

(i) IN GENERAL.—In determining whether a building (hereinafter in this subparagraph referred to as the 'prior building') is a qualified low-income building, the taxpayer may take into account 1 or more additional buildings placed in service during the 12-month period described in subparagraph (A) with respect to the prior building only if the taxpayer elects to apply clause (ii) with respect to each additional building taken into account.

(ii) TREATMENT OF ELECTED BUILDINGS.—In the case of a building which the taxpayer elects to take into account under clause (i), the period under subparagraph (A) for such building shall end at the close of the 12-month period applicable to the prior building.

(iii) DATE PRIOR BUILDING IS TREATED AS PLACED IN SERVICE.—For purposes of determining the credit period and the compliance period for the prior building, the prior building shall be treated for purposes of this section as placed in service on the most recent date any additional building elected by the taxpayer (with respect to such prior building) was placed in service.

(C) SPECIAL RULE.—A building—

(i) other than the 1st building placed in service as part of a project, and

(ii) other than a building which is placed in service during the 12-month period described in subparagraph (A) with respect to a prior building which becomes a qualified low-income building,

shall in no event be treated as a qualified low-income building unless the project is a low-income housing project (without regard to such building) on the date such building is placed in service.

4 (4) CERTAIN RULES MADE APPLICABLE.—Paragraphs (2) (other than subparagraph (A) thereof), (3), (4), (5), (6), and (7) of section 142(d), and section 6652(j), shall apply for purposes of determining whether any unit is a low-income unit; except that, in applying such provisions (other than section 142(d)(4)(B)(iii)) for such purposes, the term 'gross rent' shall have the meaning given such term by paragraph (2)(B) of this subsection.

5 (5) ELECTION TO TREAT BUILDING AFTER COMPLIANCE PERIOD AS NOT PART OF A PROJECT.—For purposes of this section, the taxpayer may elect to treat any building as not part of a qualified low-income housing project for any period beginning after the compliance period for such building.

6 (6) SPECIAL RULE WHERE DE MINIMIS EQUITY CONTRIBUTION.—Property shall not be treated as failing to be residential rental property for purposes of this section merely because the occupant of a residential unit in the project pays (on a voluntary basis) to the lessor a de minimis amount to be held toward the purchase by such occupant of a residential unit in such project if—

(A) all amounts so paid are refunded to the occupant on the cessation of his occupancy of a unit in the project, and

(B) the purchase of the unit is not permitted until after the close of the compliance period with respect to the building in which the unit is located.

Any amount paid to the lessor as described in the preceding sentence shall be included in gross rent under paragraph (2) for purposes of determining whether the unit is rent-restricted.

(h) (h) LIMITATION ON AGGREGATE CREDIT ALLOWABLE WITH RESPECT TO PROJECTS LOCATED IN A STATE.—

1 (1) CREDIT MAY NOT EXCEED CREDIT AMOUNT ALLOCATED TO BUILDING.—

(A) IN GENERAL.—The amount of the credit determined under this section for any taxable year with respect to any building shall not exceed the housing credit dollar amount allocated to such building under this subsection.

(B) TIME FOR MAKING ALLOCATION.—Except in the case of an allocation which meets the requirements of subparagraph (C), (D), or (E) an allocation shall be taken into account under subparagraph (A) only if it is made not later than the close of the calendar year in which the building is placed in service.

(C) EXCEPTION WHERE BINDING COMMITMENT.—An allocation meets the requirements of this subparagraph if there is a binding commitment (not later than the close of the calendar year in which the building is placed in service) by the housing credit agency to allocate a specified housing credit dollar amount to such building beginning in a specified later taxable year.

(D) EXCEPTION WHERE INCREASE IN QUALIFIED BASIS.—

(i) IN GENERAL.—An allocation meets the requirements of this subparagraph if such allocation is made not later than the close of the calendar year in which ends the taxable year to which it will 1st apply but only to the extent the amount of such allocation does not exceed the limitation under clause (ii).

(ii) LIMITATION.—The limitation under this clause is the amount of credit allowable under this section (without regard to this subsection) for a taxable year with respect to an increase in the qualified basis of the building equal to the excess of—

(I) the qualified basis of such building as of the close of the 1st taxable year to which such allocation will apply, over

(II) the qualified basis of such building as of the close of the 1st taxable year to which the most recent prior housing credit allocation with respect to such building applied.

(iii) HOUSING CREDIT DOLLAR AMOUNT REDUCED BY FULL ALLOCATION.—Notwithstanding clause (i), the full amount of the allocation shall be taken into account under paragraph (2).

(E) EXCEPTION WHERE 10 PERCENT OF COST INCURRED.—

(i) IN GENERAL.—An allocation meets the requirements of this subparagraph if such allocation is made with respect to a qualified building which is placed in service not later than the close of the second calendar year following the calendar year in which the allocation is made.

(ii) QUALIFIED BUILDING.—For purposes of clause (i), the term 'qualified building' means any building which is part of a project if the taxpayer's basis in such project (as of the close of the calendar year in which the allocation is made) is more than 10 percent of the taxpayer's reasonably expected basis in such project (as of the close of the second calendar year referred to in clause (i)). Such term does not include any existing building unless a credit is allowable under subsection (c) for rehabilitation expenditures paid or incurred by the taxpayer with respect to such building for a taxable year ending during the second calendar year referred to in clause (i) or the prior taxable year.

2 (2) ALLOCATED CREDIT AMOUNT TO APPLY TO ALL TAXABLE YEARS ENDING DURING OR AFTER CREDIT ALLOCATION YEAR.—Any housing credit dollar amount allocated to any building for any calendar year—

(A) shall apply to such building for all taxable years in the compliance period ending during or after such calendar year, and

(B) shall reduce the aggregate housing credit dollar amount of the allocating agency only for such calendar year.

3 (3) HOUSING CREDIT DOLLAR AMOUNT FOR AGENCIES.—

(A) IN GENERAL.—The aggregate housing credit dollar amount which a housing credit agency may allocate for any calendar year is the portion of the State housing credit ceiling allocated this paragraph for such calendar year to such agency.

(B) STATE CEILING INITIALLY ALLOCATED TO STATE HOUSING CREDIT AGENCIES.—Except as provided in subparagraphs (D) and (E), the State housing credit ceiling for each calendar year shall be allocated to the housing credit agency of such State. If there is more than 1 housing credit agency of a State, all such agencies shall be treated as a single agency.

(C) STATE HOUSING CREDIT CEILING.—The State housing credit ceiling applicable to any State for any calendar year shall be an amount equal to $1.25 multiplied by the State population.

(D) SPECIAL RULE FOR STATE WITH CONSTITUTIONAL HOME RULE CITIES.—For purposes of this subsection—

(i) IN GENERAL.—The aggregate housing credit dollar amount for any constitutional home rule city for any calendar year shall be an amount which bears the same ratio to the State housing credit ceiling for such calendar year as—

(I) the population of such city, bears to

(II) the population of the entire State.

(ii) COORDINATION WITH OTHER ALLOCATIONS.—In the case of any State which contains 1 or more constitutional home rule cities, for purposes of applying this paragraph with respect to housing credit agencies in such State other than constitutional home rule cities. The State housing credit ceiling for any calendar year shall be reduced by the aggregate housing credit dollar amounts determined for such year for all constitutional home rule cities in such State.

(iii) CONSTITUTIONAL HOME RULE CITY.—For purposes of this paragraph, the term 'constitutional home rule city' has the meaning given such term by section 146(d)(3)(C).

(E) STATE MAY PROVIDE FOR DIFFERENT ALLOCATION.—Rules similar to the rules of section 146(e) (other than paragraph (2)(B) thereof) shall apply for purposes of this paragraph.

(F) POPULATIONS.—For purposes of this paragraph, population shall be determined in accordance with section 146(j).

4 (4) CREDIT FOR BUILDINGS FINANCED BY TAX-EXEMPT BONDS SUBJECT TO VOLUME CAP TAKEN INTO ACCOUNT.—

(A) IN GENERAL.—Paragraph (1) shall not apply to the portion of any credit allowable under subsection (a) which is attributable to eligible basis financed by any obligation the interest on which is exempt from tax under section 103 if—

(i) such obligation is taken into account under section 146, and

(ii) principal payments on such financing are applied within a reasonable period to redeem obligations the proceeds of which were used to provide such financing.

(B) SPECIAL RULE WHERE 70 PERCENT OR MORE OF BUILDING IS FINANCED WITH TAX-EXEMPT BONDS SUBJECT TO VOLUME CAP.—For purposes of subparagraph (A), if 70 percent or more of the aggregate basis of any building and the land on which the building is located is financed by any obligation described in subparagraph (A), paragraph (1) shall not apply to any portion of the credit allowable under subsection (a) with respect to such building.

5 (5) PORTION OF STATE CEILING SET—ASIDE FOR CERTAIN PROJECTS INVOLVING QUALIFIED NONPROFIT ORGANIZATIONS.—

(A) IN GENERAL.—Not more than 90 percent of the State housing credit ceiling for any State for any calendar year shall be allocated to projects other than qualified low-income housing projects described in subparagraphs (B).

(B) PROJECTS INVOLVING QUALIFIED NONPROFIT ORGANIZATIONS.—For purposes of subparagraph (A), a qualified low-income housing project is described in this subparagraph if a qualified nonprofit organization is to materially participate (within the meaning of section 469(h) in the development and operation of the project throughout the compliance period.

(C) QUALIFIED NONPROFIT ORGANIZATION.— For purposes of this paragraph, the term 'qualified nonprofit organization' means any organization if—

(i) such organization is described in paragraph (3) or (4) of section 501(c) and is exempt from tax under section 501(a),and

(ii) 1 of the exempt purposes of such organization includes the fostering of low-income housing.

(D) TREATMENT OF CERTAIN SUBSIDIARIES.—

(i) IN GENERAL.—For purposes of this paragraph, a qualified nonprofit organization shall be treated as satisfying the material participation test of subparagraph (B) if any qualified corporation in which such organization holds stock satisfies such test.

(ii) QUALIFIED CORPORATION.—For purposes of clause (ii), the term 'qualified corporation' means any corporation if 100 percent of the stock of such corporation is held by 1 or more qualified nonprofit organizations at all times during the period such corporation is in existence.

(E) STATE MAY NOT OVERRIDE SET-ASIDE.—Nothing in subparagraph (E) of paragraph (3) shall be construed to permit a State not to comply with subparagraph (A) of this paragraph.

6 (6) SPECIAL RULES.—

(A) BUILDING MUST BE LOCATED WITHIN JURISDICTION OF CREDIT AGENCY.—A housing credit agency may allocate its aggregate housing credit dollar amount only to buildings located in the jurisdiction of the governmental unit of which such agency is a part.

(B) HOUSING CREDIT DOLLAR AMOUNT MAY NOT BE CARRIED OVER, ETC.—

(i) NO CARRYOVER.—The portion of the aggregate housing credit dollar amount of any housing credit agency which is not allocated for any calendar year may not be carried over to any other calendar year.

(ii) [Repealed]

(C) AGENCY ALLOCATIONS IN EXCESS OF LIMIT.—If the aggregate housing credit dollar amounts allocated by a housing credit agency for any calendar year exceed the portion of the State housing credit ceiling allocated to such agency for such calendar year, the housing credit dollar amounts so allocated shall be reduced (to the extent of such excess) for buildings in the reverse of the order in which the allocations of such amounts were made.

(D) CREDIT REDUCED IF ALLOCATED CREDIT DOLLAR AMOUNT IS LESS THAN CREDIT WHICH WOULD BE ALLOWABLE WITHOUT REGARD TO PLACED IN SERVICE CONVENTION, ETC.—

(i) IN GENERAL.—The amount of the credit determined under this section with respect to any building shall not exceed the clause (ii) percentage of the amount of the credit which would (but for this subparagraph) be determined under this section with respect to such building.

(ii) DETERMINATION OF PERCENTAGE.—For purposes of clause (i), the clause (ii) percentage with respect to any building is the percentage which—

(I) the housing credit dollar amount allocated to such building bears to

(II) the credit amount determined in accordance with clause (iii).

(iii) DETERMINATION OF CREDIT AMOUNT.—The credit amount determined in accordance with this clause is the amount of the credit which would (but for this subparagraph) be determined under this section with respect to the building if—

(I) this section were applied without regard to paragraphs (2)(A) and (3)(B) of subsection (f).

(II) subsection (f)(3)(A) were applied without regard to 'the percentage equal to ⅔ of'.

(E) HOUSING CREDIT AGENCY TO SPECIFY APPLICABLE PERCENTAGE AND MAXIMUM QUALIFIED BASIS.—In allocating a housing credit dollar amount to any building, the housing credit agency shall specify the applicable percentage and the maximum qualified basis which may be taken into account under this section with respect to such building. The applicable percentage and maximum qualified basis so specified shall not exceed the applicable percentage and qualified basis determined under this section without regard to this subsection.

7 (7) OTHER DEFINITIONS.—For purposes of this subsection—

(A) HOUSING CREDIT AGENCY.—The term 'housing credit agency' means any agency authorized to carry out this subsection.

(B) POSSESSIONS TREATED AS STATES.— The term 'State' includes a possession of the United States.

(i) (i) DEFINITIONS AND SPECIAL RULES.—For purposes of this section—

1 (1) COMPLIANCE PERIOD.—The term 'compliance period' means, with respect to any building, the period of 15 taxable years beginning with the 1st taxable year of the credit period with respect thereto.

2 (2) DETERMINATION OF WHETHER BUILDING IS FEDERALLY SUBSIDIZED.—

(A) IN GENERAL.—Except as otherwise provided in this paragraph, for purposes of subsection (b)(1), a new building shall be treated as federally subsidized for any taxable year if, at any time during such taxable year or any prior taxable year, there is or was outstanding any obligation the interest on which is exempt from tax under section 103, or any below market Federal loan, the proceeds of which are or were used (directly or indirectly) with respect to such building or the operation thereof.

(B) ELECTION TO REDUCE ELIGIBLE BASIS BY BALANCE OF LOAN OR PROCEEDS OF OBLIGATIONS.—A loan or tax-exempt obligation shall not be taken into account under subparagraph (A) if the taxpayer elects to exclude from the eligible basis of the building for purposes of subsection (d)—

(i) in the case of a loan, the principal amount of such loan, and

(ii) in the case of a tax-exempt obligation, the proceeds of such obligation.

(C) SPECIAL RULE FOR SUBSIDIZED CONSTRUCTION FINANCING.— Subparagraph (A) shall not apply to any tax-exempt obligation or below market Federal loan used to provide construction financing for any building if—

(i) such obligation or loan (when issued or made) identified the building for which the proceeds of such obligation or loan would be used, and

(ii) such obligation is redeemed, and such loan is repaid, before such building is placed in service.

(D) BELOW MARKET FEDERAL LOAN.—For purposes of subparagraph (A), the term 'below market Federal loan' means any loan funded in whole or in part with Federal funds if the interest rate payable on such loan is less than the applicable Federal rate in effect under section 1274(d)(1) (as of the date on which the loan was made).

3 (3) LOW-INCOME UNIT.—

(A) IN GENERAL.—The term 'low-income unit' means any unit in a building if—

(i) such unit is rent-restricted (as defined in subsection (g)(2)), and

(ii) the individuals occupying such unit meet the income limitation applicable under subsection (g)(1) to the project of which such building is a part.

(B) EXCEPTIONS.—A unit shall not be treated as a low-income unit unless the unit is suitable for occupancy and used other than on a transient basis.

(C) SPECIAL RULE FOR BUILDINGS HAVING 4 OR FEWER UNITS.—In the case of any building which has 4 or fewer residential rental units, no unit in such building shall be treated as a low-income unit if the units in such building are owned by—

(i) any individual who occupies a residential unit in such building, or

(ii) any person who is related (as defined in subsection (d)(2)(D)(iii)) to such individual.

4 (4) NEW BUILDING.—The term 'new building' means a building the original use of which begins with the taxpayer.

(5) EXISTING BUILDING.—The term existing building' means any building which is not a new building.

(j) (j) RECAPTURE OF CREDIT.—

1 (1) IN GENERAL.—If—

(A) as of the close of any taxable year in the compliance period, the amount of the qualified basis of any building with respect to the taxpayer is less than

(B) the amount of such basis as of the close of the preceding taxable year, then the taxpayer's tax under this chapter for the taxable year shall be increased by the credit recapture amount.

2 (2) CREDIT RECAPTURE AMOUNT.—For purposes of paragraph (1), the credit recapture amount is an amount equal to the sum of—

(A) the aggregate decrease in the credits allowed to the taxpayer under section 38 for all prior taxable years which would have resulted if the accelerated portion of the credit allowable by reason of this section were not allowed for all prior taxable years with respect to the excess of the amount described in paragraph (1)(B) over the amount described in paragraph (1)(A), plus

(B) interest at the overpayment rate established under section 6621 on the amount determined under subparagraph (A) for each prior taxable year for the period beginning on the due date for filing the return for the prior taxable year involved.

No deduction shall be allowed under this chapter for interest described in subparagraph (B).

3 (3) ACCELERATED PORTION OF CREDIT.—For purposes of paragraph (2), the accelerated portion of the credit for the prior taxable years with respect to any amount of basis is the excess of—

(A) the aggregate credit allowed by reason of this section (without regard to this subsection) for such years with respect to such basis, over

(B) the aggregate credit which would be allowable by reason of this section for such years with respect to such basis if the aggregate credit which would (but for this subsection) have been allowable for the entire compliance period were allowable ratably over 15 years.

4 (4) SPECIAL RULES.—

(A) TAX BENEFIT RULE.—The tax for the taxable year shall be increased under paragraph (1) only with respect to credits allowed by reason of this section which were used to reduce tax liability. In the case of credits not so used to reduce tax liability, the carryforwards and carrybacks under section 39 shall be appropriately adjusted.

(B) ONLY BASIS FOR WHICH CREDIT ALLOWED TAKEN INTO ACCOUNT.—Qualified basis shall be taken into account under paragraph (1)(B) only to the extent such basis was taken into account in determining the credit under subsection (a) for the preceding taxable year referred to in such paragraph.

(C) NO RECAPTURE OF ADDITIONAL CREDIT ALLOWABLE BY REASON OF SUBSECTION (f)(3).—Paragraph (1) shall apply to a decrease in qualified basis only to the extent such decrease exceeds the amount of qualified basis with respect to which a credit was allowable for the taxable year referred to in paragraph (1)(B) by reason of subsection (f)(3).

(D) NO CREDITS AGAINST TAX.—Any increase in tax under this subsection shall not be treated as a tax imposed by this chapter for purposes of determining the amount of any credit under subpart A, B, or D of this part.

(E) NO RECAPTURE BY REASON OF CASUALTY LOSS.—The increase in tax under this subsection shall not apply to a reduction in qualified basis by reason of a casualty loss to the extent such loss is restored by reconstruction or replacement within a reasonable period established by the Secretary.

(F) NO RECAPTURE WHERE DE MINIMIS CHANGES IN FLOOR SPACE.—The Secretary may provide that the increase in tax under this subsection shall not apply with respect to any building if—

(i) such increase results from a de minimis change in the floor space fraction under subsection (c)(1), and

(ii) the building is a qualified low-income building after such change.

5 (5) CERTAIN PARTNERSHIPS TREATED AS THE TAXPAYER.—

(A) IN GENERAL.—For purposes of applying this subsection to a partnership to which this paragraph applies—

(i) such partnership shall be treated as the taxpayer to which the credit allowable under subsection (a) was allowed,

(ii) the amount of such credit allowed shall be treated as the amount which would have been allowed to the partnership were such credit allowable to such partnership,

(iii) paragraph (4)(A) shall not apply, and

(iv) the amount of the increase in tax under this subsection for any taxable year shall be allocated among the partners of such partnership in the same manner as such partnership's taxable income for such year is allocated among such partners.

(B) PARTNERSHIPS TO WHICH PARAGRAPH APPLIES.—This paragraph shall apply to any partnership which has 35 or more partners unless the partnership elects not to have this paragraph apply.

(C) SPECIAL RULES.—

(i) Husband and Wife Treated as 1 Partner.—For purposes of subparagraph (B)(i), a husband and wife (and their estates) shall be treated as 1 partner.

(ii) ELECTION IRREVOCABLE.—Any election under subparagraph (B), once made, shall be irrevocable.

6 (6) NO RECAPTURE ON DISPOSITION OF BUILDING (OR INTEREST THEREIN) WHERE BOND POSTED.—In the case of disposition of a building or an interest therein, the taxpayer shall be discharged from liability for any additional tax under this subsection by reason of such disposition if—

(A) the taxpayer furnishes to the Secretary a bond in an amount satisfactory to the Secretary and for the period required by the Secretary, and

(B) it is reasonably expected that such building will continue to be operated as a qualified low-income building for the remaining compliance period with respect to such building.

(k) (k) APPLICATION OF AT-RISK RULES.—For purposes of this section—

1 (1) IN GENERAL.—Except as otherwise provided in this subsection, rules similar to the rules of section 46(c)(8) (other than subparagraph (D)(iv)(I) thereof), section 46(c)(9), and section 47(d)(1) shall apply in determining the qualified basis of any building in the same manner as such sections apply in determining the credit base of property.

2 (2) SPECIAL RULES FOR DETERMINING QUALIFIED PERSON.—

For purposes of paragraph (1)—

(A) IN GENERAL.—If the requirements of subparagraphs (B), (C), and (D) are met with respect to any financing borrowed from a qualified nonprofit organization (as defined in subsection (h)(5)), the determination of whether such financing is qualified commercial financing with respect to any qualified low-income building shall be made without regard to whether such organization—

(i) is actively and regularly engaged in the business of lending money, or

(ii) is a person described in section 46(c)(8)(D)(iv)(II)

(B) FINANCING SECURED BY PROPERTY.—The requirements of this subparagraph are met with respect to any financing if such financing is secured by the qualified low-income building; except that this subparagraph shall not apply in the case of a federally assisted building described in subsection (d)(6)(B) if—

(i) a security interest in such building is not permitted by a Federal agency holding or insuring the mortgage secured by such building, and

(ii) the proceeds from the financing (if any) are applied to acquire or improve such building.

(C) PORTION OF BUILDING ATTRIBUTABLE TO FINANCING.—The requirements of this subparagraph are met with respect to any financing for any taxable year in the compliance period if, as of the close of such taxable year, not more than 60 percent of the eligible basis of the qualified low-income building is attributable to such financing (reduced by the principal and interest of any governmental financing which is part of a wrap-around mortgage involving such financing).

(D) REPAYMENT OF PRINCIPAL AND INTEREST.—The requirements of this subparagraph are met with respect to any financing if such financing is fully repaid on or before the earliest of—

(i) the date on which such financing matures,

(ii) the 90th day after the close of the compliance period with respect to the qualified low-income building, or

(iii) the date of its refinancing or the sale of the building to which such financing relates.

3 (3) PRESENT VALUE OF FINANCING.—If the rate of interest on any financing described in paragraph (2)(A) is less than the rate which is 1 percentage point below the applicable Federal rate as of the time such financing is incurred, then the qualified basis (to which such financing relates) of the qualified low-income building shall be the present value of the amount of such

financing, using as the discount rate such applicable Federal rate. For purposes of the preceding sentence, the rate of interest on any financing shall be determined by treating interest to the extent of government subsidies as not payable.

4 (4) FAILURE TO FULLY REPAY.

(A) IN GENERAL.—To the extent that the requirements of paragraph (2)(D) are not met, then the taxpayer's tax under this chapter for the taxable year in which such failure occurs shall be increased by an amount equal to the applicable portion of the credit under this section with respect to such building, increased by an amount of interest for the period—

(i) beginning with the due date for the filing of the return of tax imposed by chapter 1 for the 1st taxable year for which such credit was allowable, and

(ii) ending with the due date for the taxable year in which such failure occurs, determined by using the underpayment rate and method under section 6621.

(B) APPLICABLE PORTION.—For purposes of subparagraph (A), the term "applicable portion" means the aggregate decrease in the credits allowed to a taxpayer under section 38 for all prior taxable years which would have resulted if the eligible basis of the building were reduced by the amount of financing which does not meet requirements of paragraph (2)(D).

(C) CERTAIN RULES TO APPLY.—Rules similar to the rules of subparagraphs (A) and (D)j of subsection (j)(4) shall apply for purposes of this subsection.

(1) (l) CERTIFICATIONS AND OTHER REPORTS TO SECRETARY—

1 (1) CERTIFICATION WITH RESPECT TO 1ST YEAR OF CREDIT PERIOD.—Not later than the 90th day following the close of the 1st taxable year in the credit period with respect to any qualified low-income building, the taxpayer shall certify to the Secretary (in such form and in such manner as the Secretary prescribes)—

(A) the taxable year, and calendar year, in which such building was placed in service,

(B) the adjusted basis and eligible basis of such building as of the close of the 1st year of the credit period.

(C) the maximum applicable percentage and qualified basis permitted to be taken into account by the appropriate housing credit agency under subsection (h),

(D) the election made under subsection (g) with respect to the qualified low-income housing project of which such building is a part, and

(E) such other information as the Secretary may require. In the case of a failure to make the certification required by the preceding sentence on the date prescribed therefor, unless it is shown that such failure is due to reasonable cause and not to willful neglect, no credit shall be allowable by reason of subsection (a) with respect to such building for any taxable year ending before such certification is made.

2 (2) ANNUAL REPORTS TO THE SECRETARY.—The Secretary may require taxpayers to submit an information return (at such time and in such form and manner as the Secretary prescribes) for each taxable year setting forth—

(A) the qualified basis for the taxable year of each qualified low-income building of the taxpayer,

(B) the information described in paragraph (1)(C) for the taxable year, and

(C) such other information as the Secretary may require.

3 (3) ANNUAL REPORTS FROM HOUSING CREDIT AGENCIES.—Each agency which allocates any housing credit amount to any building for any calendar year shall submit to the Secretary (at such time and in such manner as the Secretary shall prescribe) an annual report specifying—

(A) the amount of housing credit amount allocated to each building for such year, and

(B) sufficient information to identify each such building and the taxpayer with respect thereto, and

(C) such other information as the Secretary may require. The penalty under section 6652(j) shall apply to any failure to submit the report required by the preceding sentence on the date prescribed therefor.

(m) (m) REGULATIONS.—The Secretary shall prescribe such regulations as may be necessary or appropriate to carry out the purposes of this section, including regulations—

(1) dealing with—

(A) projects which include more than 1 building or only a portion of a building.

(B) buildings which are placed in service in portions.

(2) providing for the application of this section to short taxable years, and

(3) preventing the avoidance of the rules of this section.

(n) (n) TERMINATION.—The State housing credit ceiling under subsection (h) shall be zero for any calendar year after 1989 and subsection (h)(4) shall not apply to any building placed in service after 1989.

1 (1) IN GENERAL.—Except as provided in paragraph (2), the State housing credit ceiling under subsection (h) shall be zero for any calendar year after 1989 and, except for any building described in paragraph (2)(B), subsec-

tion (h)(4) shall not apply to any building placed in service after 1989.

* * *

SECTION 252(b) OF THE TAX REFORM ACT OF 1986*

(b) LOW-INCOME HOUSING CREDIT TREATED AS OTHER BUSINESS CREDITS.—

(1) Subsection (b) of section 38 (relating to current year business credits), as amended by this Act, is amended by striking out "plus" at the end of paragraph (3), but striking out the period at the end of paragraph (4) and inserting in lieu thereof "plus", and by adding at the end thereof the following new paragraph:

"(5) the low-income housing credit determined under section 42(a)."

(2) Subsection (d) of section 38 is amended by inserting "42(a)," before "46(a)"

(c) RECAPTURE TAX NOT TO REDUCE MINIMUM TAX.—Paragraph (1) of section 55(c), as amended by section 701 of this Act, is amended by inserting "or section 42(j)" after "section 47".

(d) Clerical Amendment.—The table of sections for subpart D of part IV of subchapter A of chapter 1 is amended by adding at the end thereof the following new item:

"Sec. 42 Low-Income Housing Credit."

(e) EFFECTIVE DATE.—

(1) IN GENERAL.—The amendments made by this section shall apply to buildings placed in service after December 31, 1986, in taxable years ending after such date.

(2) SPECIAL RULE FOR REHABILITATION EXPENDITURES.—Subsection (e) of section 42 of the Internal Revenue Code of 1986 (as added by this section) shall apply for purposes of paragraph (1).

(f) TRANSITIONAL RULES—

(1) LIMITATION TO NON-ACRS BUILDINGS NOT TO APPLY TO CERTAIN BUILDINGS, ETC.—

(A) IN GENERAL.—In the case of a building which is part of a project described in subparagraph (B)—

(i) section 42(c)(2)(B) of the Internal Revenue Code of 1986 (as added by this section) shall not apply,

(ii) such building shall be treated as not federally subsidized for purposes of section 42(b)(1)(A) of such Code,

(iii) the eligible basis of such building shall be treated, for purposes of section 42(h)(4)(A) of such Code, as if it were financed by an obligation the interest on which is exempt from tax under section 103 of such Code and which is taken into account under section 146 of such Code, and

(iv) the amendments made by section 803 shall not apply.

(B) PROJECT DESCRIBED.—A project is described in this subparagraph if—

(i) an urban development action grant application with respect to such project was submitted on September 13, 1984,

(ii) a zoning commission map amendment related to such project was granted on July 17, 1985,and

(iii) the number assigned to such project by the Federal Housing Administration is 023-36602.

(C) ADDITIONAL UNITS ELIGIBLE FOR CREDIT.—In the case of a building to which subparagraph (A) applies and which is part of a project which meets the requirements of subparagraph (D), for each low-income unit in such building which is occupied by individuals whose income is 30 percent or less of area median gross income, one additional unit (not otherwise a low-income unit) in such building shall be treated as a low-income unit for purposes of such section 42.

(D) PROJECT DESCRIBED.—A project is described in this subparagraph if—

(i) rents charged for units in such project are restricted by State regulations,

(ii) the annual cash flow of such project are restricted by State law,

* Amended by the Technical and Miscellaneous Revenue Act of 1988, Public Law 100-647, November 10, 1988.

(iii) the project is located on land owned by or ground leased from a public housing authority,

(iv) construction of such project begins on or before December 31, 1986, and units within such project are placed in service on or before June 1, 1990, and

(v) for a 20-year period, 20 percent or more of the residential units in such project are occupied by individuals whose income is 50 percent or less of area median gross income.

(E) MAXIMUM ADDITIONAL CREDIT.—The maximum present value of additional credits allowable under section 42 of such Code by reason of subparagraph (C) shall not exceed 25 percent of the eligible basis of the building.

(2) ADDITIONAL ALLOCATION OF HOUSING CREDIT CEILING.—

(A) IN GENERAL.—There is hereby allocated to each housing credit agency described in subparagraph (B) an additional housing credit dollar amount determined in accordance with the following table:

For calendar year:	The additional allocation is:
1987	$3,900,000
1988	$7,600,000
1989	$1,300,000

(B) HOUSING CREDIT AGENCIES DESCRIBED.—The housing credit agencies described in this subparagraph are:

(i) A corporate governmental agency constituted as a public benefit corporation and established in 1971 under the provisions of Article XII of the Private Housing Finance Law of the State.

(ii) A city department established on December 20, 1979, pursuant to chapter XVIII of a municipal code of such city for the purpose of supervising and coordinating the formation and execution of projects and programs affecting housing within such city.

(iii) The State housing finance agency referred to in subparagraph (C), but only with respect to projects described in subparagraph (C).

(C) PROJECT DESCRIBED.—A project is described in this subparagraph if such project is a qualified low-income housing project which—

(i) receives financing from a State housing finance agency from the proceeds of bonds issued pursuant to chapter 708 of the Acts of 1966 of such State pursuant to loan commitments from such agency made between May 8, 1984, and July 8, 1986, and

(ii) is subject to subsidy commitments issued pursuant to a program established under chapter 574 of the Acts of 1983 of such State having award dates from such agency between May 31, 1984, and June 11, 1985.

(D) SPECIAL RULES.—

(i) Any building—

(I) which is allocated any housing credit dollar amount by a housing credit agency described in clause (iii) of subparagraph (B), and

(II) which is placed in service after June 30, 1986, and before January 1, 1987, shall be treated for purposes of the amendments made by this section as placed in service on January 1, 1987.

(ii) Section 42(c)(2)(B) of the Internal Revenue Code of 1986 shall not apply to any building which is allocated any housing credit dollar amount by any agency described in subparagraph (B).

(E) ALL UNITS TREATED AS LOW INCOME UNITS IN CERTAIN CASES.—In the case of any building—

(i) which is allocated any housing credit dollar amount by any agency described in subparagraph (B), and

(ii) which after the application of subparagraph (D)(ii) is a qualified low-income building at all times during any taxable year,

such building shall be treated as described in section 42(b)(1)(B) of such Code and having an applicable fraction for such year of 1.

The preceding sentence shall apply to any building only to the extent of the portion of the additional housing credit dollar amount (allocated to such agency under subparagraph (A)) allocated to such building.

(3) CERTAIN PROJECTS PLACED IN SERVICE BEFORE 1987.—

(A) IN GENERAL.—In the case of a building which is part of a project described in subparagraph (B)—

(i) section 42(c)(2)(B) of such Code shall not apply,

(ii) such building shall be treated as placed in service during the first calendar year after 1968 and before 1990 in which such building is a qualified low-income building (determined after the application of clause (i)), and

(iii) for purposes of section 42(h) of such Code such building shall be treated as having allocated to it a housing credit dollar amount equal to the dollar amount appearing in the clause of subparagraph (B) in which such building is described.

(B) PROJECT DESCRIBED. A project is described in this subparagraph if the Code number assigned to such project by the Farmers' Home Administration appears in the following table:

The code number is:	The housing credit dollar amount is:
(i) 49284553664	$16,000
(ii) 4927742022446	$22,000
(iii) 492707422769087	$64,000
(iv) 490270742387293	$48,000
(v) 4927074218234	$32,000
(vi) 49270742274019	$36,000
(vii) 51460742345074	$53,000

(C) DETERMINATION OF ADJUSTED BASIS.—The adjusted basis of any building to which this paragraph applies for purposes of section 42 of such Code shall be its adjusted basis as of the close of the taxable year ending before the first taxable year of the credit period for such building.

(D) CERTAIN RULES TO APPLY.—Rules similar to the rules of subparagraph (E) of paragraph (2) shall apply for purposes of this paragraph.

(4) DEFINITIONS.—For purposes of this subsection, terms used in such subsection which are also used in section 42 of the Internal Revenue Code of 1986 (as added by this section) shall have the meanings given such terms by such section 42.

(5) TRANSITIONAL RULE.—In the case of any rehabilitation expenditures incurred with respect to units located in the neighborhood strategy area within the community development block grant program in Ft. Wayne, Indiana—

(A) the amendments made by this section shall not apply, and

(B) paragraph (1) of section 167 (k) of the Internal Revenue Code of 1986, shall be applied as if it did not contain the phrase 'and before January 1, 1987'.

The number of units to which the preceding sentence applies shall not exceed 150.

* * *

SECTION 39(d) OF THE INTERNAL REVENUE CODE OF 1986*

(d) NO CARRYBACK OF LOW-INCOME HOUSING CREDIT BEFORE 1987.—No portion of the unused business credit for any taxable year which is attributable to the credit determined under section 42 (relating to low-income housing credit) may be carried back to a taxable year ending before January 1, 1987.

---

* Added by Section 1002(1)(26) of the Technical and Miscellaneous Revenue Act of 1988 Public Law 100-647, November 10, 1988.

APPENDIX 6

THE "BLUE BOOK": GENERAL EXPLANATION OF THE TAX REFORM ACT OF 1986: LOW INCOME HOUSING TAX CREDIT PROVISIONS

2. Tax credit for low-income rental housing (sec. 252 of the Act and sec. 42 of the Code)[1]

Prior Law

No low-income rental housing tax credit was provided under prior law, but other tax incentives for low-income housing were available. These tax incentives consisted principally of special accelerated depreciation, five-year amortization of rehabilitation expenses, expensing of construction period interest and taxes, and tax-exempt bond financing for multifamily residential rental property.

Reasons for Change

Congress was concerned that the tax preferences for low-income rental housing available under prior law were not effective in providing affordable housing for low-income individuals. Congress believed a more efficient mechanism for encouraging the production of low-income rental housing could be provided through the low-income rental housing tax credit.

The primary tax preferences provided for low-income housing under prior law were tax-exempt bond financing, accelerated cost recovery deductions, five-year amortization of rehabilitation expenditures, and special deductions for construction period interest and taxes. These preferences operated in an uncoordinated manner, resulted in subsidies unrelated to the number of low-income individuals served, and failed to guarantee that affordable housing would be provided to the most needy low-income individuals.

A major shortcoming of the prior-law tax subsidies was that, beyond a minimum threshold requirement of low-income housing units that were required to be served, the degree of subsidy was not directly linked to the number of units serving low-income persons. As a result, there was no incentive to provide low-income units beyond the minimum required. Under the tax credit, however, the amount of the low-income housing tax credit which an owner may receive is directly related to the number of rental units made available to low-income individuals. By providing tax credits which are based on the number of units serving low-income persons, an incentive exists to provide a greater number of housing units for more low-income individuals.

Another weakness of the Federal tax subsidies available under prior law was that they were not targeted to persons of truly low-income. For example, a study by the General Accounting Office[2] (GAO) of tax-exempt bond financed residential rental projects found that above-average income renters could qualify under prior law as "low" or "moderate" income for two reasons. First, persons with incomes as high as 80 percent of area median income were eligible to occupy units reserved for low- and moderate-income tenants. This income ceiling was relatively high, particularly when compared with the median income of renters. Second, the Treasury Department did not require household incomes to be adjusted for family size until after 1985. Congress believed that the low-income housing tax credit (as well as tax-exempt bond financing for low-income housing, discussed in Title XIII) should be provided only for households with incomes not exceeding 50 percent or 60 percent of area median income. Congress further believed that these income limits should be adjusted for family size. These provisions better target affordable housing to those persons most in need of assistance.

Another shortcoming of the tax subsidies under prior law was that none limited the rents that could be charged to low-income individuals. The same GAO study found, for example, that while 96 percent of individuals with incomes over 80 percent of area median income (the prior-law ceiling on "low" or "moderate" income) paid rents of less than 30 percent of their income, only 37 percent of individuals with incomes below 80 percent of area median paid rents of less than 30 percent of their income. The low-income housing tax credit limits the rent that may be charged to a low-income tenant, and therefore ensures that the subsidized housing is affordable to low-income individuals. In return for providing housing at reduced rents, owners of rental housing receive a tax credit designed to compensate them for the rent reduction.

Congress believed that the low-income housing tax credit (and tax-exempt bonds, as retargeted) will more effectively serve both low-income individuals and owners willing to provide affordable low-income housing than the multiple, uncoordinated tax preferences for low-income housing under prior law.

Explanation of Provisions

Overview

The Act provides a tax credit that may be claimed by owners of residential rental property used for low-income housing. The credit is claimed annually, generally for a period of ten years. New construction and rehabilitation expenditures for low-income housing projects placed in service in 1987 are eligible for a maximum nine percent credit, paid annually for ten years. The acquisition cost of existing projects and the cost of newly constructed projects receiv-

[1] For legislative background of the provision, see: H.R. 3838, as reported by the Senate Committee on Finance on May 29, 1986, sec. 1413; S.Rep. 99-313, pp. 757-768; Senate floor amendment, 132 Cong. Rec. S8146-8158 (June 23, 1986); and H.Rep. 99-841, Vol. II (September 18, 1986), pp. 85-103 (Conference Report).

[2] United States General Accounting Office, *Report to the Chairman, Joint Committee on Taxation, Rental Housing: Costs and Benefits of Financing with Tax-Exempt Bonds* (GAO/RCED-86-2), February 1986.

ing other Federal subsidies placed in service in 1987 are eligible for a maximum four percent credit, also paid annually for ten years. For buildings placed in service after 1987, these credit percentages will be adjusted to maintain a present value of 70 percent and 30 percent for the two types of credits.

The credit amount is based on the qualified basis (defined below) of the housing units serving the low-income tenants. Low-income tenants for purposes of the low-income housing tax credit are defined as tenants having incomes equal to or less than either 50 percent or 60 percent of area median income, adjusted for family size. The qualifying income for a particular property depends on the minimum percentage of units that the owner elects to provide for low-income tenants. Rents that may be charged families in units on which a credit is claimed may not exceed 30 percent of the applicable income qualifying as "low", also adjusted for family size.

To qualify for the credit, residential rental property must comply continuously with all requirements of the credit throughout a 15-year compliance period. A credit allocation from the appropriate State or local credit authority must be received by the owner of property eligible for the low-income housing tax credit, unless the property is substantially financed with the proceeds of tax-exempt bonds subject to the new private activity bond volume limitation. These provisions are further explained in the following sections.

Credit amount and credit period

The Act provides two separate credit amounts: (1) a 70-percent present value credit for qualified new construction and rehabilitation expenditures (in excess of specified minimum amounts per unit) that are not federally subsidized and (2) a 30-percent present value credit for other qualifying expenditures. Expenditures qualifying for the 30-percent present value credit consist of the cost of acquisition of an existing building (including certain rehabilitation expenditures which are incurred in connection with acquisition and which do not exceed prescribed minimum amounts), and federally subsidized new construction or rehabilitation expenditures.

A taxpayer's credit amount in any taxable year is computed by applying the appropriate credit percentage to the appropriate qualified basis amount in such year, as defined below.[3] Except as described below, both credits are claimed annually over a 10-year period.

The credit period is the 10-year period beginning with the taxable year in which the building is placed in service or, at the election of the taxpayer, the succeeding taxable year. The credit may not be claimed for a taxable year in which the building is not in compliance with all requirements of the credit.

[3] Congress understood that in certain cases low-income rental housing tax credit projects would be owned indirectly through partnerships. Congress intended that Treasury Department regulations will include rules treating partnerships as if they were taxpayers where appropriate to carry out the objectives of the tax credit. Congress intended, for example, that the partnership be treated as the taxpayer for purposes of determining whether a building is new (sec. 42(i)(4)). Where a partner's interest changes during a taxable year, it is intended that each partner's distributive share of the tax credit be determined under general partnership allocation rules (*see* sec. 706), i.e., by the use of a method prescribed in Treasury Department regulations that takes into account the varying interests of the partners in the partnership during such taxable year.

Credit percentage

For buildings placed in service in 1987, the credit percentages are 9 percent annually over 10 years for the 70-percent present value credit, and 4 percent annually over 10 years for the 30-percent present value credit.

For buildings placed in service after 1987, these credit percentages are to be adjusted monthly by the Treasury Department to reflect the present values of 70 percent and 30 percent at the time the building is placed in service. Treasury's monthly adjustments of the credit percentages are to be determined on a discounted after-tax basis, based on the average of the annual applicable Federal rates (AFR) for mid-term and long-term obligations for the month the building is placed in service. The after-tax interest rate is to be computed as the product of (1) the average AFR and (2) .72 (one minus the maximum individual Federal income tax rate). The discounting formula assumes each credit is received on the last day of each year and that the present value is computed as of the last day of the first year. For example, if 72 percent of the average AFR for a given month were 5.85 percent, the 70-percent and 30-percent present value credit percentages for buildings placed in service in that month would be 8.92 percent and 3.82 percent. (For the 70-percent present value credit, this is derived as $.0892 = (.70)(.0585)/[1.0585-1/(1.0585)^9]$.) In a project consisting of two or more buildings placed in service in different months, a separate credit percentage may apply to each building.[4]

For buildings originally placed in service after 1987, Congress intended that the taxpayer, with the consent of the housing credit agency, may irrevocably elect to use the credit percentage determined using the above method for the month in which the taxpayer receives a binding commitment for a credit allocation from the credit agency or, in the case of a tax-exempt bond financed project for which no allocation is required, the month in which the tax-exempt bonds are issued.[5]

The credit percentage for rehabilitation expenditures (in excess of a prescribed minimum amount) is determined when rehabilitation is completed and the rehabilitated property is placed in service, but no later than the end of the 24-month period for which such expenditures may be aggregated.[6] These rehabilitation expenditures are treated as a separate new building for purposes of the credit.

The credit percentage for rehabilitation expenditures that are incurred in connection with the acquisition of an existing building (and which do not exceed prescribed minimum amounts) is the same percentage as is used for the acquired building, i.e., the per-

[4] As discussed below, a credit percentage equal to two-thirds of the credit percentage for the initial qualified basis is applicable to additions to qualified basis.

[5] A technical amendment may be needed so that the statute reflects this intent and the intent of Congress that such an election would be binding on the taxpayer and all successors in interest.

[6] Congress intended that the election to determine the credit percentage at the time a binding commitment for a credit allocation is received, described above, also apply in the case of credits attributable to rehabilitation expenditures (in excess of a prescribed minimum amount). A technical amendment may be needed so that the statute reflects this intent.

centage determined when the acquired building is placed in service.

Qualified basis

In general

The qualified basis amounts with respect to which the credit amount is computed are determined as the proportion of eligible basis in a qualified low-income building attributable to the low-income rental units. This proportion is the lesser of (1) the proportion of low-income units to all residential rental units or (2) the proportion of floor space of the low-income units to the floor space of all residential rental units. Generally, in these calculations, low-income units are those units presently occupied by qualifying tenants, whereas residential rental units are all housing units, whether or not presently occupied.

The qualified basis for each building is determined on the last day of each taxable year, beginning in the taxable year in which the building is placed in service or, if the taxpayer elects, the following taxable year.

Special rules for determining qualified basis

The Treasury Department may provide regulations for projects consisting of two or more buildings. Unless prescribed in regulations, the qualified basis of a project consisting of two or more buildings is determined separately for each building. Common facilities in such a project must be allocated in an appropriate manner to all buildings (whether existing or to be constructed) in the project.

The first year the credit is claimed, the allowable credit amount is determined using an averaging convention to reflect the number of months units comprising the qualified basis were occupied by low-income individuals during the year. For example, if half of the low-income units included in qualified basis were first occupied in October and the remaining half were occupied in December, a calendar year taxpayer would adjust the allowable first-year credit to reflect that these units were occupied on average only one-sixth of the year. To the extent there is such a reduction of the credit amount in the first year, an additional credit in the amount of such reduction is available in the eleventh taxable year. (This first-year adjustment does not affect the amount of qualified basis with respect to which the credit is claimed in subsequent years of the 10-year credit period.)

Additions to qualified basis

The qualified basis of a building may be increased subsequent to the initial determination only by reason of an increase in the number of low-income units or in the floor space of the low-income units (as opposed to by reason of increases in the eligible basis). Credits claimed on such additional qualified basis are determined using a credit percentage equal to two-thirds of the applicable credit percentage allowable for the initial qualified basis. As described below under the description of the State credit ceiling, an allocation of credit authority must be received for credits claimed

on additions to qualified basis, in the same manner as for credits claimed on the initial qualified basis. Unlike credits claimed on the initial qualified basis, credits claimed on additions to qualified basis are allowable annually for the portion of the required 15-year compliance period remaining after eligibility for such credits arises, regardless of the year such additional qualified basis is determined. The additional qualified basis is determined by reference to the original adjusted basis (before deductions for depreciation) of the property.

The credit amount on the additional qualified basis is adjusted in the first year such additions are made using an averaging convention to reflect the number of months units comprising the additional qualified basis were occupied by low-income individuals during the year. Any reduction of the credit amount in the first year may not be claimed in a later year. (This first-year adjustment does not affect the amount of additional qualified basis with respect to which the credit is claimed in subsequent years of the compliance period.)

Eligible basis

Eligible basis consists of (1) the cost of new construction, (2) the cost of rehabilitation, or (3) the cost of acquisition of existing buildings acquired by purchase (including the cost of rehabilitation, if any, to such buildings incurred before the close of the first taxable year of the credit period which do not exceed a prescribed minimum amount). Only the adjusted basis of the depreciable property may be included in eligible basis.[7] The cost of land is not included in adjusted basis.

Generally, the eligible basis of a building is determined at the time the building is placed in service. For this purpose, rehabilitation expenditures (in excess of $2,000 per unit) are treated as placed in service at the close of the period for which rehabilitation expenditures are aggregated, not to exceed 24 months. In the case of rehabilitation expenditures incurred in connection with the acquisition of an existing building (and which do not exceed a prescribed minimum amount), the capital expenditures incurred through the end of the first year of the credit period may be included in eligible basis.

For purposes of the low-income housing credit, the term residential rental property generally has the same meaning as residential rental property within Code section 142(d).[8] Thus, residential rental property includes residential rental units, facilities for use by the tenants, and other facilities reasonably required by the project. Eligible basis may include the cost of such facilities and amenities (e.g., stoves, refrigerators, air conditioning units, etc.) only if the included amenities are comparable to the cost of the amenities in the low-income units. Additionally, the allocable cost of tenant facilities, such as swimming pools, other recreational fa-

---

[7] The adjusted basis is determined by taking into account the adjustments described in section 1016 (other than paragraphs (2) and (3) of sec. 1016(a), relating to depreciation deductions), including, for example, the basis adjustment provided in section 48(q) for any rehabilitation credits allowed under section 38.

[8] See, however, the discussion below on single room occupancy housing as property eligible for the low-income housing credit.

cilities, and parking areas, may be included provided there is no separate fee for the use of these facilities and they are made available on a comparable basis to all tenants in the project. (*See generally*, Treas. Reg. sec. 1.103-8(b)(4)(iii).)

Except as described below, costs of the residential rental units in a building which are not low-income units may be included in eligible basis only if such units are not above the average quality standard of the low-income units. Similarly, rehabilitation expenditures may not be included in eligible basis if such expenditures improve any unit in the building beyond comparability with the low-income units. Units are of comparable quality if the construction or acquisition costs are comparable and if such units are provided in a similar proportion for both the low-income and other tenants. Congress intended that, at the election of the taxpayer, the cost of a unit which would otherwise be excluded from eligible basis may be included in eligible basis if (1) the excess cost of such unit over the average cost of the low-income units does not exceed 15 percent of the average cost of the low-income units and (2) the excess cost is excluded from eligible basis.[9]

Residential rental property may qualify for the credit even though a portion of the building in which the residential rental units are located is used for a commercial use. No portion of the cost of such nonresidential rental property included in a project may be included in eligible basis. Congress intended that the costs of such a mixed-use facility be allocated according to any reasonable method that properly reflects the proportionate benefit to be derived, directly or indirectly, by the nonresidential rental property and the residential rental units. (*See*, e.g., Prop. Treas. Reg. sec. 1.103-8(b)(4)(v).)

Certain rehabilitation expenditures.—The qualified basis attributable to rehabilitation expenditures, unless incurred in connection with the acquisition of an existing building, must equal at least $2,000 per low-income unit.[10] The $2,000 minimum is computed as an average based on all qualifying expenditures in the building, rather than on a unit-by-unit determination. Qualified basis is determined in the same fractional manner as for new construction or acquisition costs even if all rehabilitation expenditures are made only to low-income units. Rehabilitation expenditures may be included in eligible basis without a transfer of property. Rehabilitation expenditures may be aggregated only for such expenditures incurred during any 24-month period. Where rehabilitation is limited to a group of units, Treasury may provide regulations treating a group of units as a separate new building.

Where rehabilitation expenditures are paid or incurred by a person (or persons) and the taxpayer acquires the property attributable to such expenditures (or an interest therein) before such property is placed in service, the taxpayer will be treated as having paid or incurred the expenditures (*see* Treas. Reg. sec. 1.167(k)-1(b)(1) and (2)). The portion of the basis of the property not attributable to rehabilitation expenditures may not be included in the eligible basis relating to the rehabilitated property, but may be includable in the eligible basis relating to acquisition costs, as described below.

[9] A technical amendment may be needed so that the statute reflects this intent.

[10] See, below, in the case of rehabilitation expenditures incurred in connection with the acquisition of an existing building that do not exceed the $2,000 per unit minimium.

Acquisition of existing buildings.—The cost of acquisition of an existing building may be included in eligible basis and any rehabilitation expenditures to such a building incurred before the close of the first year of the credit period may at the election of the taxpayer also be included in eligible basis, without a minimum rehabilitation requirement. These costs may be included in eligible basis, however, only if the building or a substantial improvement (a capital expenditure of 25 percent or more of the adjusted basis of the building to which five-year rapid amortization was elected or to which ACRS applied (as in effect before the enactment of this Act)) to the building has not been previously placed in service within 10 years and if the building (or rehabilitated property within the building) is not subject to the 15-year compliance period.

A building that is transferred in a transfer where the basis of the property in the hands of the new owner is determined in whole or part by the adjusted basis of the previous owner (for example, by a gift of property) is considered not to have been newly placed in service for purposes of the 10-year requirement.[11] Further, Congress intended that a building which has been acquired by a governmental unit or certain qualified 501(c)(3) or 501(c)(4) organizations would not be treated as placed in service by that governmental unit or organization for purposes of the 10-year requirement if the acquisition occurs more than 10 years from the date the building or a substantial improvement to the building has last been placed in service.[12] Congress also intended that a building acquired by foreclosure by taxpayers other than a governmental unit or 501(c)(3) organization would not be treated as newly placed in service by that taxpayer for purposes of the 10-year requirement if the foreclosure occurs more than 10 years from the date the building or a substantial improvement to the building has last been placed in service and the property is resold within a short period.[13] Any other transfer will begin a new 10-year period.

The Treasury Department may waive the 10-year requirement for any building substantially assisted, financed or operated under the HUD section 8, section 221(d)(3), or section 236 programs, or under the Farmers' Home Administration section 515 program when an assignment of the mortgage secured by property in the project to HUD or the Farmers Home Administration otherwise would occur or when a claim against a Federal mortgage insurance fund would occur.

Federal grants and other subsidies.—Eligible basis may not include in any taxable year the amount of any Federal grant, regardless of whether such grant is included in gross income. A Federal grant includes any grant funded in whole or in part by the Federal government, to the extent funded with Federal funds. Examples of grants which may not be included in eligible basis include grants

[11] Congress intended that inherited property not be treated as being newly placed in service for purposes of the 10-year requirement. A technical amendment may be needed so that the statute reflects this intent.

[12] A technical amendment may be needed so that the statute reflects this intent.

[13] A technical amendment may be needed so that the statute reflects this intent.

funded by Community Development Block Grants, Urban Development Action Grants, Rental Rehabilitation Grants, and Housing Development Grants.

If any portion of the eligible basis attributable to new construction or to rehabilitation expenditures is financed with Federal subsidies, the qualified basis is eligible only for the 30-percent present value credit, unless such Federal subsidies are excluded from eligible basis. A Federal subsidy is defined as any obligation the interest on which is exempt from tax under section 103 or a direct or indirect Federal loan, if the interest rate on such loan is less than the applicable Federal rate. A Federal loan under the Farmers' Home Administration section 515 program is an example of such a Federal subsidy, as is a reduced interest rate loan attributable in part to Federal grant funds lent to a building owner.

The determination of whether rehabilitation expenditures are federally subsidized is made without regard to the source of financing for the construction or acquisition of the building to which the rehabilitation expenditures are made. For example, a Federal loan or tax-exempt bond financing that is continued or assumed upon purchase of existing housing is disregarded for purposes of the credit on rehabilitation expenditures. Congress intended that tax-exempt financing or a below market loan to provide construction financing for any building will not be treated as a Federal subsidy if such loan is repaid and any underlying obligation (e.g., tax-exempt bond) is redeemed before the building is placed in service.[14]

Minimum set-aside requirement for low-income individuals

In general

A residential rental project providing low-income housing qualifies for the credit only if (1) 20 percent or more of the aggregate residential rental units in the project are occupied by individuals with incomes of 50 percent or less of area median income, as adjusted for family size, or (2) 40 percent or more of the aggregate residential rental units in the project are occupied by individuals with incomes of 60 percent or less of area median income, as adjusted for family size.[15] (This requirement is referred to as the "minimum set-aside" requirement.)

A special set-aside may be elected for projects that satisfy a stricter requirement and that significantly restrict the rents on the low-income units relative to the other residential units in the building (the "deep-rent skewing" set-aside). Projects qualify for this rule only if, as part of the general set-aside requirement, 15 percent or more of all low-income units are occupied by individuals having incomes of 40 percent (rather than 50 percent or 60 percent) or less of area median income, and the average rent charged to tenants in the residential rental units which are not low-income units is at least 300 percent of the average rent charged to low-income tenants for comparable units. Under this special rule, a low-income

[14] A technical amendment may be needed so that the statute reflects this intent.

[15] A special set-aside requirement providing that 25 percent or more of the units are occupied by individuals with incomes of 60 percent or less of area median income is provided for New York City (*see* sec. 142(d)(6)).

tenant will continue to qualify as such, as long as the tenant's income does not exceed 170 percent of the qualifying income. Additionally, if a project to which this special set-aside requirement applies ceases to comply with the requirement because of increases in existing tenants' incomes, no penalties are imposed if each available low-income unit is rented to tenants having incomes of 40 percent or less of area median income, until the project is again in compliance.[16]

All units comprising the minimum set-aside in a project must be suitable for occupancy and used on a nontransient basis, and are subject to the limitation on gross rent charged to residents of set-aside units. (See the discussion of the gross rent limitation, below.)

The owner of each project must irrevocably elect the minimum set-aside requirement (including the deep-rent skewing set-aside described above) at the time the project is placed in service. In the case of a project consisting of a single building, the set-aside requirement must be met within 12 months of the date the building (or rehabilitated property) is placed in service, and complied with continuously thereafter for a period ending 15 years after the first day of the first taxable year in which the credit is claimed.

Special rules apply to projects consisting of multiple buildings placed in service on different dates. Unless prescribed by regulations, the initial building, within 12 months of being placed in service, must meet the set-aside requirement determined only by reference to those units in the initial building. When a second or subsequent building is placed in service, the project must meet the set-aside requirement with respect to the units in all buildings placed-in-service up to that time within 12 months of the date the second or subsequent building is placed in service.[17] The project must comply with this expanded requirement continuously thereafter for a period ending 15 years after the later of (1) the first day of the taxable year in which the expanded requirement is met or (2) if a credit is claimed with respect to the building, the first day of the taxable year in which the credit period begins with such building.[18] Subsequent buildings are subject to separate 15-year compliance periods. After the 15-year period has expired on an initial building, but while other buildings in the same project are still subject to the compliance period, the project must continue to meet the set-aside requirement determined by reference to all buildings in the project or, at the taxpayer's election, all buildings subject to the compliance period.

[16] Congress intended that for projects electing this stricter set-aside requirement the definition of gross rent is that used generally for purposes of the low-income credit. A technical amendment may be needed so that the statute reflects this intent.

[17] Congress intended that if within 12 months of the date a first building is placed in service, (1) the first building does not meet the set-aside requirement with respect to the first building and (2) a second building is placed in service, then the project is a qualified low-income project if the set-aside requirement is satisfied with respect to both buildings within 12 months of the placed-in-service date of the first building. A technical amendment may be needed so that the statute reflects this intent. Congress intended that similar rules apply by Treasury Department regulations in the case of projects with more than two buildings.

[18] Until the expanded requirement is met, the set-aside requirements determined by reference to all previously existing buildings must be continuously satisfied.

Continuous compliance required

The determination of whether a tenant qualifies for purposes of the low-income set-aside is made on a continuing basis, both with regard to the tenant's income and the qualifying area income, rather than only on the date the tenant initially occupies the unit. An increase in a tenant's income may result, therefore, in a unit ceasing to qualify as occupied by a low-income person. However, a qualified low-income tenant is treated as continuing to be such notwithstanding *de minimis* increases in his or her income. Under this rule, a tenant qualifying when initially occupying a rental unit will be treated as continuing to have such an income provided his or her income does not increase to a level more than 40 percent in excess of the maximum qualifying income, adjusted for family size. If the tenant's income increases to a level more than 40 percent above the otherwise applicable ceiling (or if the tenant's family size decreases so that a lower maximum family income applies to the tenant) that tenant is no longer counted in determining whether the project satisfies the set-aside requirement.[19] No penalty is assessed in such an event, however, provided that each residential rental unit that becomes vacant (of comparable or smaller size to the units no longer satisfying the applicable income requirement) is rented to tenants satisfying the qualifying income until the project is again in compliance. (For a discussion of the rules for complying with the set-aside requirements, see the discussion of the compliance period and penalty for noncompliance, below.)

Vacant units, formerly occupied by low-income individuals, may continue to be treated as occupied by a qualified low-income individual for purposes of the set-aside requirement (as well as for determining qualified basis) provided reasonable attempts are made to rent the unit and no other units of comparable or smaller size in the project are rented to nonqualifying individuals (see the section "Compliance period and penalty for noncompliance," below).

In no case is a unit considered to be occupied by low-income individuals if all of the occupants of such unit are students (as determined under sec. 151(c)(4)), no one of whom is entitled to file a joint income tax return.

Adjustments for family size

As stated above, the Act requires that adjustments for family size be made in determining the incomes used to qualify tenants as having low income. In general, these adjustments are the same as the adjustments presently made under section 8 of the United States Housing Act of 1937. Thus, for a project which qualifies by setting aside 20 percent of the units for tenants having incomes of 50 percent or less of area median income, a family of four generally will be treated as meeting this standard if the family has an income of 50 percent or less of the area median income; a family of three having an income of 45 percent or less generally will qualify; a family of two having an income of 40 percent or less generally

[19] In the case of projects electing the deep-rent skewing set-aside, a tenant's income may increase to 70 percent more than the maximum qualifying income.

will qualify; and, a single individual having an income of 35 percent or less generally will qualify.

Congress was aware that, in certain cases, the use of section 8 guidelines may result in qualifying incomes below the amounts reflected by these percentages because of dollar ceilings that are applied under the section 8 program. Income limits may be adjusted by the Treasury Department for areas with unusually low family income or high housing costs relative to family income in a manner consistent with determinations of very low income families and area median gross income under section 8 to reflect the 50-percent and 60-percent income levels.

Gross rent limitation

The gross rent paid by families in units included in qualified basis may not exceed 30 percent of the applicable qualifying income, adjusted for family size. Gross rent includes the cost of any utilities, other than telephone. If any utilities are paid directly by the tenant, the maximum rent that may be paid by the tenant is to be reduced by a utility allowance prescribed by the Treasury Department, after taking into consideration the procedures for making such adjustments under section 8 of the United States Housing Act of 1937.

The gross rent limitation applies only to payments made directly by the tenant. Any rental assistance payments made on behalf of the tenant, such as through section 8 of the United States Housing Act of 1937 or any comparable Federal rental assistance, are not included in gross rent. Congress further intended that any comparable State or local government rental assistance not be included in gross rent.[20]

Low-income unit

A low-income unit includes any unit in a qualified low-income building if the individuals occupying such unit meet the income limitation elected for the project for purposes of the minimum set-aside requirement and if the unit meets the gross rent requirement, as well as meeting all other requirements applicable to units satisfying the minimum set-aside requirement.

Qualified low-income housing projects and qualified low-income buildings

A qualified low-income building is a building subject to the 15-year compliance period and which is part of a qualified low-income housing project.

A qualified low-income housing project is a project that meets the minimum set-aside requirement and other requirements with respect to the set-aside units at all times that buildings comprising the project are subject to the 15-year compliance period. A qualified low-income housing project includes a qualified low-income building containing residential rental units and other property that is functionally related and subordinate to the function of providing

[20] A technical amendment may be needed so that the statute reflects this intent. Such an amendment was included in the versions of H. Con. Res. 395 which passed the House of Representatives and Senate in the 99th Congress.

residential rental units. A project may include multiple buildings having similarly constructed housing units, provided the buildings are located on the same tract of land, are owned by the same person for Federal income tax purposes, and are financed pursuant to a common plan of financing.

Residential rental units must be for use by the general public and all of the units in a project must be used on a nontransient basis. Residential rental units are not for use by the general public, for example, if the units are provided only for members of a social organization or provided by an employer for its employees. Generally, a unit is considered to be used on a nontransient basis if the initial lease term is six months or greater. Additionally, no hospital, nursing home, sanitarium, lifecare facility, retirement home providing significant services other than housing, dormitory, or trailer park may be a qualified low-income project. Factory-made housing which is permanently fixed to real property may be a qualified low-income building (see Treas. Reg. sec. 6a.103A-2(d)(4)(i) on factory-made housing).

Unlike the requirements for units in projects financed with tax-exempt bonds, certain single room occupancy housing used on a nontransient basis may qualify for the credit, even though such housing may provide eating, cooking, and sanitation facilities on a shared basis. An example of housing that may qualify for the credit is a residential hotel used on a nontransient basis that is available to all members of the public.

Compliance period and penalty for noncompliance

Qualified residential rental projects must remain as rental property and must satisfy the minimum set-aside requirement, described above, throughout a prescribed compliance period. Low-income units comprising the qualified basis on which additional credits are based are required to comply continuously with all requirements in the same manner as units satisfying the minimum set-aside requirement. Units in addition to those meeting the minimum set-aside requirement on which a credit is allowable also must continuously comply with this requirement.

The Act defines the compliance period for any building as the period beginning on the first day of the first taxable year of the credit period of such building and ending 15 years from such date. The minimum set-aside requirement must be met, in all cases, within 1 year of the date the building (or rehabilitated property) is placed in service.

Within 90 days of the end of the first taxable year for which the credit is claimed and annually for each taxable year thereafter during the compliance period, the taxpayer must certify to the Secretary that the project has continuously complied throughout the year with the set-aside requirement and report the dollar amount of the qualified basis of the building and the maximum applicable percentage and qualified basis permitted to be taken into account by the housing credit agency. Additionally, the certification must include the date (including the taxable year) in which the building

was placed in service and any other information required by Treasury.[21]

The penalty for any building subject to the 15-year compliance period failing to remain part of a qualified low-income project (due, for example, to noncompliance with the minimum set-aside requirement or the gross rent requirement or other requirements with respect to the units comprising the set-aside) is recapture of the accelerated portion of the credit, with interest, for all prior years.

Generally, any change in ownership by a taxpayer of a building subject to the compliance period is also a recapture event. An exception is provided if the seller posts a bond with the Treasury Department (in an amount prescribed by Treasury) and provided it can reasonably be expected that such building will continue to be operated as a qualified low-income building for the remainder of the compliance period. For partnerships consisting of more than 35 individual taxpayers, at the partnership's election, no change in ownership will be deemed to occur provided within a 12-month period at least 50 percent (in value) of the original ownership is unchanged.[22]

In the year of a recapture event, no credit is allowable for the taxpayer subject to recapture. Additionally, the accelerated portion of credits paid in earlier years is recaptured with interest, from the date the recaptured amount was claimed, at the overpayment rate established under section 6621. The accelerated portion of the credit in any year is the amount of credits determined for the year, less the amount which would have been determined for the year if all credits had been allowed ratably over the 15-year compliance period (with no further discounting). Because credits on the initial qualified basis of a building are claimed ratably over a 10-year credit period rather than the 15-year compliance period, the amount of credit recaptured for noncompliance during the first 11 years is one-third of the credit determined for the year, plus interest. In the absence of additions to qualified basis and previous recapture events, the credits are recaptured in the following amounts (in addition to interest): one-third for violations after year 1 and before expiration of year 11; four-fifteenths for violations after year 11 but before expiration of year 12; three-fifteenths for violations after year 12 but before expiration of year 13; two-fifteenths for violations after year 13 but before expiration of year 14; and one-fifteenth for violations after year 14 but before expiration of year 15.

Because credits claimed on additions to qualified basis are paid ratably over the remainder of the compliance period (the credit percentage is two-thirds of the otherwise applicable percentage), there is no accelerated portion of credits attributable to additions to qualified basis and, therefore, no recapture of these amounts.

---

[21] Congress intended that the penalty under sec. 6652(j) shall apply for failure to provide such information. A technical amendment may be needed so that the statute reflects this intent.

[22] Congress intended that the presence of corporate partners not disqualify the partnership from this special exception provided the partnership is at least 50 percent owned by at least 35 individual taxpayers. A technical amendment may be needed so that the statute reflects this intent.

The penalty for a decrease in the qualified basis of a building, while still remaining part of a qualified low-income project, is recapture of the credits with respect to the accelerated amount claimed for all previous years on the amount of the reduction in qualified basis.

Owners and operators of low-income housing projects on which a credit has been claimed must correct any noncompliance with the set-aside requirement or with a reduction in qualified basis within a reasonable period after the noncompliance is discovered or reasonably should have been discovered. If any noncompliance is corrected within a reasonable period, there is no recapture. Congress did not intend, however, that tenants be evicted to return a project to compliance. Rather, Congress intended that each residential rental unit of comparable or smaller size that becomes vacant while a project is not in compliance must be rented to a tenant having a qualifying income before any units in the project are rented to tenants not so qualifying until the project again is in compliance. In general, therefore, the event that gives rise to the penalty for noncompliance (i.e., recapture or a reduction in the allowable credit) will be rental of a unit to other than a low-income tenant (on other than a temporary basis) during any period when the project does not comply with the set-aside requirement or with the qualified basis amounts on which the credit is computed (or would not qualify as a result of that rental).

An example of how the recapture provisions operate follows:

Example.— Assume credits are claimed for a project based on a qualified basis of 30 percent of the basis of the project being allocable to units occupied by individuals with incomes of 50 percent or less of area median income and, at a later date, a qualified basis of only 25 percent of the basis of the project is allocable to units occupied by individuals with incomes of 50 percent or less of median income due to vacancies filled by tenants with nonqualifying incomes. Because the minimum set-aside requirement is not violated, recapture occurs only on the accelerated portion of the credit amounts allocable to the 5-percent basis of the project no longer eligible for the credit.

If the maximum credit for which a project is eligible increases and subsequently decreases, a last-in, first-out rule is applied in determining which credits are recaptured. For example, consider a building that initially claimed a credit based on a qualified basis of 25 percent of the basis of the building allocable to units occupied by individuals with incomes of 50 percent or less of area median income, and in year 3 began receiving a credit based on an additional 10 percent of the basis of the building (i.e., a total of 35 percent). The credit amount on the additions to qualified basis is computed by reference to two-thirds of the credit percentage. If in year 5 only 30 percent of the basis of the building qualifies, there is no recapture of previous years' credits because there is no accelerated portion of the credit amounts attributable to the 5 percent of the additions to qualified basis claimed since year 3.

Congress intended that there be no recapture for *de minimis* changes in the qualified basis by reason of changes in the floor

space fraction.[23] A reduction in qualified basis by reason of a casualty loss is not a recapture event provided such property is restored by reconstruction or replacement within a reasonable period.

State low-income housing credit authority limitation

Generally, any building eligible for the credit must receive an allocation of credit authority from the State or local credit agency in whose jurisdiction the qualifying low-income housing project is located. (An exception is provided for buildings financed with the proceeds of tax-exempt bonds that received an allocation pursuant to the new private activity bond volume limitation.) The aggregate amount of such credits allocated within the State is limited by the State annual low-income credit authority limitation. In all cases, credit allocations are counted against a State's annual credit authority limitation for the calendar year in which the credits are allocated. Congress intended that credits may be allocated only during the calendar year in which the building or rehabilitated property is placed in service, except in the case of (1) credits claimed on additions to qualified basis and (2) credits allocated in a later year pursuant to an earlier binding commitment made no later than the year in which the building is placed in service.[24] Under this latter exception, for example, a building placed in service in 1987 may receive a binding commitment in 1987 to receive a credit allocation of a specified amount in 1989. In 1989 this amount is subtracted from the State credit authority limitation. The credit period and compliance period with respect to the building begin in the taxable year in which the building is placed in service or, by an irrevocable election of the taxpayer, the succeeding taxable year.

An election by the taxpayer to defer the start of the credit period for one year does not affect when the allocation must occur. (See also, the discussion below for credits claimed on additions to qualified basis). The credit amount allocated to a building applies for the year the allocation is made and for all future years of the compliance period.

Allowable credit authority

General rules.—The annual credit authority limitation for each State is equal to $1.25 for every individual who is a resident of the State (as determined by the most recent estimate of the State's population released by the Bureau of the Census before the beginning of the year to which the limitation applies). For purposes of the credit authority limitation, the District of Columbia and U.S. possessions (e.g., Puerto Rico, the Virgin Islands, Guam, and American Samoa) are treated as States.

Special set-aside for qualified nonprofit organizations.—A portion of each State's credit authority limitation is set aside for exclusive use by qualified nonprofit organizations. This set-aside is equal to $0.125 per resident of the State. This set-aside amount may not be changed by State action, either legislative or gubernatorial. In ad-

[23] A technical amendment may be needed so that the statute reflects this intent.

[24] A technical amendment may be needed so that the statute reflects this intent. Credits allocated pursuant to an earlier binding commitment are counted against the State's annual credit authority limitation in the calendar year of the allocation.

dition to the special set-aside, qualified nonprofit organization projects may be allocated any additional amount of a State's remaining credit authority.

To qualify for allocations from this set-aside, an organization must be a section 501(c)(3) or 501(c)(4) organization, one of the exempt purposes of which includes the fostering of low-income housing, and the qualifying project with respect to which the credits are allocated must be one in which such organization materially participates (within the meaning of the passive loss rule). Among the operations in which the organization must be involved in on a regular, continuous, and substantial basis, in addition to the continuing operation of the project, is the development of the project.

Credits subject to the credit authority limitation

Generally, credits subject to the State credit authority limitation include any credits attributable to expenditures not financed with tax-exempt bonds subject to the new private activity bond volume limitation.

In the case of a building financed with the proceeds of tax-exempt bonds subject to the bond volume limitation (Code sec. 146), if 70 percent or more of the aggregate basis of the building and land on which the building is located is financed with such proceeds, no portion of the credits attributable to such building is subject to the credit authority limitation.

If less than 70 percent of the aggregate basis of the building and land on which the building is located is financed with tax-exempt bonds subject to the bond volume limitation, only credits attributable to those bond-financed expenditures are not subject to the credit authority limitation.

Allocation of credit authority limitation among the State and other qualified governmental units therein

In general.—Each State's credit authority limitation is allocated among the various governmental units within the State pursuant to three alternative procedures.

Under the first procedure, each State's credit authority limitation is allocated in its entirety to the State housing agency until either the governor or the legislature makes a different allocation. If more than one such agency exists, they are treated as one agency. In the absence of a qualified State agency, no allocation may occur until provided by either the governor or the legislature.

Under the second procedure, the governor of each State is provided authority to allocate the State's credit authority limitation among all of the governmental units and other issuing authorities. This authority and any allocation rules established by the governor terminate as of the effective date of any overriding State legislation.

Under the third procedure, the State legislature may enact a law providing for a different allocation than that provided under the first or second procedures. Under this authority, the State legislature may allocate all or any portion of the State limitation to any governmental unit or other issuing authority in the State.

Congress intended that any allocation procedure established by the governor or State legislature give balanced consideration to the low-income housing needs of the entire State.

Congress desired to clarify that gubernatorial proclamations issued before the date of enactment of the Act (October 22, 1986) or State legislation enacted before that date is recognized for purposes of allocating the credit authority limitations, provided that the proclamation or legislation refers to the low-income housing tax credit authority limitation.

Congress further intended that a State be permitted to allocate available credit authority to a local issuer until a specified date during each year (e.g., November 1) at which time the authority, if unused, may revert to the State for reallocation. Similarly, a State statute may provide discretionary authority to a public official (e.g., the governor) to allocate the State's credit authority limitation. Because the credit authority limitation is an annual amount, however, any authority that has not been used for credits issued before the end of the calendar year expires.

Special rule for constitutional home rule subdivisions.—The Act provides a special allocation rule for certain political subdivisions with home rule powers under a State constitution (Illinois). The home rule subdivisions to which the special allocation rule applies are those home rule subdivisions that are granted home rule powers by the beginning of the calendar year in which the credits are issued pursuant to a State constitution that was adopted in 1970 and became effective on July 1, 1971. In that State, a full portion of the State credit authority limitation is allocated to each home rule subdivision based upon the ratio that the population of that home rule subdivision bears to the population of the entire State. As is true of the other credit authority limitation determinations, this allocation is made using the most recent population estimate from the Bureau of the Census released before the beginning of the calendar year to which the credits relate. The amount so allocated to home rule subdivisions may not be altered by the power to provide a different allocation otherwise granted by the Act to the governor or the State legislature. However, a home rule subdivision may agree to a different allocation.

The portion of a State's credit authority limitation not allocated to constitutional home rule subdivisions then is allocated under essentially the same three procedures described in the previous section. Thus, under the first procedure, the remaining State credit authority limitation is allocated to the State housing agency. Under the second and third procedures described above, the governor or the State legislature may allocate the State limitation other than that allocated to home rule subdivisions to any governmental units (including home rule subdivisions).

For purposes of the rules on State action establishing allocation rules for the credit authority limitation, a mayor of a constitutional home rule subdivision is treated as a governor, and a city council is treated as a State legislature.

Constitutional home rule subdivisions are treated as States for purposes of the credit authority limitation set-aside for qualified nonprofit organizations. Pursuant to their general authority to alter credit allocation, described above, these subdivisions may agree with the State in which they are located to exchange authority to allocate credits for qualified nonprofit organizations for authority to allocate credits for other projects.

Allocation of set-aside amount for qualified nonprofit organizations.—As described above, a portion of each State's credit authority limitation is set aside exclusively for projects of qualified nonprofit organizations. Although the overall amount of credit authority set aside for these credits may not be reduced by any State action, a State may enact a statute determining which credit authorities in the State may allocate these credits and may allocate the entire set-aside amount to those authorities. Similarly, before any legislation, a governor may determine which authorities may allocate credits under the set-aside. The amount of the remaining credit authority limitation allocated to all other authorities must, of course, be adjusted to take into account any reallocation of the set-aside amount.

Determination of credit amount allocation

A building must receive low-income credit authority from the credit agency in whose jurisdiction the qualifying low-income building is located. The credit agency's remaining authority is reduced by the credit percentage multiplied by the amount of qualified basis granted by the credit agency for the building. The credit agency may grant a smaller credit percentage and a smaller qualified basis amount at the time the allocation is made than the maximum percentage and amount that would otherwise be allowed. Congress intended that the credit agencies reduce the maximum available credit percentage when the financing and rental assistance for a project from all sources is sufficient to provide the continuing operation of the qualifying low-income building without the maximum credit.

A credit agency's credit authority is reduced by the maximum amount of credit granted, whether or not the property ultimately is eligible for this maximum amount, and without regard to the averaging convention used in the first year of the credit period.

If a building is granted more credits than would be claimed in the first year of the credit period, without regard to the averaging convention, such amounts are not restored to the credit agency's authority. Such amounts may, however, be used in a later year by the owner of the building to the extent the credit determined with respect to the building is increased as a result of additions to qualified basis (but not beyond the amount allocated by the agency, and without regard to the reduced percentage applicable to such additions). (See also, the discussion on additions to qualified basis, above.)

Example 1.—Assume in calendar year 1987 a newly constructed building is placed in service and that the building's qualified basis, before consideration of the credit authority limitation, is determined to be $100,000 in that year. The credit agency may allocate any amount of qualified basis to the building, but the taxpayer may treat as his qualified basis only the lesser of (1) the qualified basis of the building, before consideration of the credit authority limitation, or (2) the qualified basis allocated to the building by the credit agency. If the credit agency allocated $100,000 of qualified

basis and the maximum 9 percent credit percentage to the building, the agency's remaining 1987 credit authority would be reduced by $9,000.

Example 2.—Assume $120,000 in qualified basis and a credit percentage of 9 percent were initially authorized by a credit agency in 1987 for a qualified low-income building and that in 1987, the first year of the credit period, the building's qualified basis was $100,000. The credit agency's remaining 1987 credit authority is reduced by $10,800. If in year two of the credit period the qualified basis of the building increases by up to $20,000 due to an increase in the number of low-income units, additional credits may be claimed with respect to this addition to qualified basis without requiring additional credit authority from the credit agency. The credit percentage applicable to the additional qualified basis is two-thirds of the credit percentage applicable to the initial qualified basis. Credits on the additions to qualified basis may be claimed over the remainder of the compliance period.

If the qualified basis of a building is greater than the qualified basis allocated to it by the credit agency, credits may not be claimed on the excess portion unless additional low-income housing credits are allocated to the building by the credit agency. The credit authority of the credit agency is reduced for the calendar year of any such additional allocations.

Generally, no carryover authority for unused credit authority is permitted. A limited exception is provided for buildings placed in service in 1990, if expenditures of 10 percent or more of total project costs are incurred before January 1, 1989. Credit authority for such property may be carried over from the 1989 credit allocation for the credit agency. Congress intended that, for allocations made after 1987, if a building cannot be placed in service in the year for which the allocation was made for reasons beyond the control of the taxpayer, then upon approval by the Treasury Department, the credit allocation will be valid if the building is placed in service in the succeeding year.[25]

Credit agencies are permitted to enter into binding commitments to allocate future credit authority for years before the sunset date to buildings not yet placed in service by binding contracts or other means.

Should a credit agency issue more credits than its credit authority limitation provides, credits will be denied to those buildings last allocated credits until the credit authority limitation is not exceeded.

Credit administration

Credit agencies allocating credits may not condition allocation of credits to the source of financing for the qualifying low-income building. The Act authorizes the Treasury Department to prescribe regulations that may require credit recipients to pay a reasonable fee to cover administrative expenses of the credit agency. The fact that credits must be allocated on a building-by-building basis does not preclude a credit agency from charging a single fee for process-

[25] A technical amendment may be needed so that the statute reflects this intent.

ing credits for a single project with multiple buildings or for multiple projects of a common taxpayer.

Agencies allocating credits must file reports with the Treasury Department containing (1) the maximum applicable percentage and qualified basis of each building, (2) the fees, if any, charged to credit recipients, (3) the aggregate amount of credits issued, and (4) other information required by Treasury. The time and manner of filing such reports and other information required are to be specified by the Treasury Department.

Transferability

A new owner of a building during its 15-year compliance period is eligible to continue to receive the credit as if the new owner were the original owner, using the same qualified basis and credit percentages as used by the original owner. Rehabilitation expenditures on such property may qualify for a credit in the same manner as rehabilitation expenditures on other qualifying property. The accelerated portion of credits claimed in previous years will be recaptured upon a transfer, subject to the election of the original owner to post a bond. All dispositions of ownership interests in buildings are treated as transfers for purposes of recapture, except for a special rule for certain partnerships. (There is no election for the new owner to assume the recapture liability for prior year credits.)

At-risk limitation

Property with respect to which a low-income housing tax credit is claimed is subject to an at-risk limitation similar to the investment tax credit at-risk rules in the case of nonqualified nonrecourse financing. An exception is provided for lenders related to the buyer of the low-income housing property. Another exception provides that the general investment tax credit at-risk rule, limiting the amount of nonrecourse financing to 80 percent of the credit base of the property, does not apply in the case of the low-income housing tax credit.[26]

A further exception is provided for financing (including seller financing) not in excess of 60 percent of the basis of the property that is lent by 501(c)(3) and 501(c)(4) organizations whose exempt purpose includes fostering low-income housing. Further, if the rate of interest for any financing qualifying for this exception is below the applicable Federal rate at the time the financing is incurred, less 1 percentage point, then the qualified basis to which such financing relates shall be reduced to reflect the present value of the payments of principal and interest, using as the discount rate such applicable Federal rate. The credit is recaptured if the financing provided by such organizations is not repaid with interest by the end of the 15-year credit compliance period.

Coordination with other provisions

The credit is subject to the rules of the general business credit, including the maximum amount of income tax liability that may

[26] This exception was enacted in the Omnibus Budget Reconciliation Act of 1986, P.L. 99-509.

be reduced by a general business tax credit in any year. Unused credits for any taxable year may be carried back to each of the 3 preceding taxable years and then carried forward to each of the 15 following taxable years. Congress intended that no credits be carried back to taxable years ending prior to January 1, 1987.[27]

For purposes of the rules in the Act limiting passive loss deductions, the credit (but not losses) is treated as arising from rental real estate activities in which the taxpayer actively participates. Credits may be used to offset tax on up to $25,000 of nonpassive income, subject to a phaseout between $200,000 and $250,000 of adjusted gross income (disregarding passive losses).

The basis of property for purposes of depreciation is not reduced by the amount of low-income credits claimed.

Effective Date

The credit is effective for buildings placed in service after December 31, 1986, and before January 1, 1991, other than (1) property to which the depreciation rules of prior-law apply or (2) property with respect to which any investor is eligible for passive losses under the special transitional exception contained in section 502 of the Act. Congress further intended that no property to which the provision of prior law allowing five-year amortization of rehabilitation expenditures applies may be included in eligible basis.[28] As stated above, all buildings eligible for the credit must be placed in service before January 1, 1991.[29] A building placed in service in 1990 is eligible for the credit, however, only if expenditures of 10 percent or more of the reasonably expected cost of the building are incurred before January 1, 1989. Under a special rule, described above, credit authority for such property placed in service in 1990 may be carried over from the 1989 volume allocation for any credit agency.

Revenue Effect

The low-income rental housing tax credit is estimated to reduce fiscal year budget receipts by $67 million in 1987, $324 million in 1988, $705 million in 1989, $1,011 million in 1990, and $1,139 million in 1991.

[27] A technical amendment may be needed so that the statute reflects this intent.

[28] A technical amendment may be needed so that the statute reflects this intent.

[29] The Act contains a general rule preventing the allocation of credit authority to buildings placed in service after 1990. Congress intended that tax-exempt bond-financed projects be treated in the same manner as other projects, and are not eligible for the credit if placed in service after 1990. A technical amendment may be needed so that the statute reflects this intent. Such an amendment was included in the versions of H. Con. Res. 395 which passed the House of Representatives and Senate in the 99th Congress.

APPENDIX 7

EXPLANATION OF 1988 TECHNICAL AND MISCELLANEOUS REVENUE ACT: LOW INCOME HOUSING TAX CREDIT AMENDMENTS

A. Explanation of Enacted Sections of Committee Bill

Explanation of Provisions

Election to determine credit percentage early

The bill provides that, in addition to the method of determining the credit percentage under present law, for buildings placed in service by a taxpayer after 1987 the taxpayer (with the consent of the housing credit agency) may irrevocably elect to determine the credit percentage applicable to the building in advance of the building's placed-in-service date. Such an election will be binding for Federal income tax purposes on the taxpayer, the credit agency, and all successors in interest. The election must be made at the time a binding commitment is received by the taxpayer from the credit agency as to the housing credit dollar amount to be allocated to the building. In the case of a building financed with the proceeds of tax-exempt bonds for which no allocation from a credit agency is required, the election must be made by the taxpayer at the time the tax-exempt bonds are issued. The election must be filed with the Treasury Department by the fifth day of the month following the date the binding commitment is made or the bonds are issued. This election is applicable to credits attributable to new construction, rehabilitation, and acquisition expenditures.

Determination of gross rent

The bill provides that in determining the gross rent that may be paid by a tenant in a low-income unit, payments of State and local rental assistance programs comparable to section 8 of the United States Housing Act of 1937 are not considered. The bill further provides that this definition of gross rent is used for purposes of determining the rent that may be charged to a low-income tenant when applying the elective deep-rent skewing set-aside requirement for certain projects (*see* sec. 142(d)(4)). (The bill retains the definition of gross rent, which includes all rental assistance payments, used in the determinination of the 3:1 rent skewing test also provided for those projects.)

The bill further provides that if a Federal rental assistance payment is made with respect to a low-income unit and the Federal statute (as in effect on October 22, 1986) governing that assistance payment requires that the gross rent paid by the occupants for that unit increase as the income of the occupants increases and that any such increase in the occupants' gross rent reduce equally the Federal rental assistance payment, then the gross rent paid by the tenant may exceed 30 percent of the applicable income limit to the extent required under the applicable Federal housing program statute.

Special rules for multiple building projects

The bill provides new rules for determining whether a building is part of a qualified low-income housing project in the case of multiple building projects. In such a project, buildings need not meet the minimum low-income set-aside requirement only by reference to the order that the buildings are placed in service. If within 12 months of the placed-in-service date of a prior building the project meets the set-aside requirement with respect to the first building and any subsequent buildings placed in service within the 12-month period, then the first building and included subsequent buildings are part of a qualified low-income project. Subsequent buildings not included in determining whether the project satisfies the set-aside requirement with respect to prior buildings have their own 12-month period before they are required to be included in the set-aside determination for the project.

De minimis exception to disproportionate cost limit

The bill permits a portion of the basis of housing units whose cost is disproportionate to that of the low-income units to be included in eligible basis. Unless otherwise provided by Treasury regulations, to be eligible for this exception, the cost per square foot of the disproportionate unit may not exceed by 15 percent the average cost per square foot of the low-income units. If cost differentials exceed 15 percent, the cost of the entire disproportionate unit must be excluded from eligible basis, as under present law.

The bill further provides that costs with respect to which an election was made by the taxpayer to deduct rehabilitation expenditures under prior law section 167(k) may not be included in eligible basis.

Exceptions to 10-year rule

The bill provides several exceptions to the restriction that buildings eligible for an aquisition credit may not have been previously placed in service within 10 years of the date of acquisition. Under these exceptions, a placement in service is disregarded if it is as a result of (1) death, (2) acquisition by a governmental unit or certain qualified 501(c)(3) or 501(c)(4) organizations whose acquisition of the property was at least 10 years after it was previously placed in service, or (3) a foreclosure occurring at least 10 years after the previous placed-in-service date, provided the property is resold within 12 months of such foreclosure.

Amendments affecting State credit authority

The bill provides that the State low-income housing credit authority must allocate credits to a building in the calendar year it is placed in service, unless (1) credits are allocated as the result of additions to qualified basis or (2) the authority makes a binding commitment no later than the last day of such year to allocate a specified amount of credits to the building in a later year. An allocation in a later calendar year pursuant to a binding commitment is counted against the State's credit authority limitation in such later year. Such later allocation does not defer the start of the credit period or the compliance period.

The bill provides that if a corporation is wholly owned by one or more qualified nonprofit organizations and such corporation materially participates in the development and operation of a qualified low-income project, the qualified nonprofit organization(s) will be treated as materially participating in the development and operation of such project for purposes of this section.

Recapture

The bill makes several modifications to the rules regarding recapture of the credit. First, the bill provides that there will be no recapture for certain *de minimis* changes in the qualified basis by reason of changes in floor space of low-income housing units. Second, for partnerships more than 50 percent of which are owned by 35 or more natural persons or estates, the presence of a corporate partner will not exclude the partnership from a special rule under which recapture is determined at the partnership, rather than the partner, level.

Other amendments

The bill clarifies that, similar to other Federally subsidized loans, the proceeds of an issue of tax-exempt obligations used to finance a building may be excluded from eligible basis and the building will not be treated as federally subsidized.

The bill provides that tax-exempt financing or a below market loan used to provide construction financing for a building will not be treated as a Federal subsidy if such loan is repaid and any underlying obligation (e.g., tax-exempt bond) is redeemed before the building is placed in service.

The bill modifies the at-risk provisions applicable to certain financing from qualified nonprofit organizations in the case of certain federally assisted buildings in which a security interest is not permitted by a Federal agency.

The bill provides certain information reporting requirements on owners of qualified low-income housing projects and imposes a penalty for failure to provide required information.

The bill provides that credits may not be carried back to taxable years ending before January 1, 1987.

The bill makes clarifying amendments to certain transitional rules of limited application.

The bill also corrects other minor clerical and technical errors.

B. Explanation from Conference Report

House Bill

The House bill provides that changes in family size resulting from death, divorce, separation, and abandonment are disregarded in determining the maximum gross rent that may be charged an existing low-income tenant.

The House bill removes the restriction on corporate ownership for certain large partnerships qualifying for special recapture treatment. The bill also reverses the election of prior law, making large partnerships subject to recapture at the partnership level rather than the partner level, unless they elect otherwise.

Committee report language is provided to clarify that a housing project is not disqualified from receiving a credit allocation solely because the developer undertook the project as a condition of receiving zoning variances for other, non-low-income rental housing property.

Senate Amendment

The Senate amendment permits a building to be placed in service in the year in which the credit allocation is received or in either of the two succeeding years provided that at least 10 percent of the expected project costs were paid by the end of the year in which the credit allocation was received. Project costs are the total costs budgeted to acquire and develop the project. These costs include costs budgeted by the taxpayer to acquire the land and any existing structure. The amendment applies only to credit allocations for new construction and substantial rehabilitations.

Conference Agreement

The conference agreement generally follows the Senate amendment with three modifications. First, the determination of whether the taxpayer has incurred at least ten percent of the total project costs is measured by calculating the following fraction. The numerator of the fraction is the taxpayer's basis (land and depreciable basis) in the property as of the close of the calendar year in which the credit allocation is made by the State authority. The denominator of the fraction is the taxpayer's reasonably expected basis (land and depreciable basis) in the property at the time the property is placed in service.

Second, the conference agreement adopts the House provision removing the restriction on corporate ownership for certain large partnerships and reversing the election of current law to recapture at the partnership rather than the partner level.

Third, the conferees concur with the House committee report regarding low-income property developed in return for the receipt of zoning variances.[1]

APPENDIX 8

TEXT OF THE INTERNAL REVENUE SERVICE TEMPORARY REGULATIONS ON THE LOW INCOME HOUSING TAX CREDIT: JUNE 22, 1987

DEPARTMENT OF THE TREASURY

Internal Revenue Service

26 CFR Parts 1 and 602

[T.D. 8144]

Income Taxes; Low-Income Housing Credit

AGENCY: Internal Revenue Service, Treasury.

ACTION: Temporary regulations.

SUMMARY: This document provides temporary regulations concerning the low-income housing credit under section 42 of the Internal Revenue Code of 1986, as enacted by the Tax Reform Act of 1986 (Pub. L. 99–514). These regulations provide guidance concerning the State low-income housing credit authority limitation. In addition, the text of the temporary regulations set forth in this document serves as the comment document for the proposed regulations cross-referenced in the notice of proposed rulemaking in the Proposed Rules section of this issue of the **Federal Register.**

EFFECTIVE DATE: The regulations apply to buildings placed in service after December 31, 1986, in taxable years ending after that date.

FOR FURTHER INFORMATION CONTACT: Robert Beatson of the Legislation and Regulations Division, Office of Chief Counsel, Internal Revenue Service, 1111 Constitution Avenue NW., Washington, DC 20224 (Attention: CC:LR:T LR–82–86) (202–566–3829, not a toll-free call).

SUPPLEMENTARY INFORMATION:

Background

This document contains temporary regulations relating to the low-income housing credit under section 42 of the Internal Revenue Code of 1986 as enacted by section 252 of the Tax Reform Act of 1986 (Pub. L. 99–514). New § 1.42–1T is added by this document to Part 1 of Title 26 of the Code of Federal Regulations. The temporary regulations provided by this document will remain in effect until superseded by final regulations on this subject.

Explanation of Provisions

Section 252 of the Tax Reform Act of 1986 enacted a new low-income housing credit equal to the applicable percentage of the qualified basis of each qualified low-income building. The temporary regulations provide guidance with respect to the State housing credit ceiling, the special set-aside for qualified nonprofit organization projects, apportionment of housing credit dollar amounts among housing credit agencies within each State, the time and manner for making housing credit allocations to qualified low-income buildings, the manner in which housing credit allocations are taken into account by owners of qualified low-income buildings, rules for low-income housing financed in whole or in part with tax-exempt bonds, termination of authority to make housing credit allocations, information reporting, and certain definitional issues.

Non-Applicability of Executive Order 12291

The Commission of Internal Revenue has determined that these temporary regulations are not a major rule as defined in Executive Order 12291 and that a regulatory impact analysis therefore is not required.

Regulatory Flexibility Act

No general notice of proposed rulemaking is required by 5 U.S.C. 553(b) because these are temporary regulations, and there is a need to provide the public with immediate guidance. Accordingly, the Regulatory Flexibility Act does not apply and no Regulatory Flexibility Analysis is required for this rule.

Paperwork Reduction Act

The collection of information contained in these regulations has been submitted to the Office of Management and Budget (OMB) in accordance with the requirements of the Paperwork Reduction Act of 1980. These requirements have been approved by OMB (Control no. 1545–0988).

Drafting Information

The principal author of these regulations is Robert Beatson of the Legislation and Regulations Division of the Office of Chief Counsel, Internal Revenue Service. However, personnel from other offices of the Internal Revenue Service and the Treasury Department participated in developing the regulations on matters of both substance and style.

List of Subjects

26 CFR 1.0–1—1.58–8

Income taxes, Tax liability, Tax rates, Credits.

26 CFR Part 602

Reporting and recordkeeping requirements.

Amendments to the Regulations

The amendments to 26 CFR Parts 1 and 602 are as follows:

PART 1—INCOME TAX REGULATIONS

Paragraph 1. The authority for Part 1 is amended by adding the following citation:

Authority: 26 U.S.C. 7805. * * * Section 1.42–1T also issued under 26 U.S.C. 42 (m).

Par. 2. A new § 1.42–1T is added immediately following § 1.41–8 to read as follows:

§ 1.42–1T Limitation on low-income housing credit allowed with respect to qualified low-income buildings receiving housing credit allocations from a State or local housing credit agency (temporary).

(a) *In general*—(1) *Determination of amount of low-income housing credit.* Section 42 provides that, for purposes of section 38, a low-income housing credit is determined for a building in an amount equal to the applicable percentage of the qualified basis of the qualified low-income building. In general, the credit may be claimed annually for a 10—year credit period, beginning with the taxable year in which the building is placed in service or, at the election of the taxpayer, the succeeding taxable year. If, after the first year of the credit period, the qualified basis of a building is increased in excess of the qualified basis upon which the credit was initially determined, the allowable credit with respect to such additional qualified basis is determined using a credit percentage equal to two-thirds of the applicable percentage for the initial qualified basis. The credit for additions to qualified basis is generally allowable for the remaining years in the 15-year compliance period which begins with the first taxable year of the credit period for the building. In general, the low-income housing credit is available with respect to buildings placed in service after December 31, 1986, in taxable years ending after that date. *See* section 42 for the definitions of "qualified low-income building", "applicable percentage", "qualified basis", "credit period", "compliance period", and for other rules relating to determination of the amount of the low-income housing credit.

(2) *Limitation on low-income housing credit allowed.* Generally, the low-income housing credit determined under section 42 is allowed and may be claimed for any taxable year if, and to the extent that, the owner of a qualified low-income building receives a housing credit allocation from a State or local housing credit agency. The aggregate amount of housing credit allocations that may be made in any calendar year by all housing credit agencies within a State is limited by a State housing credit ceiling, or volume cap, described in paragraph (b) of this section. The authority to make housing credit allocations within the State housing credit ceiling may be apportioned among the State and local housing credit agencies, under the rules prescribed in paragraph (c) of this section. Upon apportionment of the State housing credit volume cap, each State or local housing credit agency receives an aggregate housing credit dollar amount that may be used to make housing credit allocations among qualified low-income buildings located within an agency's geographic jurisdiction. The rules governing the making of housing credit allocations by any state or local housing credit agency are provided in paragraph (d) of this section. Housing credit allocations are required to be taken into account by owners of qualified low-income buildings under the rules prescribed in paragraph (e) of this section. Exceptions to the requirement that a qualified low-income building receive a housing credit allocation from a State or local housing credit agency are provided in paragraph (f) of this section. Rules regarding termination of the authority of State and local housing credit agencies to make housing credit allocations after December 31, 1989, are specified in paragraph (g) of this section. Rules concerning information reporting by State and local housing credit agencies and owners of qualified low-income buildings are provided in paragraph (h) of this section. Special statutory transitional rules are incorporated into this section of the regulations as described in paragraph (i) of this section.

(b) *The State housing credit ceiling.* The aggregate amount of housing credit allocations that may be made in any calendar year by all State and local housing credit agencies within a State may not exceed the State's housing credit ceiling for such calendar year. The State housing credit ceiling for each State for any calendar year is equal to $1.25 multiplied by the State's population. A State's population for any calendar year is determined by reference to the most recent census estimate (whether final or provisional) of the resident population of the State released by the Bureau of the Census before the beginning of the calendar year for which the State's housing credit ceiling is set. Unless otherwise prescribed by applicable revenue procedure, determinations of population are based on the most recent estimates of population contained in the Bureau of the Census publication, "Current Population Reports, Series P–25: Population Estimates and Projections, Estimates of the Population of States". For purposes of this section, the District of Columbia and United States possessions are treated as States.

(c) *Apportionment of State housing credit ceiling among State and local housing credit agencies*—(1) *In general.* A State's housing credit ceiling for any calendar year is apportioned among the State and local housing credit agencies within such State under the rules prescribed in this paragraph. A "State housing credit agency" is any State agency specifically authorized by gubernatorial act or State statute to make housing credit allocations on behalf of the State and to carry out the provisions of section 42(h). A "local housing credit agency" is any agency of a political subdivision of the State that is specifically authorized by a State enabling act to make housing credit allocations on behalf of the State or political subdivision and to carry out the provisions of section 42(h). A "State enabling act" is any gubernatorial act, State statute, or State housing credit agency regulation (if authorized by gubernatorial act or State statute). A State enabling act enacted on or before October 22, 1986, the date of enactment of the Tax Reform Act of 1986, shall be given effect for purposes of this paragraph if such State enabling act expressly carries out the provisions of section 42(h).

(2) *Primary apportionment.* Except as otherwise provided in paragraphs (c) (3) and (4) of this section, a State's housing credit ceiling is apportioned in its entirety to the State housing credit agency. Such an apportionment is the "primary apportionment" of a State's housing credit ceiling. There shall be no primary apportionment of the State housing credit ceiling and no grants of housing credit allocations in such State until a State housing credit agency is authorized by gubernatorial act or State statute. If a State has more than one State housing credit agency, such agencies shall be treated as a single agency for purposes of the primary apportionment. In such a case, the State housing credit ceiling may be divided among the multiple State housing credit agencies pursuant to gubernatorial act or State statute.

(3) *States with 1 or more constitutional home rule cities*—(i) *In general.* Notwithstanding paragraph (c)(2) of this section, in any State with 1 or more constitutional home rule cities, a portion of the State housing credit ceiling is apportioned to each constitutional home rule city. In such a State, except as provided in paragraph (c)(4) of this section, the remainder of the State housing credit ceiling is apportioned to the State housing credit agency under paragraph (c)(2) of this section. *See* paragraph (c)(3)(iii) of this section. The term "constitutional home rule city" means, with respect to any calendar year, any political subdivision of a State that, under a State constitution that was adopted in 1970 and effective on July 1, 1971, had home rule powers on the first day of the calendar year.

(ii) *Amount of apportionment to a constitutional home rule city.* The amount of the State housing credit ceiling apportioned to a constitutional home rule city for any calendar year is an amount that bears the same ratio to the State housing credit ceiling for that year as the population of the constitutional home rule city bears to the population of the entire State. The population of any constitutional home rule city for any calendar year is determined by reference to the most recent census estimate (whether final or provisional) of the resident population of the constitutional home rule city released by the Bureau of the Census before the beginning of the calendar year for which the State housing credit ceiling is apportioned. However, determinations of the population of a constitutional home rule city may not be based on Bureau of the Census estimates that do not contain estimates for all of the constitutional home rule cities within the State. If no Bureau of the Census estimate is available for all such constitutional home rule cities, the most recent decennial census of population shall be relied on. Unless otherwise prescribed by applicable revenue procedure, determinations of population for constitutional home rule cities are based on estimates of population contained in the Bureau of the Census publication, "Current Population Reports, Series P-26: Local Population Estimates".

(iii) *Effect of apportionments to constitutional home rule cities on apportionments to other housing credit agencies.* The aggregate amounts of the State housing credit ceiling apportioned to constitutional home rule cities under this paragraph (c)(3) reduce the State housing credit ceiling available for apportionment under paragraph (c) (2) or (4) of this section. Unless otherwise provided in a State constitutional amendment or by law changing the home rule provisions adopted in a manner provided by the State constitution, the power of the governor or State legislature to apportion the State housing credit ceiling among local housing credit agencies under paragraph (c)(4) of this section shall not be construed as allowing any reduction of the portion of the State housing credit ceiling apportioned to a constitutional home rule city under this paragraph (c)(3). However, any constitutional home rule city may agree to a reduction in its apportionment of the State housing credit ceiling under this paragraph (c)(3), in which case the amount of the State housing credit ceiling not apportioned to the constitutional home rule city shall be available for apportionment under paragraph (c) (2) or (4) of this section.

(iv) *Treatment of governmental authority within constitutional home rule city.* For purposes of determining which agency within a constitutional home rule city receives the apportionment of the State housing credit ceiling under this paragraph (c)(3), the rules of this paragraph (c) shall be applied by treating the constitutional home rule city as a "State", the chief executive officer of a constitutional home rule city as a "governor", and a city council as a "State legislature". A constitutional home rule city is also treated as a "State" for purposes of the set-aside requirement for housing credit allocations to projects involving a qualified nonprofit organization. *See* paragraph (c)(5) of this section for rules governing set-aside requirements. In this connection, a constitutional home rule city may agree with the State housing credit agency to exchange an apportionment set aside for projects involving a qualified nonprofit organization for an apportionment that is not so restricted. In such a case, the authorizing gubernatorial act, State statute, or State housing credit agency regulation (if authorized by gubernatorial act or State statute) must ensure that the set-aside apportionment transferred to the State housing credit agency be used for the purposes described in paragraph (c)(5) of this section.

(4) *Apportionment to local housing credit agencies*—(i) *In general.* In lieu of the primary apportionment under paragraph (c)(2) of this section, all or a portion of the State housing credit ceiling may be apportioned among housing credit agencies of governmental subdivisions. Apportionments of the State housing credit ceiling to local housing credit agencies must be made pursuant to a State enabling act as defined in paragraph (c)(1) of this section. Apportionments of the State housing credit ceiling may be made to housing credit agencies of constitutional home rule cities under this paragraph (c)(4), in addition to apportionments made under paragraph (c)(3) of this section. Apportionments of the State housing credit ceiling under this paragraph (c)(4) need not be based on the population of political subdivisions and may, but are not required to, give balanced consideration to the low-income housing needs of the entire State.

(ii) *Change in apportionments during a calendar year.* The apportionment of the State housing credit ceiling among State and local housing credit agencies under this paragraph (c)(4) may be changed after the beginning of a calendar year, pursuant to a State enabling act. No change in apportionments shall retroactively reduce the housing credit allocations made by any agency during such year. Any change in the apportionment of the State housing credit ceiling under this paragraph (c)(4) that occurs during a calendar year is effective only to the extent housing credit agencies have not previously made housing credit allocations during such year from their original apportionments of the State housing credit ceiling for such year. To the extent apportionments of the State housing credit ceiling to local housing credit agencies made pursuant to this paragraph (c)(4) for any calendar year are not used by such local agencies before a certain date (*e.g.*, November 1) to make housing credit allocations in such year, the amount of unused apportionments may revert back to the State housing credit agency for reapportionment. Such reversion must be specifically authorized by the State enabling act.

(iii) *Exchanges of apportionments.* Any State or local housing credit agency that receives an apportionment of the State housing credit ceiling for any calendar year under this paragraph (c)(4) may exchange part or all of such apportionment with another State or local housing credit agency to the extent no housing credit allocations have been made in such year from the exchanged portions. Such exchanges must be made with another housing credit agency in the same State and must be consistent with the State enabling act. If an apportionment set aside for projects involving a qualified nonprofit organization is transferred or exchanged, the transferee housing credit agency shall be required to use the set-aside apportionment for the purposes described in paragraph (c)(5) of this section.

(iv) *Written records of apportionments.* All apportionments, exchanges of apportionments, and reapportionments of the State housing credit ceiling which are authorized by this paragraph (c)(4) must be evidenced in the written records maintained by each State and local housing credit agency.

(5) *Set-aside apportionments for projects involving a qualified nonprofit organization*—(i) *In general.* Ten percent of the State housing credit ceiling for a calendar year must be set aside exclusively for projects involving a qualified nonprofit organization (as defined in paragraph (c)(5)(ii) of this section). Thus, at least 10 percent of apportionments of the State housing credit ceiling under paragraphs (c) (2) and (3) of this section must be used only to make housing credit allocations to buildings that are part of projects involving a qualified nonprofit organization. In the case of apportionments of the State housing credit ceiling under paragraph (c)(4) of this section, the State enabling act must ensure that the apportionment of at least 10 percent of the State housing credit ceiling be used exclusively to make housing credit allocations to buildings that are part of projects involving a qualified nonprofit organization. The State enabling act shall prescribe which housing credit agencies in the State receive apportionments that must be set aside for making housing credit allocations to buildings that are part of projects involving a qualified nonprofit organization. These set-aside apportionments may be distributed disproportionately among the State or local housing credit agencies receiving apportionments under paragraph (c)(4) of this section. The 10-percent set-aside requirement of this paragraph (c)(4) is a minimum requirement, and the State enabling act may set aside more than 10 percent of the State housing credit ceiling for apportionment to housing credit agencies for exclusive use in making housing credit allocations to buildings that are part of projects involving a qualified nonprofit organization.

(ii) *Projects involving a qualified nonprofit organization.* The term "projects involving a qualified nonprofit organization" means projects with respect to which a qualified nonprofit organization is to materially participate (within the meaning of section 469(h)) in the development and continuing operation of the project throughout the 15-year compliance period. The term "qualified nonprofit organization" means any organization that is described in section 501(c) (3) or (4), is exempt from tax under section 501(a), and includes as one of its exempt purposes the fostering of low-income housing.

(6) *Expiration of unused apportionments.* Apportionments of the State housing credit ceiling under this paragraph (c) for any calendar year may be used by housing credit agencies to make housing credit allocations only in such calendar year. Any part of an apportionment of the State housing credit ceiling for any calendar year that is not used for housing credit allocations in such year expires as of the end of such year and does not carry over to any other year. However, any part of an apportionment for 1989 that is not used to make a housing credit allocation in 1989 may be carried over to 1990 and used to make a housing credit allocation to a qualified low-income building described in section 42(n)(2)(B). *See* paragraph (g)(2) of this section.

(d) *Housing credit allocations made by State and local housing credit agencies*—(1) *In general.* This paragraph governs State and local housing credit agencies in making housing credit allocations to qualified low-income buildings. The amount of the apportionment of the State housing credit ceiling for any calendar year received by any State or local housing credit agency under paragraph (c) of this section constitutes the agency's aggregate housing credit dollar amount for such year. The aggregate amount of housing credit allocations made in any calendar year by a State or local housing credit agency may not exceed such agency's aggregate housing credit dollar amount for such year. A State or local housing credit agency may make housing credit allocations only to qualified low-income buildings located within the agency's geographic jurisdiction.

(2) *Amount of a housing credit allocation.* In making a housing credit allocation, a State or local housing credit agency must specify a credit percentage, not to exceed the building's applicable percentage determined under section 42(b), and a qualified basis amount. The amount of the housing credit allocation for any building is the product of the specified credit percentage and the specified qualified basis amount. In specifying the credit percentage and qualified basis amount, the State or local housing credit agency shall not take account of the first-year conventions described in section 42(f)(2)(A) and (3)(B). A State or local housing credit agency may adopt rules or regulations governing conditions for specification of less than the maximum credit percentage and qualified basis amount allowable under section 42 (b) and (c), respectively. For example, an agency may specify a credit percentage and a qualified basis amount of less than the maximum credit percentage and qualified basis amount allowable under section 42 (b) and (c), respectively, when the financing and rental assistance from all sources for the project of which the building is a part is sufficient to provide the continuing operation of the building without the maximum credit amount allowable under section 42.

(3) *Counting housing credit allocations against an agency's aggregate housing credit dollar amount.* The aggregate amount of housing credit allocations made in any calendar year by a State or local housing credit agency may not exceed such agency's aggregate housing credit dollar amount (*i.e.*, the agency's apportionment of the State housing credit ceiling for such year). This limitation on the aggregate dollar amount of housing credit allocations shall be computed separately for set-aside apportionments received pursuant to paragraph (c)(5) of this section. Housing credit allocations count against an agency's aggregate housing credit dollar amount without regard to the amount of credit allowable to or claimed by an owner of a building in the taxable year in which the allocation is made or in any subsequent year. Thus, housing

credit allocations (which are computed without regard to the first-year conventions as provided in paragraph (d)(2) of this section) count in full against an agency's aggregate housing credit dollar amount, even though the first-year conventions described in section 42(f) (2)(A) and (3)(B) may reduce the amount of credit claimed by a taxpayer in the first year in which a credit is allowable. *See also* paragraph (e)(2) of this section. Housing credit allocations count against an agency's aggregate housing credit dollar amount only in the calendar year in which made and not in subsequent taxable years in the credit period or compliance period during which a taxpayer may claim a credit based on the original housing credit allocation. Since the aggregate amount of housing credit allocations made in any calendar year by a State or local housing credit agency may not exceed such agency's aggregate housing credit dollar amount, an agency shall at all times during a calendar year maintain a record of its cumulative allocations made during such year and its remaining unused aggregate housing credit dollar amount.

(4) *Rules for when applications for housing credit allocations exceed an agency's aggregate housing credit dollar amount.* A State or local housing credit agency may adopt rules or regulations governing the awarding of housing credit allocations when an agency expects that applicants during a calendar year will seek aggregate allocations in excess of the agency's aggregate housing credit dollar amount. The State enabling act may provide uniform standards for the awarding of housing credit allocations when there is actual or anticipated excess demand from applicants in any calendar year.

(5) *Reduced or additional housing credit allocations*—(i) *In general.* A State or local housing credit agency may not reduce or rescind a housing credit allocation made to a qualified low-income building in the manner prescribed in paragraph (d)(8) of this section. Thus, a housing credit agency may not reduce or rescind a housing credit allocation made to a qualified low-income building which is acquired by a new owner who is entitled to a carryover of the allowable credit for such building under section 42(d)(7). A housing credit agency may make additional housing credit allocations to a building in any year in the building's compliance period, whether or not there are additions to qualified basis for which an increased credit is allowable under section 42(f)(3). Each additional housing credit allocation made to a building is treated as a separate allocation and is subject to the rules and requirements of this section. However, in the case of an additional housing credit allocation made with respect to additions to qualified basis for which an increased credit is allowable under section 42(f)(3), the amount of the allocation that counts against the agency's aggregate housing credit dollar amount shall be computed as if the specified credit percentage were unreduced in the manner prescribed in section 42(f)(3)(A) and the specified qualified basis amount were unreduced by the first-year convention prescribed in section 42(f)(3)(B).

(ii) *Examples.* The rules of paragraph (d)(5)(i) of this section may be illustrated by the following examples:

Example (1). For 1987, the County L Housing Credit Agency has an aggregate housing credit dollar amount of $2 million. D, an individual, places in service on July 1, 1987, a new qualified low-income building. As of the close of each month in 1987 in which the building is in service, the building consists of 100 residential rental units, of which 20 units are both rent-restricted and occupied by individuals whose income is 50 percent or less of area median gross income. The total floor space of the residential rental units is 120,000 square feet, and the total floor space of the low-income units is 20,000 square feet. The building is not Federally subsidized within the meaning of section 42(i)(2). As of the end of 1987, the building has eligible basis under section 42(d) of $1 million. Thus, the qualified basis of the building determined without regard to the first-year convention provided in section 42(f) is $166,666.67 (*i.e.*, $1 million eligible basis times ⅙, the floor space fraction which is required to be used instead of the larger unit fraction). However, the amount of the low-income housing credit determined for 1987 under section 42 reflects the first-year convention provided in section 42(f)(2). Since the building has the same floor space and unit fractions as of the close of each of the six months in 1987 during which it is in service, upon applying the first-year convention in section 42(f)(2), the qualified basis of the building in 1987 is $83,333.33 (*i.e.*, $1 million eligible basis times 1/12, the fraction determined under section 42(f)(2)(A)). Under paragraph (d)(2) of this section, the County L Housing Credit Agency may make a housing credit allocation by specifying a credit percentage, not to exceed 9 percent, and a qualified basis amount, which may be greater or less than the qualified basis of the building in 1987 as determined under section 42(c), without regard to the first-year convention provided in section 42(f)(2). If the County L Housing Credit Agency specifies a credit percentage of 8 percent and a qualified basis amount of $100,000, the amount of the housing credit allocation is $8,000. Under paragraph (d)(3) of this section, the County L Housing Credit Agency's aggregate housing credit dollar amount for 1987 is reduced by $8,000, notwithstanding that D is entitled to claim less than $8,000 of the credit in 1987 under the rules in paragraph (e) of this section. Under paragraph (e)(2) of this section, in 1987 D is entitled to claim only $4,000 of the credit, determined by applying the first-year convention of 6/12 to the specified qualified basis amount contained in the housing credit allocation (*i.e.*, .08 x $100,000 x (6/12)).

Example (2). The facts are the same as in *Example (1)* except that on July 1, 1988, the number of occupied low-income units increases to 50 units and the floor space of the occupied low-income units increases to 48,000 square feet. These occupancy fractions remain unchanged as of the close of each month remaining in 1988. Under section 42(c), the qualified basis of the building in 1988, without regard to the first-year convention in section 42(f)(3)(B), is $400,000 (*i.e.*, $1 million eligible basis times .4, the floor space fraction which is required to be used instead of the larger unit fraction). D's 1987 housing credit allocation from the County L Housing Credit Agency remains effective in 1988 and entitles D to a credit of $8,000 (*i.e.*, .08, the specified credit percentage, times $100,000, the specified qualified basis amount). With respect to the additional $300,000 of qualified basis which the 1987 housing credit allocation does not cover, D must apply to the County L Housing Credit Agency for an additional housing credit allocation. Assume that the County L Housing Credit Agency has a sufficient aggregate housing credit dollar amount for 1988 to make a housing credit allocation to D in 1988 by specifying a credit percentage of 9 percent and a qualified basis amount of $300,000. The amount of the housing credit allocation that counts against the County L Housing Credit Agency's aggregate housing credit dollar amount is $27,000 (*i.e.*, the amount counted (.09 times $300,000) is unreduced in the manner prescribed in section 42(f)(3) (A) and (B)). Since D's qualified basis in 1987 was $166,666.67, D is entitled to claim a credit in 1988 with respect to such basis of $14,000 (*i.e.*, .08 x $100,000, the 1987 credit allocation, +.09 x $66,666.67, the 1988 credit allocation). In addition, D is entitled to claim a credit in 1988 and subsequent years in the 15-year compliance period with respect to the additional $233,333.33 of qualified basis covered by the 1988 housing credit allocation. However, the allowable credit for 1988 with respect to this amount of additional qualified basis is subject to reductions prescribed in section 42(f)(3) (A) and (B). Thus, D is entitled in 1988 to a credit at a 6-percent rate applied to $116,666.67 of additional qualified basis, which is reduced to reflect the first-year convention. D's total allowable low-income housing credit in 1988 is $21,000 (*i.e.*, $14,000 with respect to original qualified basis + $7,000 with respect to 1988 additions to qualified basis). If the County L Housing Credit Agency had specified an 8-percent credit percentage in 1988 with respect to the qualified basis not covered by the 1987 housing credit allocation to D, D's allowable credit with respect to the $233,333.33 of additions to qualified basis would not exceed, in 1988 and subsequent years, an amount determined by applying a specified credit percentage of 5.33 percent (*i.e.*, two-thirds of 8 percent). In 1988, D's specified qualified basis amount would be adjusted for the first-year convention.

(6) *No carryover of unused aggregate housing credit dollar amount.* Any portion of a State or local housing credit agency's aggregate housing credit dollar amount for any calendar year that is not used to make a housing credit allocation in such year may not be carried over to any other year, except as provided in paragraph (g) of this section. An agency may not permit owners of qualified low-income buildings to transfer housing credit allocations to other buildings. However, an agency may provide a procedure whereby owners may return to the agency, prior to the end of the calendar year in which housing credit allocations are made, unusable portions of such allocations. In such a case, an owner's housing credit allocation is deemed reduced by the amount of the allocation returned to the agency, and the agency may reallocate such amount to other qualified low-income buildings prior to the end of the year.

(7) *Effect of housing credit allocations in excess of an agency's aggregate housing credit dollar amount.* In the event that a State or local housing credit agency makes housing credit allocations in excess of its aggregate housing credit dollar amount for any calendar year, the allocations shall be deemed reduced (to the extent of such excess) for buildings in the reverse order in which such allocations were made during such year.

(8) *Time and manner for making housing credit allocations.*—(i) *Time.* Housing credit allocations are effective for the calendar year in which made in the manner prescribed in paragraph (d)(8)(ii) of this section. A State or local housing credit agency may not make a housing credit allocation to a qualified low-income building prior to the calendar year in which such building is placed in service. An agency may adopt its own procedures for receiving applications for housing credit allocations from owners of qualified low-income buildings. An agency may provide a procedure for making, in advance of a building's being placed in service, a binding commitment (*e.g.*, by contract, inducement resolution, or other means) to make a housing credit allocation in the calendar year in which a qualified low-income building is placed in service or in a subsequent calendar year. Any advance commitment shall constitute a housing credit allocation for purposes of this section.

(ii) *Manner.* Housing credit allocations are deemed made when Part I of IRS Form 8609, Low-Income Housing Credit Allocation Certification, is completed and signed by an authorized official of the housing credit agency and mailed to the owner of the qualified low-income building. A copy of all completed (as to Part I) Form 8609 allocations along with a single completed Form 8610, Annual Low-Income Housing Credit Agencies Report, must also be mailed to the Internal Revenue Service not later than the 28th day of the second calendar month after the close of the calendar year in which the housing credit was allocated to the qualified low-income building. Housing credit allocations to a qualified low-income building must be made on Form 8609 and must include—

(A) The address of the building;

(B) The name, address, and taxpayer identification number of the housing credit agency making housing credit allocation;

(C) The name, address, and taxpayer identification number of the owner of the qualified low-income building;

(D) The date of the allocation of housing credit;

(E) The housing credit dollar amount allocated to the building on such date;

(F) The specified maximum applicable credit percentage allocated to the building on such date;

(G) The specified maximum qualified basis amount;

(H) The percentage of the aggregate basis financed by tax-exempt bonds taken into account for purposes of the volume cap under section 146;

(I) A certification under penalties of perjury by an authorized State or local housing credit agency official that the allocation is made in compliance with the requirements of section 42(h); and

(J) Any additional information that may be required by Form 8609 or by an applicable revenue procedure.

See paragraph (h) of this section for additional rules concerning filing of forms.

(iii) *Certification.* The certifying official for the State or local housing credit agency need not perform an independent investigation of the qualified low-income building in order to certify on Part I of Form 8609 that the housing credit allocation meets the requirements of section 42(h). For example, the certifying official may rely on information contained in an application for a low-income housing credit allocation submitted by the building owner which sets forth facts necessary to determine that the building is eligible for the low-income housing credit under section 42.

(iv) *Fee.* A State or local housing credit agency may charge building owners applying for housing credit allocations a reasonable fee to cover the agency's administrative expenses for processing applications.

(v) *No continuing agency responsibility.* The State or local housing credit agency need not monitor or investigate the continued compliance of a qualified low-income building with the requirements of section 42 throughout the applicable compliance period.

(e) *Housing credit allocation taken into account by owner of a qualified low-income building*—(1) *Time and manner for taking housing credit allocation into account.* An owner of a qualified low-income building may not claim a low-income housing credit determined under section 42 in any year in excess of an effective housing credit allocation received from a State or local housing credit agency. A housing credit allocation made to a qualified low-income building is effective with respect to any owner of the building beginning with the owner's taxable year in which the housing credit allocation is received. A housing credit allocation is deemed received in a taxable year, except as modified in the succeeding sentence, if that allocation is made (in the manner described in paragraph (d)(8) of this section) not later than the earlier of (i) the 60th day after the close of the taxable year, or (ii) the close of the calender year in which such taxable year ends. A housing credit allocation is deemed received in a taxable year ending in 1987, if such allocation is made (in the manner described in paragraph (d)(8) of this section) on or before December 31, 1987. A housing credit allocation is not effective for any taxable year if received in a calendar year which ends prior to when the qualified low-income building is placed in service. A housing credit allocation made to a qualified low-income building remains effective for all taxable years in the compliance period. A taxpayer is required to complete the Form 8609 on which a housing credit agency made the applicable housing credit allocation and submit a copy of such Form 8609 with its Federal income tax return for each year in the compliance period. Failure to comply with the requirement of the preceding sentence with respect to any taxable year after the first taxable year in the credit period shall be treated as a mathematical or clerical error for purposes of the provisions of section 6213 (b)(1) and (g)(2).

(2) *First-year convention limitation on housing credit allocation taken into account.* For purposes of the limitation that the allowable low-income housing

credit may not exceed the effective housing credit allocation received from a State or local housing credit agency, as provided in paragraph (e)(1) of this section, the amount of the effective housing credit allocation shall be adjusted by applying the first-year convention provided in section 42(f)(2)(A) and (3)(B) and the percentage credit reduction provided in section 42(f)(3)(A). Under paragraphs (d) (2) and (5) of this section, the State of local housing credit agency must specify the credit percentage and qualified basis amount, the product of which is the amount of the housing credit allocation, without taking account of the first-year convention described in section 42(f)(2)(A) and (3)(B) or the percentage credit reduction prescribed in section 42(f)(3)(A). However, for purposes of the limitation on the amount of the allowable low-income housing credit, as provided in paragraph (e)(2) of this section, in a taxable year in which the first-year convention applies to the amount of credit determined under section 42(a), the specified qualified basis amount shall be adjusted by the first-year convention fraction which is equal to the number of full months (during the first taxable year) in which the building was in service divided by 12. In addition, for purposes of the limitation on the amount of the allowable low-income housing credit, as provided in paragraph (e)(1) of this section, in a taxable year in which the reduction in credit percentage applies to additions to qualified basis, as prescribed in section 42(f)(3), the specified credit percentage shall be reduced by one-third. *See* examples in paragraphs (d)(5)(ii) and (e)(3)(ii) of this section.

(3) *Use of excess housing credit allocation for increases in qualified basis*—(i) *In general.* If the housing credit allocation made to a qualified low-income building exceeds the amount of credit allowable with respect to such building in any taxable year (without regard to the first-year conventions under section 42(f)), such excess is not transferable to another qualified low-income building. However, if in a subsequent year there are increases in the qualified basis for which an increased credit is allowable under section 42(f)(3) at a reduced credit percentage, the original housing credit allocation (including the specified credit percentage and qualified basis amount) would be effective with respect to such increased credit.

(ii) *Example.* The provisions of this paragraph (e)(3) may be illustrated by the following example:

Example. In 1987, a newly-constructed qualified low-income building receives a housing credit allocation of $90,000 based on a specified credit percentage of 9 percent and a specified qualified basis amount of $1,000,000. The building is placed in service in 1987, but the qualified basis in such year is only $800,000, resulting in an allowable credit in 1987 (determined without regard to the first-year conventions) of $72,000. In 1988, the qualified basis is increased to $1,100,000, resulting in an additional credit allowable under section 42(f)(3) (without regard to the first-year conventions) of $18,000 (*i.e.*, $300,000 × .06, or ⅔ of .09). The unused portion of the 1987 housing credit allocation ($18,000) is effective in 1988 and in each subsequent year in the compliance period only with respect to the specified qualified basis for the 1987 housing credit allocation ($1,000,000). Thus, the owner is allowed to claim a credit in 1988 and in each subsequent year (without regard to the first-year conventions), based on the effective housing credit allocation from 1987, of $84,000 (*i.e.*, $72,000 + ($200,000 × .06)). The owner of the qualified low-income building must obtain a new housing credit allocation in 1988 with respect to the additional $100,000 of qualified basis in order to claim a credit on such basis in 1988 and in each subsequent year. If the applicable first-year convention under section 42(f)(3)(B) entitled the owner in 1988 to only ½ of the otherwise applicable credit for the additions to qualified basis, under paragraph (e)(2) of this section the owner is allowed to claim a credit in 1988, based on the effective housing credit allocation from 1987, of $78,000 (*i.e.*, $72,000 + ($200,000 × .06 × .5)).

(4) *Separate housing credit allocations for new buildings and increases in qualified basis.* Separate housing credit allocations must be received for each building with respect to which a housing credit may be claimed. Rehabilitation expenditures with respect to a qualified low-income building are treated as a separate new building under section 42(e) and must receive a separate housing credit allocation. Increases in qualified basis in a qualified low-income building are not generally treated as a new building for purposes of section 42. To the extent that a prior housing credit allocation received with respect to a qualified low-income building does not allow an increased credit with respect to an increase in the qualified basis of such building, an additional housing credit allocation must be received in order to claim a credit with respect to that portion of increase in qualified basis. *See* paragraph (e)(3) of this section. The amount of credit allowable with respect to an increase in qualified basis is subject to the credit percentage limitation of section 42(f)(3)(A) and the first-year convention of section 42(f)(3)(B). *See* paragraph (d)(5) of this section for a rule requiring that the State or local housing credit agency count a housing credit allocation made with respect to an increase in qualified basis as if the specified credit percentage were unreduced in the manner prescribed in section 42(f)(3) and the specified basis amount were unreduced by the first-year convention prescribed in section 42(f)(3)(B).

(5) *Acquisition of building for which a prior housing credit allocation has been made.* If a carryover credit would be allowable to an acquirer of a qualified low-income building under section 42(d)(7), such acquirer need not obtain a new housing credit allocation with respect to such building. Under section 42(d)(7), the acquirer would be entitled to claim only such credits as would have been allowable to the prior owner of the building.

(6) *Multiple housing credit allocations.* A qualified low-income building may receive multiple housing credit allocations from different housing credit agencies having overlapping jurisdictions. A qualified low-income building that receives a housing credit allocation set aside exclusively for projects involving a qualified nonprofit organization may also receive a housing credit allocation from a housing credit agency's aggregate housing credit dollar amount that is not so set aside.

(f) *Exception to housing credit allocation requirement*—(1) *Tax-exempt bond financing*—(i) *In general.* No housing credit allocation is required in order to claim a credit under section 42 with respect to that portion of the eligible basis (as defined in section 42(d)) of a qualified low-income building that is financed with the proceeds of an obligation described in section 103(a) ("tax-exempt bond") which is taken into account for purposes of the volume cap under section 146. In addition, no housing credit allocation is required in order to claim a credit under section 42 with respect to the entire qualified basis (as defined in section 42(c)) of a qualified low-income building if 70 percent or more of the aggregate basis of the building and the land on which the building is located is financed with the proceeds of tax-exempt bonds which are taken into account for purposes of the volume cap under section 146. For purposes of this paragraph, "land on which the building is located" includes only land that is functionally related and subordinate to the qualified low-income building. *See* § 1.103–8(b)(4)(iii) for the meaning of the term "functionally related and subordinate". For purposes of this paragraph, the basis of the land shall be determined using principles that are consistent with the rules contained in section 42(d).

(ii) *Determining use of bond proceeds.* For purposes of determining the portion of proceeds of an issue of tax-exempt bonds used to finance (A) the eligible basis of a qualified low-income building, and (B) the aggregate basis of the building and the land on which the building is located, the proceeds of the issue must be allocated in the bond indenture or a related document (as defined in § 1.103–13(b)(8)) in a manner consistent with the method used to allocate the net proceeds of the issue for purposes of determining whether 95 percent or more of the net proceeds of the issue are to be used for the exempt purpose of the issue. If the issuer is not consistent in making this allocation throughout the bond indenture and related documents, or if neither the bond indenture nor a related document provides an allocation, the proceeds of the issue will be allocated on a pro rata basis to all of the property financed by the issue, based on the relative cost of the property.

(iii) *Example.* The provisions of this paragraph may be illustrated by the following example:

Example. In 1987, County K assigns $500,000 of its volume cap for private activity bonds under section 146 to a $500,000 issue of exempt facility bonds to provide a qualified residential rental project to be owned by A, an individual. The aggregate basis of the building and the land on which the building is located is $700,000. Under the terms of the bond indenture, the net proceeds of the issue are to be used to finance $490,000 of the eligible basis of the building. More than 70 percent of the aggregate basis of the qualified low-income building and the land on which the building is located is financed with the proceeds of tax-exempt bonds to which a portion of the volume cap under section 146 was allocated. Accordingly, A may claim a credit under section 42 without regard to whether any housing credit dollar amount was allocated to that building. If, instead, the aggregate basis of the building and land were $800,000, A would be able to claim the credit under section 42 without receiving a housing credit allocation for the building only to the extent that the credit was attributable to eligible basis of the building financed with tax-exempt bonds.

(g) *Termination of authority to make housing credit allocation*—(1) *In general.* No State or local housing credit agency shall receive an apportionment of a State housing credit ceiling for calendar years after 1989. Consequently, no housing credit allocations may be made after 1989, except as provided in paragraph (g)(2) of this section. Housing credit allocations made prior to January 1, 1990, remain effective after such date.

(2) *Carryover of unused 1989 apportionment.* Any State or local housing credit agency that has an unused portion of its apportionment of the State housing credit ceiling for 1989 from which housing credit allocations have not been made in 1989 may carry over such unused portion into 1990. Such carryover portion of the 1989 apportionment shall be treated as the agency's apportionment for 1990. From this 1990 apportionment, the State or local housing credit agency may make housing credit allocations only to a qualified low-income building meeting the following requirements:

(i) The building must be constructed, reconstructed, or rehabilitated by the taxpayer seeking the allocation;

(ii) More than 10 percent of the reasonably anticipated cost of such construction, reconstruction, or rehabilitation must have been incurred as of January 1, 1989; and

(iii) The building must be placed in service before January 1, 1991.

(3) *Expiration of exception for tax-exempt bond financed projects.* The exception to the requirement that a housing credit allocation be received with respect to any portion of the eligible basis of a qualified low-income building, as provided in paragraph (f) of this section, shall not apply to any building placed in service after 1989, unless such building is described in paragraph (g)(2) (i), (ii), and (iii) of this section.

(h) *Filing of forms and special rules*—(1) *Completed form.* For purposes of this section, a form shall be treated as completed if the State or local housing credit agency or the building owner has made a good faith effort to complete the form in accordance with the form and the instructions for the form.

(2) *Manner of filing.* A completed Form 8586, Low-Income Housing Credit, shall be filed with the owner's Federal income tax return for each taxable year the owner of a qualified low-income building is claiming the low-income housing credit during the 10-year credit period. A completed Form 8609 (or copy thereof) shall be filed with the owner's Federal income tax return for each of the 15 taxable years in the compliance period. If a housing credit allocation is not required to be received by an owner under paragraph (f) of this section, the owner shall obtain a blank copy of Form 8609 and fill in the address of the building and the name and address of the owner in Part I. Part II of Form 8609 shall be completed by the owner of the qualified low-income building only for the first year the low-income housing credit is claimed by the building owner. Part III of Form 8609 (Statement of Qualification) shall be completed by the owner of the qualified low-income building for each year of the 15-year compliance period.

(3) *Revised or renumbered forms.* If any form is revised or renumbered, any reference in this section to the form shall be treated as a reference to the revised or renumbered form.

(i) *Transitional rules.* The transitional rules contained in section 252(f)(1) of the Tax Reform Act of 1986 are incorporated into this section of the regulations for purposes of determining whether a qualified low-income building is entitled to receive a housing credit allocation or is excepted from the requirement that a housing credit allocation be received. Housing credit allocations made to qualified low-income buildings described in section 252(f)(1) shall not count against the State or local housing credit agency's aggregate housing credit dollar amount. The transitional rules contained in section 252(f)(2) of the Tax Reform Act of 1986 are incorporated into this section of the regulations for purposes of determining amounts available to certain State or local housing credit agencies for the making of housing credit allocations to certain qualified low-income housing projects. Amounts available to housing credit agencies under section 252(f)(2) shall be treated as special apportionments unavailable for housing credit allocations to qualified low-income buildings not described in section 252(f)(2). Housing credit allocations made from the special apportionments shall not count against the State or local credit agency's aggregate housing credit dollar amount. The set-aside requirements shall not apply to these special apportionments. The transitional rules contained in section 252(f)(3) of the Tax Reform Act 1986 are incorporated in this section of the regulations for purposes of determining the amount of housing credit allocations received by certain qualified low-income buildings. Housing credit allocations deemed received under section 252(f)(3) shall not count against the State or local housing credit agency's aggregate housing credit dollar amount.

APPENDIX 9

IRS TEMPORARY REGULATIONS ON THE LOW INCOME HOUSING TAX CREDIT:

DEPARTMENT OF THE TREASURY

Internal Revenue Service

26 CFR Parts 1 and 602

[T.D. 8162]

Low-Income Housing Credit for Federally-Assisted Buildings and OMB Control Numbers Under the Paperwork Reduction Act

AGENCY: Internal Revenue Service, Treasury.

ACTION: Temporary regulations.

SUMMARY: This document provides temporary regulations concerning the low-income housing credit for certain Federally-assisted buildings under section 42 of the Internal Revenue Code of 1986, as enacted by the Tax Reform Act of 1986. These regulations provide guidance concerning the low-income housing credit allowable for certain Federally-assisted buildings acquired during a 10-year period. In addition, the text of the temporary regulations set forth in this document serves as the comment document for the proposed regulations cross-referenced in the notice of proposed rulemaking in the Proposed Rules section of this issue of the **Federal Register.**

EFFECTIVE DATE: The regulations are effective for buildings placed in service by a taxpayer after December 31, 1986.

FOR FURTHER INFORMATION CONTACT: Robert Beatson of the Legislation and Regulations Division, Office of Chief Counsel, Internal Revenue Service, 1111 Constitution Avenue NW., Washington, DC 20224 (Attention: CC:LR:T LR-61-87) (202-566-3829, not a toll-free call).

SUPPLEMENTARY INFORMATION:

Background

This document contains temporary regulations relating to the low-income housing credit allowable under section 42(d)(6) of the Internal Revenue Code of 1986 for certain Federally-assisted buildings described in section 42(d)(2)(B)(ii), as enacted by section 252 of the Tax Reform Act of 1986 (Pub. L. 99-514). New § 1.42-2T is added by this document to Part 1 of Title 26 of the Code of Federal Regulations. The temporary regulations provided by this document will remain in effect until superseded by final regulation on this subject.

Explanation of Provisions

Section 252 of the Tax Reform Act of 1986 enacted a new low-income housing credit equal to the applicable percentage of the qualified basis of each qualified low-income building. The temporary regulations provide guidance with respect to the credit allowable for certain Federally-assisted buildings acquired during a 10-year period. The low-income housing credit is available to the acquirer of a qualified low-income building for which a special waiver is granted by the Internal Revenue Service in order to avert an assignment of the mortgage secured by the building to the Department of Housing and Urban Development or the Farmers' Home Administration, or to avert a claim against a Federal mortgage insurance fund with respect to a mortgage which is so secured.

Special Analyses

The Commissioner of Internal Revenue has determined that these temporary regulations are not a major rule as defined in Executive Order 12291 and that a regulatory impact analysis therefore is not required.

No general notice of proposed rulemaking is required by 5 U.S.C. 553 (b) because these are temporary regulations, and there is a need to provide the public with immediate guidance. Accordingly, the Regulatory Flexibility Act does not apply and no Regulatory Flexibility Analysis is required for this rule.

Paperwork Reduction Act

The collection of information requirements contained in these regulations have been submitted to the Office of Management and Budget (OMB) in accordance with the requirements of the Paperwork Reduction Act of 1980. These requirements have been approved by OMB (Control no. 1545-1005).

Drafting Information

The principal author of these regulations is Robert Beatson of the Legislation and Regulations Division of the Office of Chief Counsel, Internal Revenue Service. However, personnel from other offices of the Internal Revenue Service and the Treasury Department participated in developing the regulations on matters of both substance and style.

List of Subjects

26 CFR 1.0-1—1.58-8

Income taxes, Tax liability, Tax rates, Credits.

26 CFR Part 602

Reporting and recordkeeping requirements.

Amendments to the Regulations

The amendments to 26 CFR Parts 1 and 602 are as follows:

PART 1—INCOME TAX REGULATIONS

Paragraph 1. The authority for Part 1 is amended by adding the following citation:

Authority: 26 U.S.C. 7805. * * * Section 1.42-2T also issued under 26 U.S.C. 42 (m).

Par. 2. A new § 1.42-2T is added immediately following § 1.42-1T to read as follows:

§ 1.42-2T Waiver of requirement that an existing building eligible for the low-income housing credit has been held for 10 years prior to acquisition by the taxpayer (temporary).

(a) *Low-income housing credit for existing building.* Section 42 provides that, for purposes of section 38, new and existing qualified low-income buildings are eligible for a low-income housing credit. The eligibility rules for new and existing buildings differ. Under section 42(d)(2), the acquisition cost (to the extent properly included in basis) of an existing building may be eligible for the low-income housing credit if—

(1) The taxpayer acquires the building by purchase (as defined in section 179(d)(2), as applicable under section 42(d)(2)(D)(iii)(I)),

(2) There is a period of at least 10 years between the date of the building's acquisition by the taxpayer and the later of—

(i) The date the building was last placed in service, or

(ii) The date of the most recent nonqualified substantial improvement of the building, and

(3) The building was not previously placed in service by the taxpayer, or by a person who was a related person (as defined in section 42(d)(2)(D)(iii)(II)) with respect to the taxpayer as of the time the building was last previously placed in service.

(b) *Waiver of 10-year holding period requirement.* Section 42(d)(6) provides that a taxpayer may apply for a waiver of the 10-year holding period requirement specified in paragraph (a)(2) of this section. The Internal Revenue Service will grant a waiver only if—

(1) The existing building satisfies all of the requirements in paragraph (c) of this section, and

(2) The taxpayer makes an application in conformity with the requirements in paragraph (d) of this section.

(c) *Waiver requirements*—(1) *Federally-assisted building.* To satisfy the requirement of this paragraph (c)(1), a building must be a Federally-assisted building. The term "Federally-assisted building" means any building which is substantially assisted, financed, or operated under section 8 of the United States Housing Act of 1937, section 221(d)(3) or 236 of the National Housing Act of 1934, or section 515 of the Housing Act of 1949, as such acts were in effect on October 22, 1986.

(2) *Federal mortgage funds at risk.* To satisfy the requirement of this paragraph (c)(2), Federal mortgage funds must be at risk with respect to a mortgage that is secured by the building or a project of which the building is a part. For purposes of this paragraph (c)(2), Federal mortgage funds are at risk if, in the event of a default by the mortgagor on the mortgage secured by the building or the project of which the building is a part—

(i) The mortgage could be assigned to the Department of Housing and Urban Development or the Farmers' Home Administration, or

(ii) There could arise a claim against a Federal mortgage insurance fund (or such Department or Administration).

(3) *Action by the Department of Housing and Urban Development or the Farmers' Home Administration.* To satisfy the requirement of this paragraph (c)(3), specified Federal action must have been taken by either the Department of Housing and Urban Development or the Farmers' Home Administration ("the Federal agency") with respect to the building or the project of which the building is a part that demonstrates that a waiver of the 10-year holding period requirement is necessary to avert Federal mortgage funds being at risk within the meaning of paragraph (c)(2) of this section. The following specified Federal actions shall be the only means of satisfying the requirement of this paragraph (c)(3):

(i) The federal agency intends to accept an assignment of a mortgage secured by the building or the project of which the building is a part, and such assignment requires payments by the agency or a mortgage insurance fund maintained by the agency to the prior mortgagee;

(ii) The Federal agency or a mortgage insurance fund maintained by the agency intends to accept, as a consequence of foreclosure proceedings or otherwise, conveyance of the building or the project of which the building is a part;

(iii) The Federal agency or a mortgage insurance fund maintained by the agency intends, as a consequence of default, to take possession of, hold title to, or otherwise assume ownership of the building or the project of which the building is a part; or

(iv) The Federal agency has designated the building or the project of which the building is a part as a troubled building or project. A designation of a troubled building or project must satisfy the following requirements:

(A) Designation of troubled status must be based on a review by the Federal agency of the financial condition of the building or project and on a determination by the agency of a history of financial distress and mortgage defaults;

(B) Designation of troubled status must be made or received and approved by the national office of the Federal agency; and

(C) Federal agency regulations or procedures must provide that, in the event of transfer of the ownership of a designated troubled building or project, the building or project may be subject to review by the Federal agency.

Each Federal agency may prescribe its own standards and procedures for designating a troubled building or project so long as such standards are consistent with the requirements of this paragraph (c)(3)(iv).

(4) *No prior credit allowed.* The requirement of this paragraph (c)(4) is satisfied only if no prior owner was allowed a low-income housing credit under section 42 for the building.

(d) *Application for Waiver*—(1) *Time and manner.* In order to receive a waiver of the 10-year holding period requirement specified in paragraph (a)(2) of this section, a taxpayer must file an application that complies with the requirement of this paragraph (d) and applicable procedural rules set forth in paragraph (e) of § 601.201 (Statement of Procedural Rules). The application must be filed by a taxpayer who has acquired the building by purchase or who has a binding contract to purchase the building. Such binding contract may be conditioned upon the granting of a waiver under this section. The application may be filed at any time after a binding contract has been entered into, but no later than 12 months after the taxpayer's acquisition of the building. An application for a waiver of the 10-year holding period requirement must not contain a request for a ruling on any other issue arising under section 42 or other sections of the Internal Revenue Code. An application for a waiver of the 10-year holding period requirement must be mailed or delivered to the Internal Revenue Service, Associate Chief Counsel (Technical and International), Attention CC:IND:D:C, Room 6545, 1111 Constitution Avenue, NW., Washington, DC 20224.

(2) *Information required.* An application for a waiver of the 10-year holding period requirement must contain the following information:

(i) The taxpayer's name, address and taxpayer identification number;

(ii) The name (if any) and address of the acquired building and the project (if any) of which it is a part;

(iii) The date of acquisition or of the binding contract for acquisition of the building by the taxpayer, the amount of consideration paid or to be paid for the acquisition (including the value of any liabilities assumed by the taxpayer), and the taxpayer's certification that such acquisition is by purchase (as defined in section 179(d)(2), as applicable under section 42(d)(2)(D)(iii)(I));

(iv) The identity of the person from whom the building is acquired, and whether such person is a Federal agency, a mortgagee holding title to the building, or the mortgagor or prior owner;

(v) The date the building was last placed in service and the date of the most recent (if any) nonqualified substantial improvement of the building (as defined in section 42(d)(2)(D)(i));

(vi) The taxpayer's certification that the building was not previously placed in service by the taxpayer, or by a person who was a related person (as defined in section 42(d)(2)(D)(iii)(II)) with respect to the taxpayer as of the time the building was last placed in service;

(vii) The source of Federal assistance received by the building (for purposes of paragraph (c)(1) of this section);

(viii) The taxpayer's certification that, as of the earlier of the time of acquisition of the building or the time of application for the waiver, the building is a Federally-assisted building (as defined in paragraph (c)(1) of this section);

(ix) The amount and disposition (*e.g.*, discharge, assignment, assumption, or refinance) of any outstanding mortgage, if any, at the time of acquisition and the identities of the mortgagee and mortgagor;

(x) The taxpayer's certification that, as of the earlier of the time of acquisition of the building or the time of application for the waiver, Federal mortgage funds are at risk within the meaning of paragraph (c)(2) of this section;

(xi) Documentation of specified Federal agency action within the meaning of paragraph (c)(3) of this section; and

(xii) The taxpayer's certification that no prior owner was allowed a low-income housing credit under section 42 of the building.

(3) *Other rules.* (i) In the event that an acquired building will be owned by more than one taxpayer, a single application for waiver may be filed by one taxpayer on behalf of the co-owners, if the application contains the names, addresses and taxpayer identification numbers of the other owners. A general partner or a designated limited partner may file an application for waiver on behalf of a partnership.

(ii) With respect to the requirement in paragraph (d)(2)(xi) of this section for documentation of specified Federal agency action, in the case of Federal agency designation of a troubled building or project (as described in paragraph (c)(3)(iv) of this section), a letter or other written statement is required from an appropriate official in the national office of the Federal agency verifying designation of troubled status and compliance with the requirements in paragraph (c)(3)(iv) of this section.

(iii) With respect to the certifications required in paragraphs (d)(2) (x) and (xii) of this section, the taxpayer may make the certifications to the best of its knowledge, and no documentation from other persons need be submitted with the application.

(4) *Effective date of waiver.* A waiver will be effective when granted but in no event later than 60 days after a taxpayer files a substantially complete application for waiver under this paragraph (d). If a taxpayer has filed a substantially complete application but the Internal Revenue Service requires additional information or materials, any waiver granted will be effective no later than 60 days after the initial application was filed.

(5) *Attachment to return.* A waiver letter granted by the Internal Revenue Service shall be filed with the taxpayer's Federal income tax return for the first taxable year the low-income housing credit is claimed by the taxpayer.

(e) *Effective date of regulations.* The provisions of § 1.42-2T are effective for buildings placed in service by the taxpayer after December 31, 1986.

APPENDIX 10

INTERNAL REVENUE SERVICE NOTICE 88-80

Low-Income Housing Tax Credit—Determination of Income for Purposes of Section 42(g)(1)

Notice 88-80

The purpose of this Notice is to inform taxpayers that regulations to be issued under section 42(g)(1) of the Internal Revenue Code of 1986 (the "Code") (relating to the determination of a qualified low-income housing project) will provide that the income of individuals and area median gross income (adjusted for family size) are to be made in a manner consistent with the determination of annual income and the estimates for median family income under section 8 of the United States Housing Act of 1937 (H.U.D. section 8).

For purposes of H.U.D. section 8, annual income is defined under 24 CFR 813.106 (1987). HUD section 8 median family income estimates (*i.e.*, area median gross income estimates) are based on decennial Census data updated with Bureau of the Census P-60 income data and Department of Commerce County Business Patterns employment and earnings data. The determination of annual income and median family income estimates are based on definitions of income that include some items of income that are not included in a taxpayer's gross income for purposes of computing Federal Income Tax liability. Thus, the income of individuals and area median gross income (adjusted for family size) for purposes of section 42(g)(1) of the Code will *not* be made by reference to items of income used in determining gross income for purposes of computing Federal Income Tax liability.

This document serves as an "administrative pronouncement" as that term is described in section 1.6661-3(b)(2) of the Income Tax Regulations and may be relied upon to the same extent as a revenue ruling or revenue procedure.

The principal author of this Notice is Christopher J. Wilson of the Legislation and Regulations Division. For further information regarding this Notice contact Mr. Wilson on (202) 566-4336 (not a toll-free call).

H.U.D. DEFINITION OF ANNUAL INCOME 24 CFR 813.106

§ 813.106 Annual Income.

(a) Annual income is the anticipated total income from all sources received by the Family head and spouse (even if temporarily absent) and by each additional member of the Family, including all net income derived from assets for the 12-month period following the effective date of certification of income, exclusive of certain types of income as provided in paragraph (c) of this section.

(b) Annual Income includes, but is not limited to:

(1) The full amount, before any payroll deductions, of wages and salaries, overtime pay, commissions, fees, tips and bonuses, and other compensation for personal services;

(2) The net income from operation of a business or profession. Expenditures for business expansion or amortization of capital indebtness shall not be used as deductions in determining net income. An allowance for depreciation of assets used in a business or profession may be deducted, based on straight line depreciation, as provided in Internal Revenue Service regulations. Any withdrawal of cash or assets from the operation of a business or profession will be included in income, except to the extent the withdrawal is reimbursement of cash or assets invested in the operation by the Family;

(3) Interest, dividends, and other net income of any kind from real or personal property. Expenditures for amortization of capital indebtedness shall not be used as a deduction in determining net income. An allowance for depreciation is permitted only as authorized in paragraph (b)(2) of this section. Any withdrawal of cash or assets from an investment will be included in income, except to the extent the withdrawal is reimbursement of cash or assets invested by the Family. Where the Family has Net Family Assets in excess of $5,000, Annual Income shall include the greater of the actual income derived from all Net Family Assets or a percentage of the value of such Assets based on the current passbook savings rate, as determined by HUD;

(4) The full amount of periodic payments received from social security, annuities, insurance policies, retirement funds, pensions, disability or death benefits and other similar types of periodic receipts, including a lump-sum payment for the delayed start of a periodic payment;

(5) Payments in lieu of earnings, such as unemployment and disability compensation, worker's compensation and severance pay (but see paragraph (c)(3) of this section);

(6) Welfare Assistance. If the Welfare Assistance payment includes an amount specifically designated for shelter and utilities that is subject to adjustment by the Welfare Assistance agency in accordance with the actual cost of shelter and utilities, the amount of Welfare Assistance income to be included as income shall consist of:

(i) The amount of the allowance or grant exclusive of the amount specifically designated for shelter or utilities, plus

(ii) The maximum amount that the Welfare Assistance agency could in fact allow the Family for shelter and utilities. If the Family's Welfare Assistance is ratably reduced from the standard of need by applying a percentage, the amount calculated under this paragraph (b)(6)(ii) shall be the amount resulting from one application of the percentage;

(7) Periodic and determinable allowances, such as alimony and child support payments, and regular contributions or gifts received from persons not residing in the dwelling;

(8) All regular pay, special pay and allowances of a member of the Armed Forces (but see paragraph (c)(7) of this section); and

(9) Any earned income tax credit to the extent it exceeds income tax liability.

(c) Annual income does not include the following:

(1) Income from employment of children (including foster children) under the age of 18 years;

(2) Payments received for the care of foster children;

(3) Lump-sum additions to Family assets, such as inheritances, insurance payments (including payments under health and accident insurance and worker's compensation), capital gains and settlement for personal or property losses (but see paragraph (b)(5) of this section);

(4) Amounts received by the Family, that are specifically for, or in reimbursement of, the cost of medical expenses for any Family member;

(5) Income of a live-in aide, as defined in § 813.102;

(6) Amounts of educational scholarships paid directly to the student or to the educational institution, and amounts paid by the Government to a veteran, for use in meeting the costs of tuition, fees, books, equipment, materials, supplies, transportation, and miscellaneous personal expenses of the student. Any amount of such scholarship or payment to a veteran not used for the above purposes that is available for subsistence is to be included in income;

(7) The special pay to a Family member serving in the Armed Forces who is exposed to hostile fire;

(8)(i) Amounts received under training programs funded by HUD;

(ii) Amounts received by a Disabled person that are disregarded for a limited time for purposes of Supplemental Security Income eligibility and benefits because they are set aside for use under a Plan to Attain Self-Sufficiency (PASS); or

(iii) Amounts received by a participant in other publicly assisted programs which are specifically for or in reimbursement of out-of-pocket expenses incurred (special equipment, clothing, transportation, child care, etc.) and which are made solely to allow participation in a specific program;

(9) Temporary, nonrecurring or sporadic income (including gifts); or

(10) Amounts specifically excluded by any other Federal statute from consideration as income for purposes of determining eligibility or benefits under a category of assistance programs that includes assistance under the United States Housing Act of 1937. A notice will be published in the FEDERAL REGISTER and distributed to PHAs and owners identifying the benefits that qualify for this exclusion. Updates will be published and distributed when necessary.

(d) If it is not feasible to anticipate a level of income over a 12-month period, the income anticipated for a shorter period may be annualized, subject to a redetermination at the end of the shorter period.

[49 FR 19936, May 10, 1984, as amended at 50 FR 29591, June 24, 1985; 50 FR 39097, Sept. 27, 1985; 51 FR 21308, June 11, 1986; 52 FR 34113, Sept. 9, 1987; 53 FR 4388, Feb. 16, 1988; 53 FR 7734, Mar. 10, 1988]

APPENDIX 11
INTERNAL REVENUE SERVICE NOTICE 88-91

Low-Income Housing Tax Credit—Additional Certification Requirements

Notice 88-91

The purpose of this Notice is to inform owners of low-income housing that buildings that have been or will be allocated a low-income housing tax credit under section 42 of the Internal Revenue Code of 1986 (the "Code") must be assigned a building identification number (BIN). Buildings described in section 42(h)(4) of the Code (relating to buildings financed by tax-exempt bonds subject to the volume cap under section 146) must also receive a BIN from the applicable housing credit agency whether or not a separate housing credit allocation is required.

Section 42(l) of the Code requires owners of qualified low income buildings and housing credit agencies to provide certain information to the Secretary. Forms 8586 and 8609 were developed, in part, to satisfy these requirements. Form 8586 is used by owners of qualified low-income buildings to claim the low-income housing credit. Form 8609 is used to obtain a housing credit allocation and serves as an annual statement from the building owner to the Secretary that the building continues to qualify as a qualified low-income building.

Forms 8586 and 8609 will be revised to provide the Service with information needed to identify buildings and transfers and to monitor compliance with the low-income housing tax credit requirements. The BIN is essential for this monitoring process. At the time a credit is allocated to a building, that building must be assigned a BIN by the applicable housing credit agency. BINs must be assigned retroactively to buildings that previously were allocated a tax credit during 1987 or 1988. The retroactive assignment of a BIN will not require any building owner to file an amended return. However, the revised Forms must be attached to the owner's next-filed Federal income tax return and all subsequent income tax returns in accordance with the instructions on the Forms. In addition, all owners of buildings that have been allocated a low-income housing tax credit (including owners of buildings subject to the rules of section 42(h)(4)) must complete the revised Form 8609, including Part II of revised Form 8609, the first year certification requirement.

The BIN will consist of a two character state designation (identical to a postal state abbreviation) followed by a two digit designation representing the year the credit is allocated, and a five digit numbering designation. For example, the identification number for one of 25 buildings allocated a credit in 1987 by the Connecticut Housing Finance Authority (the only housing credit allocating agency in the state) might read CT-87-00023. The BIN will be assigned by the housing credit agency that is authorized to make the credit allocation and will be applicable throughout the building's 15-year compliance period. The BIN must be entered on all forms requesting a BIN.

Rehabilitation expenditures treated as a separate new building under section 42(e) of the Code will not be required to have a separate BIN if the building to which the rehabilitation expenditures were made has a BIN. In this case, the BIN used for such expenditures shall be the BIN previously assigned to the building.

It is imperative that agencies in states with multiple housing credit agencies coordinate to ensure that each building receiving a low-income housing credit allocation have a separate and distinct BIN. It is suggested that the state housing authority having primary oversight for administration of the tax credit act as a clearing house to avoid duplication of BINs.

Housing credit agencies will be provided revised Forms 8609 and 8586. In the case of a building to which a credit was allocated previously (including buildings described in section 42(h)(4) of the Code), the housing credit agency must supply the building owners with revised Forms by completing Part I of revised Form 8609 (including the assignment of a BIN) and forwarding the Form (along with revised Form 8586) to the owner. The suggested letter in Part II of this Notice may be used by the housing credit agency to accompany both revised Forms. The suggested letter explains the purpose of the new Forms and the responsibilities of the building owner.

A revised Form 8609 is required for *each* building eligible for a credit. Accordingly, housing credit agencies that have provided credits on a Form 8609 to a low-income housing project consisting of more than one building must reallocate those credits among the buildings in the project and provide a separate Form 8609 for each building. In no event may reallocation of credits to all buildings in a project be less than or exceed the amount of credits previously allocated to the project. In addition, the credit may only be taken to the extent of a building's qualified basis.

Final regulations will provide that the term "qualified low-income building" includes residential rental property that is either an apartment building, a single family dwelling, a townhouse, a rowhouse, a duplex, or a condominium. A qualified low-income building does not include residential rental property owned or leased by a cooperative housing corporation or a tenant-stockholder, as those terms are defined under section 216(b)(1) and (2) of the Code.

Part II. SUGGESTED LETTER FOR USE BY STATE HOUSING AGENCIES TO NOTIFY OWNERS OF LOW-INCOME HOUSING OF NEW BUILDING IDENTIFICATION NUMBER REQUIREMENT AND CHANGES TO FORMS 8609 AND 8586.

[The following is suggested language that may be used by agencies when notifying building owners of the building identification number (BIN) assigned to such owner.]

The Internal Revenue Service (the "Service") has amended Form 8609 (Low-Income Housing Credit Allocation Certification) and Form 8586 (Low-Income Housing Credit) to monitor compliance with the low-income housing tax credit requirements. Buildings receiving a credit allocation must be assigned a building identification number (BIN). A BIN must also be assigned to buildings described in section 42(h)(4) of the Internal Revenue Code of 1986 (the "Code") (relating to buildings financed by tax-exempt bonds subject to the volume cap under section 146), whether or not a separate housing credit allocation is required. Rehabilitation expenditures treated as a separate new building under section 42(e) of the Code will *not* be required to have a separate BIN if a BIN is assigned to the building to which the rehabilitation expenditures have been made. In this case, the BIN used for such expenditures shall be the BIN assigned to the building.

Buildings that have previously been allocated a credit (including buildings subject to the rules of 42(h)(4)) are required to have a BIN assigned retroactively. This number shall apply to the building throughout the building's compliance period and must be reported by you on all forms for which a BIN is requested.

Attached are copies of revised Forms 8609 and 8586. We have completed Part I of revised Form 8609 and have assigned a BIN to your building. This will be the building's permanent identification number for purposes of filing any forms with the Service. The retroactive assignment of a BIN will not require you to file an amended return. However, the revised Forms must be attached to your next-filed Federal income tax return and all subsequent income tax returns in accordance with the instructions on the Forms. In addition, you must complete the revised Forms 8609 and 8586, including Part II of revised Form 8609, the first year certification requirement even if Part II of old Form 8609 has previously been completed. If you are subject to the rules of section 42(h)(4) you must also complete the revised Forms, including Part II of revised Form 8609. If you have received an allocation but have not filed a tax return, you should replace the old Forms 8609 and 8586 with completed revised Forms 8609 and 8586 and include such Forms with your next-filed Federal income tax return.

A Form 8609 (and BIN) is required for *each* building that is eligible for the credit. If you previously received a single Form 8609 for a low-income housing project consisting of more than one building, we are sending you a separate revised Form 8609 for each building in the project. Credits previously allocated to the project have been reallocated to the buildings in the project based upon the information we received from you when applying for a credit allocation. Regardless of the amount of credit reallocated to each building, credits may only be taken to the extent of a building's qualified basis.

Part III. ADMINISTRATIVE PRONOUNCEMENT

This document serves as an "administrative pronouncement" as that term is described in section 1.6661-3(b)(2) of the Income Tax Regulations and may be relied upon to the same extent as a revenue ruling or revenue procedure.

The collection of information contained in this Notice has been reviewed and approved by the Office of Management and Budget in accordance with the requirements of the Paperwork Reduction Act (44 U.S.C. 3507) under control number 1545-0988. The estimated average burden associated with the collection of information in this Notice is 44 minutes per respondent.

Comments concerning the accuracy of this burden estimate and suggestions for reducing this burden should be directed to the Internal Revenue Service, Washington, D.C. 20224, Attention: IRS Reports Clearance Officer TR:FP; and the Office of Information and Regulatory Affairs, Office of Management and Budget, Washington, D.C. 20503, Attention: Desk Officer for Internal Revenue Service.

The principal author of this Notice is Christopher J. Wilson of the Legislation and Regulations Division. For further information regarding this Notice contact Mr. Wilson on (202) 566-4336 (not a toll-free call).

APPENDIX 12

INTERNAL REVENUE SERVICE'S ADVANCE NOTICE 88-116, ON THE LOW-INCOME HOUSING TAX CREDIT, ISSUED OCT. 12, 1988 (TEXT)

(Note: Notice 88-116 will appear in Internal Revenue Bulletin 1988-44, dated Oct. 31, 1988.)

Low-Income Housing Tax Credit — Carryover of 1989 Credits for Certain Projects in Progress, Description of Construction, Reconstruction or Rehabilitation, Placed in Service

Notice 88-116

Section 42(n)(1) of the Internal Revenue Code (the "Code") provides, generally, that the State housing credit ceiling under section 42(h) shall be zero for any calendar year after 1989. Thus, in general, all buildings eligible for the low-income housing credit must be placed in service before January 1, 1990. Under section 42(n)(2), however, 1989 credit amounts that are not allocated in 1989 may be applied to a building placed in service in 1990 if such building is constructed, reconstructed, or rehabilitated by the taxpayer and more than 10 percent of the reasonably anticipated cost of such construction, reconstruction, or rehabilitation has been incurred as of January 1, 1989. The purpose of this Notice is to provide guidance to taxpayers under section 42(n) of the Code regarding (1) what costs will be considered construction, reconstruction, or rehabilitation costs; and (2) when such costs will be considered to be incurred. In addition, this Notice provides guidance regarding when a building will be considered to be placed in service for purposes of section 42.

CONSTRUCTION, RECONSTRUCTION OR REHABILITATION COSTS

For purposes of section 42(n), the term construction, reconstruction, or rehabilitation costs means any amount that is (1) properly chargeable to a capital account and (2) incurred before or on January 1, 1989. Amounts are chargeable to a capital account if they are properly includible in computing eligible basis under section 42(d). Amounts treated as an expense and deducted in the year they are paid or incurred or amounts that are otherwise not added to eligible basis do not qualify. For example, the cost of acquisition of an existing building is a qualifying cost. Amounts incurred for taxes and architectural and engineering fees, site survey fees, legal expenses, insurance premiums, development fees, and other construction related costs satisfy the definition of construction, reconstruction, or rehabilitation costs if they are included in the eligible basis of the building. Production period interest (within the meaning of section 263A(f)) allocable to the construction, reconstruction, or rehabilitation of a building is a qualifying cost. The cost of land is not a qualifying cost. For purposes of section 42(n), the total anticipated costs of construction, reconstruction, or rehabilitation shall be determined by reference to a reasonable estimate, on or before January 1, 1989, of such amount.

COSTS INCURRED AS OF JANUARY 1, 1989

Construction, reconstruction, or rehabilitation costs are incurred for purposes of this section on the date such expenditures would be considered incurred under an accrual method of accounting, regardless of the method of accounting used by the taxpayer incurring the costs with respect to other items of income and expense.

PLACED IN SERVICE

For purposes of section 42, the term "placed in service" has two definitions — one for buildings and one for rehabilitation expenditures that are treated as a separate new building (section 42(e)(4)(A)). The placed-in-service date for a new or existing building used as residential rental property is the date on which the building is ready and available for its specifically assigned function, i.e., the date on which the first unit in the building is certified as being suitable for occupancy in accordance with state or local law. In general, a transfer of the building results in a new placed-in-service date if, on the date of the transfer, the building is occupied or ready for occupancy.

Under section 42(e)(4)(A) of the Code, rehabilitation expenditures that are treated as a separate new building are placed in service at the close of any 24-month period, over which such expenditures are aggregated. The placed-in-service date of section 42(e)(4)(A) applies even if the building is occupied during the rehabilitation period.

A building may be placed in service even if the rental units in the building are not currently occupied by low-income tenants.

This document serves as an "administrative pronouncement" as that term is described in section 1.661-3(b)(2) of the Income Tax Regulations and may be relied upon to the same extent as a revenue ruling or revenue procedure.

The principal author of this notice is Christopher J. Wilson of the Legislation and Regulations Division. For further information regarding this notice contact Mr. Wilson on (202) 566-4945 (not a toll-free call).

APPENDIX 13

INTERNAL REVENUE SERVICE NOTICE 89-1

ELECTION OF APPROPRIATE PERCENTAGE MONTH: CARRYOVER OF POST 1987 LOW-INCOME HOUSING CREDIT DOLLAR AMOUNTS (IRS NOTICE 89-1)*

This Notice informs taxpayers of the requirements of two of the amendments to section 42 of the Internal Revenue code (the Code) made by the Technical and Miscellaneous Revenue Act of 1988 (the 1988 Act) (Pub. L. 100-647). Those amendments relate to (1) an election by a taxpayer to use the appropriate percentage for a month other than the month in which a building is placed in service, and (2) carryover of post-1987 low-income housing credit dollar amounts.

ELECTION OF APPROPRIATE PERCENTAGE MONTH

Section 1002(1)(1)(A) of the 1988 Act amended section 42(b)(2)(A) of the Code to read as follows:

In the case of any qualified low-income building placed in service by the taxpayer after 1987, the term "applicable percentage" means the appropriate percentage prescribed by the Secretary for the earlier of—

(i) the month in which such building is placed in service, or

(ii) at the election of the taxpayer—

(I) the month in which the taxpayer and the housing credit agency enter into an agreement with respect to such building which is binding on such agency, the taxpayer, and all successors in interest as to the housing credit dollar amount to be allocated to such building, or

(II) in the case of any building to which subsection (h)(4)(B) applies, the month in which the tax-exempt obligations are issued.

A month may be elected under clause (ii) only if the election is made not later than the 5th day after the close of such month. Such an election, once made, shall be irrevocable.

For purposes of the election under section 42(b)(2)(A)(ii)(I) of the Code (as amended) as set forth above, an agreement between a taxpayer and a state housing credit agency is considered binding on the agency, the taxpayer, and all successors in interest if it:

(1) is in writing;

(2) specifies the housing credit dollar amount to be allocated to the building;

(3) specifies the type(s) of building(s) to which the housing credit dollar amount applies (e.g., newly constructed, existing, or substantial rehabilitation under section 42(e));

(4) is a binding contract under state law;

(5) is binding on all successors in interest to the taxpayer; and

(6) is dated and signed by the taxpayer and the agency during the month in which all the requirements of (1) through (5) are met.

A taxpayer may elect under section 42(b)(2)(A)(ii)(I) of the Code to use the appropriate percentage for a month other than the month in which a building is placed in service. If such an election is made, the applicable percentage will be the appropriate percentage for the month in which the binding agreement to allocate a specific housing credit dollar amount is made, assuming that the taxpayer has not previously made the election for a different month. Whether the appropriate percentage is the appropriate percentage for the 70 percent present value credit or the 30 percent present value credit will be determined under section 42(i)(2) when the building is placed in service. The election may be made either as part of the binding agreement to allocate a specific housing credit dollar amount or in a separate document. A proper election under section 42(b)(2)(A)(ii)(I) must:

(1) be in writing;

(2) reference section 42(b)(2)(A)(ii)(I) of the Code;

(3) if it is in a separate document, reference the binding agreement to allocate the specific housing credit dollar amount that meets the requirements of (1) through (6) above;

(4) be signed by the taxpayer; and

(5) be notarized by the 5th day following the month in which the binding agreement was made. The notarization must be made on the last page of the election statement and may not be made on a separate page.

The original notarized document must be given to the housing credit agency before the close of the 5th calendar day of the month following the month in which the binding agreement was made. The taxpayer must retain a copy of the binding agreement and the election statement and file an additional copy with the taxpayer's Form 8609, Low-Income Housing Credit Allocation Certification, for the first taxable year in which the credit is claimed. The agency must retain a copy of the binding agreement and the election statement and file the original with the agency's Form 8610, Annual Low-Income Housing Credit Agencies Report, for the year the allocation is actually made. If the housing credit dollar amount ultimately allocated on Form 8609 differs from

---
*From Internal Revenue Service Bulletin 1989-2, January 9, 1989.

the amount previously agreed to in the binding agreement, an explanation should be furnished.

The housing credit dollar amount ultimately allocated to the building may not be less than the amount specified in the binding agreement, unless at the time the credit is allocated, the product of the building's actual or reasonably expected qualified basis and the appropriate percentage for the month in which the agreement was made is less than the amount specified in the binding agreement. If, at the time of the allocation, the product of the building's actual or reasonably expected qualified basis and the appropriate percentage for the month in which the agreement was made is greater than the housing credit dollar amount specified in the binding agreement, the agency may allocate a greater credit dollar amount if there is any additional housing credit dollar amount available to allocate for the calendar year of the allocation.

Example 1.

In January 1989 the taxpayer and the state housing credit agency enter into an agreement that meets the requirements for an agreement to be binding for purposes of section 42(b)(2)(A)(ii)(I) of the Code. In the agreement, the state housing credit agency agrees to allocate $100,000 of housing credit dollar amount to the low-income housing building being constructed by the taxpayer. This amount will be deducted from the state housing credit ceiling only during the calendar year in which the allocation is actually made. Before February 5, 1989, an election statement that meets the requirements for an election under section 42(b)(2)(A)(ii)(I) is signed by the taxpayer and is notarized so that the applicable percentage for the building will be the appropriate percentage for the month of January 1989. When the building is placed in service in August 1989, the product of the building's qualified basis and the appropriate percentage for the month of January 1989 is $150,000, rather than $100,000. Under the agreement the agency must allocate $100,000 of housing credit dollar amount. However, the agency may also allocate an additional $50,000 of housing credit dollar amount from its state housing credit fund for calendar year 1989 if the agency has credit available to allocate. The appropriate percentage for the month of January 1989 is the appropriate percentage to be used for the building, despite the fact that more housing credit dollar amount is allocated to the building when the building is placed in service than was previously agreed. Because the allocation of the $100,000 of housing credit dollar amount under the agreement and the $50,000 of additional housing credit dollar amount are made during the same calendar year, only one Form 8609 for the total amount allocated to the building must be completed.

The election under section 42(b)(2)(A)(ii)(II) of the Code pertains to buildings that are 70 percent or more financed by tax-exempt bonds subject to the volume cap of section 146. For those buildings, taxpayers may elect to apply the appropriate percentage for the month in which the tax-exempt bonds are issued. A proper election under section 42(b)(2)(A)(ii)(II) must:

(1) be in writing;

(2) reference section 42(b)(2)(A)(ii)(II) of the Code;

(3) specify the percentage of the aggregate basis of the building and the land on which the building is located that is financed by tax-exempt bonds subject to the volume cap of section 146;

(4) state the month in which the tax-exempt bonds are issued;

(5) state that the month in which the tax-exempt bonds are issued is the month elected for the appropriate percentage with respect to the building;

(6) be signed by the taxpayer; and

(7) be notarized by the 5th day following the month in which the bonds are issued. The notarization must be made on the last page of the election statement and may not be made on a separate page.

The taxpayer must provide the original notarized statement to the state housing credit agency before the close of the 5th calendar day of the month following the month in which the bonds are issued. If an agency, other than the state housing credit agency, issues the tax-exempt bonds, the taxpayer must also provide the state housing credit agency with a signed statement from the issuing authority that certifies the material in items (3) and (4). The taxpayer must retain a copy of the election statement and file an additional copy with the taxpayer's Form 8609 for the first taxable year in which the credit is claimed. The agency must retain a copy of the election statement and file the original with the agency's Form 8610 for the year an allocation is made.

Example 2.

A taxpayer plans to rehabilitate a low-income housing building in which 60 percent of the aggregate basis of the building and the land on which such building is located is financed by tax-exempt bonds subject to the volume cap under section 146 of the Code. The building does not meet the requirements of section 42(h)(4)(B) because less than 70 percent of such aggregate basis is financed by tax-exempt bonds subject to the volume cap under section 146. Therefore, the taxpayer may not elect under section 42(b)(2)(A)(ii)(II) to have the appropriate percentage for the month the tax-exempt bonds are issued apply to the low-income housing building. However, the taxpayer may enter into a binding agreement with the state housing credit agency under section 42(b)(2)(A)(ii)(I) as to the housing credit dollar amount to be allocated to the building and may elect to have the appropriate percentage for the month of the agreement apply to the building, assuming that no previous binding agreement exists as to the housing credit dollar amount to be allocated to the building.

If, under state law, a binding agreement for a specific housing credit dollar amount becomes null and void, and the taxpayer enters into another binding agreement for a specific housing credit dollar amount, the taxpayer may elect under section 42(b)(2)(A)(ii)(I) of the Code to apply the appropriate percentage for the month of the new binding agreement, assuming no such election was made with regard to the previous binding agreement

If a taxpayer and the state housing credit agency entered into a binding agreement (which is still in effect under state law) for a specific housing credit dollar amount during calendar year 1988, the taxpayer may elect the appropriate percentage for the month in which the binding agreement was made by making an election statement in accordance with the requirements of this Notice before January 6, 1989.

If a taxpayer wishes to rely on a binding agreement or an elections statement made prior to the date of release of this Notice, the taxpayer may do so if both such agreement and election statement (or solely the election statement in the case of an election made pursuant to section 42(b)(2)(A)(ii)(II) of the Code) are modified to conform to the requirements of this Notice before January 6, 1989. Such modified agreement and election statement shall relate back to the month in which the binding agreement was originally made or the month in which tax-exempt bonds were issued, as appropriate. With respect to agreements made after December 31, 1988, and tax-exempt bonds issued after such date, the taxpayer has until the close of the 5th day after the month in which the agreement was made or the tax-exempt bonds were issued to elect to apply the appropriate percentage.

CARRYOVER OF POST-1987 LOW-INCOME HOUSING CREDIT DOLLAR AMOUNTS

Sections 1002(1)(14)(A) and 4003 of the 1988 Act amended section 42(h)(1) of the Code dealing with the allocation of housing credit dollar amounts by state housing credit agencies. Section 4003(a) provides an additional exception to the general rule in section 42(h)(1)(B) that allocations by state housing credit agencies must be made not later than the close of the taxable year in which a building is placed in service. The exception, which applies to "qualified buildings" not yet placed in service, is contained in section 42(h)(1)(E) and permits a qualified building to be placed in service in the year in which an allocation is received or in either of the 2 succeeding calendar years.

Section 42(h)(1)(E)(ii) of the Code defines a qualified building for purposes of section 42(h)(1)(E)(i) as any building that is part of a project if the taxpayer's basis in the project (as of the end of the calendar year in which the allocation is made) is more than 10 percent of the taxpayer's reasonably expected basis in the project (as of the end of the second calendar year succeeding the allocation year).

The following rules shall apply for purposes of the 10 percent basis exception in section 42(h)(1)(E) of the Code:

(1) Basis means the adjusted basis of land and depreciable real property, whether or not such amounts are includable in eligible basis; however, an allocation pursuant to section 42(h)(1)(E) of the Code is based upon items includable in eligible basis.

(2) A taxpayer has basis in land and other acquired real property when the benefits and burdens of ownership have been transferred to the taxpayer. In the case of purchased property, this transfer normally occurs at closing. For example, amounts paid to acquire an option to purchase land or a building are not includable in basis because the full benefits and burdens of ownership have not been transferred to the taxpayer; nor have the benefits and burdens of ownership been transferred merely because a nonrefundable downpayment is made.

(3) Whether a taxpayer has basis in construction costs depends upon the method of accounting used by the taxpayer. For example, the cost of construction services is included in the basis of an accrual method taxpayer when the services are performed, and in the basis of a cash method taxpayer when the bill for such services is paid.

(4) With respect to taxpayers who are members of partnerships or other flow-through entities, the accounting method of the flow-through entity shall be applied to determine whether the 10 percent exception applies.

Application of the foregoing rules may result in an answer different from that required by section 42(n) of the Code as it existed prior to the passage of the 1988 Act as interpreted by Notice 88-116. To the extent that the provisions of Notice 88-116 are inconsistent with this notice, Notice 88-116 is superseded.

Generally, an allocation is made when a state housing credit agency issues a Form 8609 to the taxpayer. However, an allocation pursuant to section 42(h)(1)(E) of the Code is an exception to this general rule. When an allocation is made pursuant to section 42(h)(1)(E), a Form 8609 is not issued by the state housing credit agency until the calendar year in which the building is placed in service. State housing credit agencies are responsible for issuing Forms 8609 to taxpayers in the calendar years that buildings are placed in service even if such years are later than the calendar years in which allocations are made pursuant to section 42(h)(1)(E). Thus, even though the state housing credit ceiling is zero for any calendar year after 1989, agencies are required to issue Forms 8609 after that date to taxpayers that received allocations pursuant to section 42(h)(1)(E) and placed buildings in service after December 31, 1989.

An allocation pursuant to section 42(h)(1)(E) of the Code reduces the state housing credit ceiling for the year in which the allocation is made, whether or not a Form 8609 is issued that year.

An allocation pursuant to section 42(h)(1)(E) of the Code is made when an allocation document containing the following information is completed:

(1) the address of the building, or if none exists, a specific description of its location;

(2) the name, address, and taxpayer identification number of the building owner receiving the allocation;

(3) the name and address of the housing credit agency;

(4) the taxpayer identification number of the agency;

(5) the date of the allocation;

(6) the housing credit dollar amount allocated to the building;

(7) the taxpayer's total reasonably expected basis in the project;

(8) the taxpayer's basis in the project as of the close of the calendar year in which the allocation is made and the percentage such basis bears to the total reasonably expected basis in the project;

(9) the expected date that the building will be placed in service; and

(10) the Building Identification Number (B.I.N.) to be assigned to the building when the building is placed in service. The B.I.N. should reflect the year the allocation is made, rather than the year the building is placed in service, unless the building is placed in service during the allocation year.

A building receiving an allocation pursuant to section 42(h)(1)(E) of the Code must be placed in service no later than the close of the second calendar year following the calendar year in which the allocation is made. If a building does not receive an allocation pursuant to section 42(h)(1)(E), the building must be placed in service by December 31, 1989, even if all or a portion of the building is financed with tax-exempt debt. Therefore, any building that is to be placed in service after December 31, 1989, must receive an allocation of credit pursuant to section 42(h)(1)(E) before the housing credit agency's authority to allocate credit expires.

When an allocation is made pursuant to section 42(h)(1)(E) of the Code, the taxpayer must retain a copy of the allocation document and file an additional copy with the Form 8609 that is issued to the taxpayer during the calendar year that the building is placed in service. Form 8609 must be filed for the first taxable year in which the credit is claimed. The agency must retain a copy of the allocation document and file the original with the agency's Form 8610, for the year an allocation is made.

If a taxpayer receives an allocation under section 42(h)(1)(E) of the Code and wishes to elect under section 42(b)(2)(A)(ii) to use the appropriate percentage for a month other than the month in which the building is placed in service, the requirements specified above for an effective election under section 42(b)(2)(A)(ii) must also be met.

This document serves as an "administrative pronouncement" as that term is described in section 1.6661-3(b)(2) of the Income Tax Regulations and may be relied upon to the same extent as a revenue ruling or revenue procedure.

The principal authors of this Notice are Donna M. Young, Christopher J. Wilson, and John J. Mattras, Jr. of the Office of Assistant Chief Counsel Passthroughs and Special Industries. For further information regarding this Notice contact one of the authors on (202) 566-4537 (not a toll-free call).

APPENDIX 14

INTERNAL REVENUE SERVICE ANNOUNCEMENT 89-3: SPECIAL STATE HOUSING CREDIT AGENCY RULES FOR 1988

Special State Housing Credit Agency Allocation Rules For 1988

Announcement 89-3

This Announcement clarifies that an allocation of 1988 low-income housing tax credits under section 42(h) of the Internal Revenue Code shall be deemed to be made by the close of the 1988 calendar year if an allocation is made during calendar year 1988 on either an old or revised copy of Form 8609, Low-Income Housing Credit Allocation Certification, that is dated prior to January 1, 1989. State housing credit agencies must, however, provide copies of the revised Form 8609 to taxpayers for use in filing with their federal income tax returns. Thus, even though the section 42(h)(1)(B) allocation requirements for calendar year 1988 may be satisfied by use of any Form 8609 that is completed on or before December 31, 1988, an allocation must be reflected on a revised Form 8609. For example, if a state housing credit agency made a timely allocation of 1988 housing credit dollar amounts using the old Form 8609, the agency must transfer the information from the old Form 8609 (including the date the old Form 8609 was completed and signed) onto the revised Form 8609 and send a copy of the revised Form 8609 to the taxpayer.

Due to the late distribution of revised Forms 8609, State housing credit agencies will have through January 31, 1989, to complete and mail the revised Form 8609 to taxpayers.

Note that when an allocation is made pursuant to section 42(h)(1)(E) of the Code, a Form 8609 is not issued by the state housing credit agency until the calendar year in which the building is placed in service. Therefore, an allocation made pursuant to section 42(h)(1)(E) shall be deemed to be made by the close of the 1988 calendar year if the allocation document that meets the requirements of Notice 89-1 is dated prior to January 1, 1989. The agency will be required to transfer the information from the allocation document (including the date the allocation document was completed and signed) onto the revised Form 8609 and send a copy of the revised Form 8609 to the taxpayer during the calendar year in which the building is placed in service.

For purposes of section 42(h)(1)(B) of the Code, allocations of housing credit dollar amounts for calendar years after calendar year 1988 will be considered timely made only if made on revised Form 8609 or in an allocation document pursuant to the requirements of Notice 89-1 by December 31 of the particular calendar year or by any alternative method of allocation to be announced by the IRS.

PROCEDURAL INFORMATION

This document serves as an "administrative pronouncement" as that term is described in section 1.6661-3(b)(2) of the Income Tax Regulations and may be relied upon to the same extent as a revenue ruling or revenue procedure.

DRAFTING INFORMATION

The principal author of this Announcement is Christopher J. Wilson of the Office of Assistant Chief Counsel (Passthroughs and Special Industries). For further information regarding this Announcement contact Mr. Wilson on (202) 566-4945 (not a toll-free call).

APPENDIX 15

INTERNAL REVENUE SERVICE NOTICE 89-6

UTILITY ALLOWANCE REQUIREMENTS, DETERMINATION OF GENERAL PUBLIC USE, AND PROVISION OF SERVICES (IRS NOTICE 89-6)*

The purpose of this Notice is to inform taxpayers that regulations under section 42 of the Internal Revenue Code of 1986 (the "Code") relating to the Low-Income Housing Tax Credit will provide that—

1. Department of Housing and Urban Development (HUD) regulated buildings shall use HUD utility allowances for purposes of section 42(g)(2) of the Code. Other housing shall use the utility rates or schedules provided for the relevant area by the applicable Public Housing Authority (PHA). Special rules apply to buildings or tenants receiving Farmers Home Administration (FmHA) housing assistance.
2. Residential rental units will be considered to be "for use by the general public" if housing is provided in a manner consistent with federal housing policy governing nondiscrimination as determined under HUD rules and regulations.
3. Any services may be provided to low-income tenants in connection with their occupancy of residential rental units. However, the cost of any services that are required to be paid by a tenant as a condition of occupancy generally must be included in gross rent for purposes of applying the gross rent limitation of section 42(g)(2) of the Code.

UTILITY ALLOWANCES.

In order to qualify as a "rent-restricted unit" within the meaning of section 42(g) of the Code, the gross rent for such unit must not exceed 30 percent of the applicable income limitation. Failure to qualify as a rent restricted unit may result in ineligibility for the section 42 credit, reduction in the amount of the credit, and/or recapture of previously allowed credits. For this purpose, gross rent includes the cost of any utilities, other than telephone. If any utilities are paid directly by the tenant, section 42(g)(2)(B)(ii) requires the inclusion in gross rent of a utility allowance determined by the Secretary, after taking into account the procedures under section 8 of the United States Housing Act of 1937.

Regulations will provide that the owner of a HUD-regulated building—a building whose rents and utility allowances are reviewed by HUD on an annual basis—must use HUD utility allowances. For other buildings occupied by one or more tenants receiving HUD rental assistance payments ("HUD tenant assistance"), an owner must use the applicable Public Housing Authority (PHA) utility allowances established for the Section 8 Existing Housing Program. A building owner must apply FmHA utility allowances to any rent-restricted unit in a building where either the building or any tenant receives FmHA housing assistance. If a building is both HUD-regulated and FmHA assisted, then FmHA utility allowances must be used. Similarly, all low-income tenants receiving HUD rental assistance are subject to FmHA utility allowances where the building or any other tenant in the building receives FmHA assistance. For example, a low-income building receiving assistance under FmHA section 515 shall use Exhibit A-5 of FmHA Instruction 1944-E (or a successor method of determining utility allowances), regardless of whether the building is HUD regulated or any low-income tenant in the building receives HUD rental assistance. These rules will apply only for the purposes of section 42(g), and will not apply to the use of utility allowances by HUD or FmHA for their own internal purposes.

Regulations will also provide that a building owner must use the applicable Public Housing Authority (PHA) utility allowance for a building where there is neither (1) HUD tenant assistance, nor (2) an applicable HUD or FmHA utility allowances. In these cases, any interested party (e.g., a low-income tenant, building owner, or state housing authority) may obtain a latter from a local utility company providing the estimated cost of that utility for each unit of similar size and construction for the geographic area in which the low-income building is located. An interested party may obtain a latter from the local utility company at any time during the building's 15-year compliance period. Costs incurred in this process must be borne by the initiating party. The interested party must furnish a copy of the letter to the owner of the building and should retain the original. If the utility estimates provided by the local utility companies differ from the utility allowances provided by the PHA, the utility company estimates shall be used in calculating the gross rent limitation. If the utility estimates provided by the local utility companies are higher for one or more rent-restricted units, the building owner must adjust the rents of any rest-restricted unit where failure to do so would result in a violation of the gross rent limitation of section 42(g)(2). Finally, if at any time during the building's 15-year compliance period the building or a low-income tenant (1) becomes subject to HUD or FmHA utility allowances, or (2) receives HUD tenant assistance, all rent-restricted units in the building become subject to the appropriate HUD, FmHA, or PHA utility allowance.

A building owner who is required to use either HUD, FmHA, or PHA utility allowances must use such allowances to compute gross rents of rent-restricted units paid more than 90 days after the date of publication of this Notice in the Internal Revenue Bulletin. These allowances shall apply throughout the building's 15-year

*From Internal Revenue Service Bulletin 1989-2, January 9, 1989.

compliance period and shall be updated at the time rents are revised. A building owner who must apply a new utility allowance during the 15-year compliance period because a building or tenant receives HUD or FmHA assistance, or because local utility company estimates become applicable, must use such new utility allowances to compute gross rents of rent-restricted units paid 90 days after the date of occupancy of the federally-assisted tenant or 90 days from the post date of the last utility company estimate. These utility allowances shall also be updated when rents are revised.

In all cases, rent paid for occupancy after the deadline for applying the correct utility allowance must reflect the correct utility allowance. If application of the correct utility allowance results in a violation of the gross rent limitation of section 42(g)(2) for any low-income tenant, then the building owner must adjust that tenant's rent to claim a credit for the unit occupied by that tenant.

GENERAL PUBLIC USE REQUIREMENT.

The legislative history of section 42 of the Code provides that "Residential rental units must be for use by the general public. . . . Residential rental units are not for use by the general public, for example, if the units are provided only for members of a social organization or provided by an employer for its employees." H.R. Conf. Rep. No. 841, 99th Cong., 2d Sess. II-95 (the "Conf. Rep."), 1986-3 (Vol. 4) C.B. 95. Regulations will provide that the term "for use by the general public" shall be determined in a manner consistent with HUD housing policy governing non-discrimination as evidenced by HUD rules and regulations. See HUD Handbook 4350.3 (or its successor). Accordingly, owners of residential rental units that give preferences to certain classes of tenants (e.g., the homeless, disabled and/or handicapped) will not violate the general public use requirement if such preferences would not violate any HUD policy governing non-discrimination expressed in the HUD handbook. However, if residential rental units are restricted to a class of residents that would violate HUD housing policy (e.g., residential rental units provided solely for members of a social organization or by an employer for its employees) then the building in which these units are located will be ineligible for the credit.

PROVISION OF SERVICES.

Regulations will provide that, solely for purposes of section 42 of the Code, the furnishing of tenants of services other than housing (whether or not such services are significant) will not prevent property from qualifying as residential rental property. Regulations will also provide that, with the exception of certain federally-assisted projects for the elderly and handicapped (see below), any charges for services that are not optional to low-income tenants must be included in gross rent for purposes of section 42(g)(2)(A). A service is optional if payment for the service is not required as a condition of occupancy. Thus, in certain circumstances, a retirement-type facility may qualify under section 42 as residential rental property, notwithstanding that significant services other than housing are furnished to tenants. However, if continual nursing medical, or psychiatric care is provided, it will be presumed that such services are mandatory. Such is generally the case with hospitals, nursing homes, sanitariums, and lifecare facilities.

For example, assume that meals and other services are provided to low-income tenants in a retirement home. Assume also that the cost of these services, when combined with rent and utility allowances, exceeds the 30 percent gross rent limitation. If any low-income tenants are required to pay for these services as a condition of occupancy, then the units occupied by these tenants are not rent-restricted units and are not included in qualified basis. However, if payment for these services is optional, then these units are rent-restricted units and are includible in qualified basis assuming that the gross rent limitation is otherwise satisfied. Where multiple services are provided, a building owner must decide which services are mandatory and included in the 30 percent gross rent limitation. All other services must be provided on an optional basis.

The cost of services must be included in the 30 percent gross rent limitation even if federal or state law requires that services be offered to tenants by project owners. A limited exception to this rule applies to existing federally-assisted projects for the elderly and handicapped that are authorized by 24 CFR 278 to provide a mandatory meals program. In these projects, mandatory meal charges will not be included in gross rent for purposes of section 42(g)(2)(A) if the provisions of 24 CFR 278 are otherwise complied with.

This document serves as an "administrative pronouncement" as that term is described in section 1.6661-3(b)(2) of the Income Tax Regulations and may be relied upon to the same extent as a revenue ruling or revenue procedure.

The principal author of this Notice is Christopher J. Wilson of the Office of Assistant Chief Counsel (Passthroughs and Special Industries). For further information regarding this Notice contact Mr. Wilson on (202) 566-4945 (not a toll-free call).

Form **8609**
(Rev. December 1988)
Department of the Treasury
Internal Revenue Service

Low-Income Housing Credit Allocation Certification

► **To be attached to return of building owner with Form 8586 (Do not file separately)**

OMB No. 1545-0988
Expires 8-31-91

Attachment Sequence No. **36**

Part I **Allocation of Credit**—To Be Completed by Housing Credit Agency

Addition to Qualified Basis ☐ Amended Form ☐

A Address of **building** (do not use P. O. box)

B Name and address of **housing credit agency**

C Name and address of **building owner** receiving allocation

D Taxpayer identification number of agency

E Building identification number (BIN)

1a	Date of allocation ► ..../..../......... **b** Housing credit dollar amount allocated	**1b**	
2	Maximum applicable credit percentage allocated	**2**	%
3	Maximum qualified basis	**3**	
4	Percentage of the aggregate basis financed by tax-exempt bonds	**4**	%

Under penalties of perjury, I declare that the allocation made is in compliance with the requirements of section 42 of the Internal Revenue Code, and that I have examined Part I of this form and to the best of my knowledge and belief, the information is true, correct, and complete.

► .... Signature of authorized official ► .... Name (please type or print) ► .... Date

Part II **First-Year Certification**—To Be Completed by Building Owner for First Year of Credit Period Only

1a	Date building placed in service ► ..../..../......... **b** Eligible basis of building (see instructions)	**1b**	
2a	Original qualified basis of the building at close of first year of credit period	**2a**	

b Is the building part of a multiple building project? ☐ Yes ☐ No

3 Check the box that describes the allocation for the building (check one only):

a ☐ Newly constructed and Federally subsidized **b** ☐ Newly constructed and **not** Federally subsidized **c** ☐ Existing building

d ☐ Sec. 42(e) rehabilitation expenditures Federally subsidized **e** ☐ Sec. 42(e) rehabilitation expenditures **not** Federally subsidized

4a If box 3a or box 3d is checked, do you elect to reduce eligible basis under section 42(i)(2)(B)? ☐ Yes ☐ No

b Do you elect to reduce eligible basis by disproportionate costs of non-low-income units (section 42(d)(3))? ☐ Yes ☐ No

5 Check the appropriate box for each election:

a Elect to begin credit period the first year after the building is placed in service (section 42 (f)(1)) ☐ Yes ☐ No

b Elect **not** to treat large partnership as taxpayer (section 42(j)(5)) ☐ Yes

c Elect minimum set-aside requirement (section 42(g)) (see instructions) ☐ 15-40 ☐ 20-50 ☐ 40-60 ☐ 25-60 (N.Y.C. only)

Note: *A separate **Schedule A (Form 8609),** Annual Statement, must be attached to Form 8609 for each year of the 15-year compliance period after 1987.*

Caution: Read the instructions under "Signature" (page 3) before signing this part.

Under penalties of perjury, I declare that: (1) the above building continues to qualify as a part of a qualified low-income housing project and meets the requirements of Internal Revenue Code section 42(g), (2) the qualified basis of the building has ►☐ /has not ►☐ decreased for this tax year, and (3) I am not claiming any relief from the passive loss rules of section 502 of the Tax Reform Act of 1986 for this property. I have examined this form and accompanying schedules, and to the best of my knowledge and belief, it is true, correct, and complete.

► .... Signature ► .... Taxpayer identification number ► .... Date

► .... Name (please type or print)

For Paperwork Reduction Act Notice, see instructions.

Paperwork Reduction Act Notice

We ask for this information to carry out the Internal Revenue laws of the United States. We need it to ensure that taxpayers are complying with these laws and to allow us to figure and collect the right amount of tax. You are required to give us this information.

The time needed to complete and file the following forms will vary depending on individual circumstances. The estimated average times are:

Form	Recordkeeping	Learning about the law or the form	Preparing and sending the form to IRS
8609	7 hrs., 25 min.	1 hr., 59 min.	2 hrs., 11 min.
Sch. A (8609)	3 hrs., 21 min.	42 min.	47 min.

If you have comments concerning the accuracy of these time estimates or suggestions for making these forms more simple, we would be happy to hear from you. You can write to the Internal Revenue Service or the Office of Management and Budget at the addresses listed in the instructions for the tax return with which this form is filed.

General Instructions

(Section references are to the Internal Revenue Code unless otherwise noted.)

Purpose of Form.—Sections 38 and 42 allow owners of residential low-income rental buildings to claim a low-income housing credit for each qualified building over a 10-year credit period. Form 8609 is used to obtain a housing credit allocation from the housing credit agency. Form 8609 and related Schedule A (Form 8609), Annual Statement, are also used to certify certain necessary information under section 42.

Section 502(a) of the Tax Reform Act of 1986 provides transitional relief from the passive loss rules for qualified investors in a qualified low-income housing project. However, if any person has been allowed any benefit under section 502(a) for the project, the low-income housing credit is not allowed for the project.

Housing Credit Agency.—"Housing Credit Agency" means any state or local agency authorized under section 42 to make low-income housing credit allocations within its jurisdiction.

Owner of Building.—Owners must complete Part II of this form and a separate Schedule A (Form 8609), even if an allocation of credit by a housing credit agency is not required, and attach both the form and the schedule to their income tax return. If an allocation is not required, the owner should enter in Part I the address of the building and the name and address of the building owner, and complete Part I, line 4. Once completed, the form must be sent to the housing credit agency so a BIN can be assigned to the building. See specific instructions before completing these parts.

Building Identification Number (BIN).—This number will be assigned by the housing credit agency when a credit allocation is made. Some buildings may have received an allocation before the numbering system was in place. In that case, a number will be assigned to each building retroactively. If this is the case with a building you own, begin associating a number with the building when a number is assigned.

If the building did not require an allocation from the housing credit agency because it was 70% or more financed by certain tax-exempt bonds, you will still need to obtain a BIN from the agency. See **Owner of Building,** above.

Rehabilitation expenditures treated as a separate new building under section 42(e) should not have a separate BIN if the building already has one. Use the number assigned to the building.

Allocation of Credit.—In order for an owner to claim a low-income housing credit on a building, the housing credit agency must make an allocation of the credit by the close of the calendar year in which the building is placed in service, unless—

- the allocation is the result of an advance binding commitment by the credit agency made not later than the close of the calendar year in which the building is placed in service (see section 42(h)(1)(C));
- the allocation relates to an increase in qualified basis (see section 42(h)(1)(D)); or
- the allocation relates to a carryover of post-1987 low-income housing credit dollar amounts (see section 42(h)(1)(E) and Notice 89-1, I.R.B. 1989-2, dated January 9, 1989).

The agency can only make an allocation to a building located within its geographical jurisdiction. Once an allocation is made, it is good for the first tax year the credit is allowable and for all future years during the 10-year credit period. A separate Form 8609 must be completed for each building to which an allocation of credit is made.

Tax-Exempt Bonds.—No housing credit allocation is required for any portion of the eligible basis of a qualified low-income building that is financed with tax-exempt bonds taken into account for purposes of the volume cap under section 146. No allocation at all is required to claim the credit if 70 percent or more of the aggregate basis of the building and the land on which the building is located is financed with such tax-exempt bonds and the building is placed in service by December 31, 1989. However, if a building is 70% or more financed with certain tax-exempt bonds and the building is to be placed in service after December 31, 1989, such building must receive an allocation of credit pursuant to section 42(h)(1)(E) before the housing credit agency's authority to allocate credit expires. "Aggregate basis" means the sum of the eligible basis of the qualified low-income building and land on which the building is located. "Land on which the building is located" includes only land that is functionally related and subordinate to the qualified low-income building (see Regulations section 1.103-8(b)(4)(iii) for the meaning of "functionally related and subordinate").

When To File.—Housing credit agencies should forward a copy of Form 8609 (Part I completed only) with instructions to the owner of the building. The housing credit agency must retain the original to send to the IRS with its annual report, **Form 8610,** Annual Low-Income Housing Credit Agencies Report.

Owners must attach completed Forms 8609 and accompanying Schedules A (Form 8609) to **Form 8586,** Low-Income Housing Credit, and file these forms with their income tax return by the due date of the return. (Do not attach Form 8609 or Schedule A (Form 8609) to Form 8586 if the credit claimed on Form 8586 is a flow-through credit from a partnership, S corporation, estate or trust because that entity will complete those forms and attach them to its return.

Recordkeeping Requirements.—To verify changes in qualified basis from year to year you must keep a copy of this Form 8609 together with all accompanying Schedule(s) A, Forms 8586, 8611, and 8693 for three years after the fifteen-year compliance period ends (unless this recordkeeping requirement is otherwise extended).

Specific Instructions

Part I—Allocation of Credit

Completed by Housing Credit Agency

Check the "Addition to Qualified Basis" box if an allocation relates to an increase in qualified basis under section 42(f)(3).

Line 1a.—Generally, the date of allocation is the date the Form 8609 is issued. However, if an allocation is made pursuant to section 42(h)(1)(E), the date of allocation is the date specified in the document used by the housing credit agency to make the allocation.

Line 1b.—Enter the housing credit dollar amount allocated to the building for each year of the 10-year credit period. If there is a change in the amount of initial allocation before the close of the calendar year, file an amended Form 8609 to be used in place of the original form and check the Amended Form box at the top of Form 8609.

Line 2.—Enter the maximum applicable credit percentage allocated to the building for the month the building was placed in service or, if applicable, for the month determined under section 42(b)(2)(A)(ii).

If an election is made under section 42(b)(2)(A)(ii) to use the applicable percentage for a month other than the month in which a building is placed in service, the requirements set forth in Notice 89-1 must be met. The agency must retain a copy of the binding agreement and the election statement and file the original with the agency's Form 8610 for the year the allocation is actually made. The maximum applicable credit percentage is published monthly by the IRS in the revenue ruling that deals with applicable Federal interest rates. For new buildings that are not federally subsidized under section 42(i)(2)(A) when placed in service, use the applicable percentage for the 70% present value credit; for new buildings that are federal subsidized when placed in service, or existing buildings, use the applicable percentage for the 30% present value credit. A taxpayer may elect under section 42(i)(2)(B) to reduce eligible basis by the principal amount of any outstanding below-market federal loan or the proceeds of any tax-exempt obligation in order to obtain the higher credit percentage (see Part II, line 4a).

For allocations to buildings covering an addition to qualified basis, do not reduce the maximum applicable credit percentage even though the building owner may only claim a credit based on 2/3 of the credit percentage allocated to the building.

Line 3.—Enter the maximum qualified basis of the building. To figure this, multiply the eligible basis of the qualified low-income building by the lesser of:

(1) the percentage of low-income units to all residential rental units (the "unit percentage"), or

(2) the percentage of floor space of the low-income units to the floor space of all residential rental units (the "floor-space percentage").

The **eligible basis** for new buildings is generally the cost of construction. For existing buildings, the eligible basis is the acquisition cost plus capital improvements (see the instructions for Part II, line 1b, and section 42(d)).

Line 4.—Enter the percentage of the aggregate basis of the building financed by certain tax-exempt bonds. If this amount is zero, enter zero (do not leave this line blank).

Part II—First-Year Certification

Completed by Building Owner for the First Year of Credit Period Only

Line 1a.—For purposes of section 42, the placed in service date for a residential rental building is the date on which the first unit in the building is ready and available for occupancy in accordance with state or local law. Rehabilitation expenditures treated as a separate new building under section 42(e)(4)(A) are placed in service at the close of any 24-month period over which such expenditures are aggregated, whether or not the building is occupied during the rehabilitation period.

Line 1b.—Enter the eligible basis (in dollar terms) of the building, figured as of the date the building is placed in service. In cases where a building is placed in service in portions, determine eligible basis at the close of the first year of the credit period (see sections 42(f)(1) and 42(g)(3)(B)(iii) for determining the start of the credit period).

You may elect to reduce eligible basis by the principal amount of any outstanding below-market federal loan or the proceeds of any tax-exempt obligation to obtain a higher credit percentage. If you make this election, check the "Yes" box in Part II, line 4a, and reduce eligible basis by the principal amount of such loan or obligation proceeds before entering the amount on line 1b. In addition, you must reduce the eligible basis by the amount of any Federal grant received.

Eligible basis must also be reduced by the entire basis allocable to non-low-income units that are above the average quality standard of the low-income units in the building. You may, however, include a portion of the basis of these non-low-income units if the cost of any of these units: (1) does not exceed by more than 15% the average cost of all low-income units in the building, and (2) you elect by checking the "Yes" box for line 4b to exclude this excess cost from eligible basis.

Finally, eligible basis may not include any portion of a building's adjusted basis for which an election is made under section 167(k).

Line 2a.—Multiply the eligible basis of the building shown on line 1b by the lesser of the unit percentage or the floor space percentage as of the close of the first year of the credit period. See the instructions for Part I, line 3, above.

Line 2b.—Check the appropriate box in line 2b to indicate whether or not the building for which basis is entered on line 2a is part of a multiple-building project. A multiple building project is a project that includes more than one qualified low-income building that must: (1) be located on the same tract of land, (2) be owned by the same person for Federal income tax purposes, (3) be financed pursuant to a common plan of financing, and (4) have similarly constructed housing units. A qualified low-income building includes residential rental property that is either an apartment building, a single family dwelling, a townhouse, a rowhouse, a duplex, or a condominium. Taxpayers electing under section 42(g)(3)(B) to aggregate buildings to satisfy the minimum set-aside requirement elected for the project under section 42(g)(1) must check the Yes box.

Line 3.—A new building is treated as Federally subsidized for any tax year if at any time during the tax year or any prior tax year there is or was outstanding any tax-exempt bond financing or any below market Federal loan, the proceeds of which are or were used (directly or indirectly) for the building or its operation.

Line 4a.—Section 42(i)(2)(B) allows an owner to elect to reduce the eligible basis by the principal amount of any outstanding below-market federal loan or the proceeds of any tax-exempt obligation and claim the 70-percent present value credit on the remaining eligible basis. However, if such an election is made, the taxpayer may not claim the 30-percent present value credit on the portion of the basis that was financed with the below-market Federal loan or the tax-exempt obligation.

Line 4b.—See the instructions for Part II, line 1b, above.

Line 5.—

(a) Section 42(f)(1) allows an owner of a building to elect to begin the credit period in the tax year after the building is placed in service.

Note: *Section 42(g)(3)(B)(iii) provides special rules for determining the start of the credit period for certain multiple building projects.*

(b) Section 42(j)(5) as amended by the Technical and Miscellaneous Revenue Act of 1988, requires partnerships with 35 or more partners to be treated as the taxpayer for purposes of recapture unless an election is made not to treat the partnership as the taxpayer. Check the "Yes" box if you do not want the partnership to be treated as the taxpayer for purposes of recapture.

(c) The owner of a qualified low-income housing project must meet the requirements under section 42(g) by electing one of the following tests: (1) 15-40 Test: 15 percent or more of the residential units in the project must be both rent restricted and occupied by individuals whose income is 40 percent or less of the area median gross income (see also section 142(d)(4)(B)), (2) 20-50 Test: 20 percent or more of the residential units in the project must be both rent restricted and occupied by individuals whose income is 50 percent or less of the area median gross income, or (3) 40-60 Test: 40 percent or more of the residential units in the project must be both rent restricted and occupied by individuals whose income is 60 percent or less of the area median gross income.

Check the appropriate box for the test you wish to elect.

Note: *Owners of buildings in projects located in New York City may not use the 40-60 test. Instead, they may use a 25-60 test: 25 percent or more of the residential units in the project must be both rent restricted and occupied by individuals whose income is 60 percent or less of the area median gross income (see also section 142(d)(6)).*

Once made, the elections under sections 42(f)(1), 42(j)(5), and 42(g) are irrevocable.

Signature.—Form 8609 must be attached to your income tax return each year during the compliance period beginning with the first year the credit is claimed. Because Form 8609 requires an original signature each year and the form is not issued annually by the housing credit agency, complete the following steps after you receive the form from the agency:

(1) Complete Part II of the form (do not sign it).

(2) After completing Part II, make a copy of the form.

(3) **SIGN THE COPY,** and keep the original copy you receive from the housing credit agency so that copies can be made from the unsigned original copy and used for filing with your future years' income tax returns.

(4) Complete separate Schedule A (Form 8609) for each building and attach it to the signed copy of Form 8609 which you attach to your income tax return. See the instructions for Schedule A for details on completing Schedule A. You can get Schedule A from most I.R.S. offices.

(5) If the maximum applicable credit percentage allocated to the building in Part I, line 2, reflects an election made under section 42(b)(2)(A)(ii), the taxpayer must attach a copy of the election statement and, if the binding agreement specifying the housing credit dollar amount is contained in a separate document, a copy of the binding agreement to Form 8609 for the first tax year in which the credit is claimed. (See Notice 89-1.)

(6) If the housing credit dollar amount allocated in Part I, line 1b, reflects an allocation made pursuant to section 42(h)(1)(E), the taxpayer must attach a copy of the allocation document to Form 8609 for the first tax year in which the credit is claimed. (See Notice 89-1.)

☆U.S. Government Printing Office: 1988-242-473/80037

Form **8586** | **Low-Income Housing Credit** | OMB No. 1545-0984 **1987**

Department of the Treasury Internal Revenue Service | ▶ **Attach to your tax return** | Attachment Sequence No. **78**

Name(s) as shown on return | Identifying number

Part I Low-Income Housing Credit

			Building A	Building B	Total (A + B)
1	Date building was placed in service (MO-YR)	1			
2	Eligible basis of building—See instructions	2			
3	Low-income portion (lesser of unit percentage or floor-space percentage—see instructions)	3			
4	Qualified basis of low-income building (multiply line 2 by line 3)	4			
5	Credit percentage—See instructions	5			
6	Multiply line 4 by line 5	6			

7 Flow-through housing credits from other entities

If you are a—	Then enter total of current year housing credit(s) from—
a Shareholder	Schedule K-1 (Form 1120S), line 11b
b Partner	Schedule K-1 (Form 1065), line 12b
c Beneficiary	Schedule K-1 (Form 1041), line 9
d Patron	Appropriate form

. . . . 7

8 Current year credit—Add line 6 (third column) and line 7 8

Note: *If you have a 1987 investment credit (Form 3468), jobs credit (Form 5884), credit for alcohol used as fuel (Form 6478), or research credit (Form 6765) in addition to your 1987 low-income housing credit, or if you have a carryback or carryforward of any general business credit, stop here and go to Form 3800,* ***General Business Credit,*** *to claim your 1987 low-income housing credit. If you have only a low-income housing credit, you may continue with lines 9 through 16 to claim your credit.*

Part II Tax Liability Limitations

9a	Individuals—From Form 1040, enter amount from line 43	
b	Corporations—From Form 1120, Schedule J, enter tax from line 3 (or Form 1120-A, Part I, line 1)	9
c	Other filers—Enter income tax before credits from return	
10a	Individuals—From Form 1040, enter credit from line 44, plus any orphan drug and nonconventional source fuel credits included on line 46	
b	Corporations—From Form 1120, Schedule J, enter credits from lines 4(a) through 4(d) (Form 1120-A filers, enter zero)	10
c	Other filers—See instructions for line 10c	
11	Income tax liability as adjusted (subtract line 10 from line 9)	11
12	Tentative minimum tax—	
a	Individuals—From Form 6251, enter amount from line 17	
b	Corporations—From Form 4626, enter amount from line 19	12
c	Estates and Trusts—From Form 8656, enter amount from line 20	
13	Excess of income tax liability over tentative minimum tax—Subtract line 12 from line 11	13
14a	Enter smaller of line 11 or $25,000 (see instructions for line 14)	14a
b	If line 11 is more than $25,000—Enter 75% of the excess	14b
15	Add lines 14a and 14b	15
16	Total allowed credit—Enter smallest of line 8, line 13, or line 15. This is your **General Business Credit** for 1987. Enter here and on Form 1040, line 45; Form 1120, Schedule J, line 4(e); Form 1120-A, Part I, line 2; or the proper line of other returns	16

Paperwork Reduction Act Notice.—We ask for this information to carry out the Internal Revenue laws of the United States. We need it to ensure that taxpayers are complying with these laws and to allow us to figure and collect the right amount of tax. You are required to give us this information.

Changes You Should Note.—The Tax Reform Act of 1986 changed the alternative minimum tax rules for the general business credits. This will require an additional computation on lines 12 and 13.

If you have credits from passive activities, see **Form 8582-CR,** Passive Activity Credit Limitations, before completing Form 8586.

Caution: *Legislation pending at the time this form was printed would affect several areas of the housing credit. It includes provisions that:*

(1) prohibit carryback of the credit to years ending before 1-1-87;

(2) clarify when a building in a multiple building project is considered to be part of a qualified low-income housing project;

(3) permit some of the basis of housing units whose cost is disproportionate to that of the low-income units to be included in eligible basis;

(4) permit an owner to obtain an advance binding commitment for a credit allocation for a later year.

General Instructions

(Section references are to the Internal Revenue Code, unless otherwise noted.)

General Business Credit.—The general business credit consists of the investment credit, jobs credit, credit for alcohol used as fuel, research credit, and low-income housing credit. If you have more than one of these credits for 1987 or a carryback or carryforward of any of these credits, attach the appropriate credit forms and summarize them on **Form 3800,** General Business Credit. If you have only a 1987 low-income housing credit, you do not have to file Form 3800 this year.

Partnerships, S corporations, estates and trusts.—Complete Part I to figure the credit to pass through to the partners, shareholders, or beneficiaries. Attach the Form 8586 to the income tax return.

Purpose of Form.—Owners of residential rental projects providing low-income housing should use Form 8586 to claim the low-income housing credit.

Caution: *You cannot claim the credit on any project for which any person was allowed relief from the passive loss rules under section 502 of the Tax Reform Act of 1986.*

Introduction

The Tax Reform Act of 1986 provides a credit of 70% of the qualified basis of each new low-income building placed in service after 1986 (30% in the case of certain Federally subsidized new buildings or certain existing buildings purchased and placed in service). This credit is taken over a 10-year period so that the present value of the 10 annual credit amounts at the beginning of the credit period equals 70% (or 30%) of the qualified basis.

You may elect to begin the 10-year credit period in the tax year **after** the year the building was placed in service. Use **Form 8609**, Low-Income Housing Credit Allocation Certification, to make this election.

Qualified low-income housing project.—The low-income housing credit can only be claimed for residential rental projects that meet the requirements of one of the following tests:

(A) 20-50 Test: 20 percent or more of the residential units in the project must be both rent restricted and occupied by individuals whose income is 50 percent or less of the area median gross income, or

(B) 40-60 Test: 40 percent or more of the residential units in the project must be both rent restricted and occupied by individuals whose income is 60 percent or less of the area median gross income.

A unit is "rent restricted" if the gross rent does not exceed 30 percent of the income limitation in (A) or (B) above for the individuals occupying the unit. You may choose to meet either test for the project, but once made, the election is irrevocable. Use Form 8609 to make this election. See section 42(g) for more details.

You must obtain a completed Form 8609 from the state or local credit agency for each building to cover the amount of the credit you wish to claim. A copy of Form 8609 must be attached to your return for each building for each year. For calendar-year 1987 filers the allocation *must* be made by December 31, 1987. For FY 1987-88 filers the allocation must be made by the earlier of: (1) 60 days after the close of your tax year, or (2) December 31, 1988.

You may not take a low-income housing credit on a building if it has not received an allocation. Similarly, no credit will be allowed in excess of the amount allocated to the building by the housing credit agency. See section 42(h). An allocation is not needed to the extent that a building is financed with certain tax-exempt bonds. If 70% or more of a building is financed with tax-exempt bonds, no allocation is needed from the agency (but you must still complete the appropriate parts of Form 8609 and attach it to your return).

Certification of first-year credit. You must certify certain first-year information to the IRS on Form 8609. If you fail to file this certification, you may not claim a credit for that building for any year ending before the certification is made.

Recapture of credit. There is a 15-year compliance period during which the rental project must continue to meet certain requirements. If, as of the close of any tax year in this period, there is a reduction of the qualified basis from the previous year, you may have to recapture all or a part of the credit you have taken. Use **Form 8611,** Recapture of Low-Income Housing Credit. See section 42(j).

Specific Instructions

Lines 1 through 6.—If you have more than two buildings, attach a schedule and enter the totals in the third column.

Line 1.—Please make sure this date agrees with the date shown on the attached Form 8609 for that building.

Line 2. Eligible Basis.—Generally, the eligible basis of a building for its entire 15-year compliance period is figured as of the date it is placed in service. For housing projects consisting of two or more buildings, figure the credit separately for each building.

For new buildings the eligible basis is generally the cost of construction.

For existing buildings the eligible basis is the cost of acquisition plus any rehabilitation expenditures incurred before the close of the first tax year of the credit period. The building must have been acquired by purchase from an unrelated person and there must have been at least 10 years since the building was last placed in service or substantially improved.

Rehabilitation expenditures that are not Federally subsidized may be treated as a separate new building eligible for the 9% credit if the expenditures incurred during any 24-month period average $2,000 or more per low-income unit in a building. If such rehabilitation expenditures are Federally subsidized they may be treated as a separate new building eligible for the 4% credit. The expenditures will be treated as placed in service at the close of the 24-month period. See section 42(e).

When figuring the eligible basis of a new or existing building, do not include the cost of land. Furthermore, you must reduce the basis by the amount of any Federal grants received and by any basis allocable to non-low-income units that are above the average quality standard of the low-income units in the building.

Residential rental property may qualify for the credit even though part of the building in which the residential units are located is used for commercial use. To figure the eligible basis of such property, do not include the cost of the nonresidential rental property. You may generally include the basis of common areas or tenant facilities, such as swimming pools or parking areas. See section 42(d).

Line 3. Low-Income Portion.—Only the portion of the basis on line 2 attributable to the low-income rental units qualifies for the credit. This is the lesser of: (1) the percentage of low-income units to all residential rental units (the "unit percentage"), or (2) the percentage of floor space of the low-income units to the floor space of all residential rental units (the "floor-space percentage"). Low-income units are those units presently occupied by qualifying tenants, while residential rental units are all units, whether or not occupied.

For the first year of the credit period you must use a modified percentage on line 3 to reflect the average portion of a 12-month period that the units in a building were occupied by low-income individuals. Find the low-income portion of each building (the lesser of the unit percentage or the floor-space percentage) as of the end of each full month that the building was in service during the year. Add these percentages together and divide by 12. Enter the result on line 3. For example, if a building was in service for the last three months of your tax year, and was half occupied as of the end of each of those three months, then you would enter .125 ([.5 + .5 + .5] ÷ 12) on line 3. This first year adjustment does not affect the amount of qualified basis on which the credit is claimed in the remaining nine years of the credit period, and the amount of the reduction may be claimed in the eleventh year.

Line 4. Qualified Basis of Low-Income Building.—This is the portion of the qualified low-income building attributable to the low-income rental units.

At-risk limitation for individuals and closely held corporations. The basis of property may be limited if you borrowed against the property and are protected against loss, or if you borrowed money from a person who has other than a creditor interest in the property. See section 42(k).

Line 5. Credit Percentage.—This is generally 9% (.09) or 4% (.04) for buildings placed in service during 1987. However, this percentage may be limited if you did not receive an allocation from the housing credit agency for the full amount of the credit.

If the agency has made an allocation on Form 8609, enter on line 5 of Form 8586 the credit percentage shown on Form(s) 8609, Part I, line 3.

If an allocation is not required to be made by an agency, enter on line 5 of Form 8586 the applicable percentage as follows:

Newly constructed buildings not Federally subsidized	9%
Rehabilitation expenditures treated as separate new building	9%
Newly constructed buildings that are Federally subsidized	4%
Existing buildings	4%

For buildings placed in service after 12/31/87 the credit percentage will be adjusted monthly to reflect the present value at the time the building is placed in service. See the revenue ruling published monthly by the IRS that deals with applicable Federal interest rates.

Line 7.—If you have flow-through credit(s) from a partnership, S corporation, cooperative, estate, or trust, add them up and enter the total on line 7.

Line 10c. Other Filers.—Before you can claim the low-income housing credit against your tax liability, you must first reduce this tax liability by the following credits:

- Personal credits.
- Foreign tax credit.
- Possessions corporation tax credit.
- Orphan drug credit.
- Nonconventional source fuel credit.

Line 14. Limitation.—See section 38(c)(4) for special rules for married couples filing separate returns, for controlled corporate groups, and for estates and trusts.

Carrybacks and carryforwards.—If you cannot use part or all of the credit because of the tax liability limitations, you may carry the excess to other years. Use Form 3800.

★U.S. Government Printing Office: 1987—506-582

APPENDIX 17

Executive Summary

Mitchell-Danforth Task Force On the Low-Income Housing Tax Credit

Members
Elizabeth Mitchell, Chairman
Leopold Adler II
William C. Apgar, Jr., Phd.
Patrick Barbolla
Herbert Collins
Terrence Duvernay
Wesley Finch
Paul S. Grogan
F. Barton Harvey III
Charles A. Henderson
A. Bruce Rozet
Peter W. Salsich, Jr.
Barry Zigas

The members of the Task Force are pleased to present to Senator George J. Mitchell (D-ME) and Senator John C. Danforth (R-MO) this report on the Low-Income Housing Tax Credit (the Credit). The Senators gave the Task Force a mandate to:

1) review the current progress of the Credit;
2) define the appropriate role of the Credit in the overall housing policy framework; and,
3) propose improvements needed to create an optimum program.

At the request of the Senators, the Task Force undertook a detailed assessment of this program, meeting on six occasions. The Task Force reviewed the progress made in implementing the program, from the perspective of the development community, tenants, and the administering states.

Created in the Tax Reform Act of 1986, the Credit provides an incentive for investors to own low-income housing. A 10 year tax credit is available for each unit set-aside for low-income use as long as a specific proportion of units in a building or project are occupied by eligible households. The rents charged on the set-aside units are restricted and the units must be occupied by eligible households for 15 years.

An assessment of the Credit by the Task Force is timely, as it coincides with on-going Congressional consideration of a new national housing policy. No true "national housing policy" exists today as a framework within which the Credit can be placed. Yet this problem does not diminish the role the Credit now plays, or its potential in an emerging national policy framework.

A number of recent studies have addressed the need for a re-invigorated national housing policy and have made recommendations to Congress on program improvements. A concept paper released in 1988 by the Senate Subcommittee on Housing and Urban Affairs cites a role for the Credit in stimulating the production and rehabilitation of low-income rental housing. The Task Force hopes that the improvements to the program herein recommended, along with a permanent extension of the program beyond its current expiration on December 31, 1989, will be incorporated within the current national housing policy formulation.

An optimum Credit program is important today given the increasing housing problems facing the nation. With evidence of housing problems ranging from declining homeownership to growing homelessness, the notion that Americans are universally well housed is being shaken. Real difficulties face low-income families and individuals who must find housing from a rental stock that is frequently unaffordable. Moreover, only a quarter of those in poverty and eligible for public assistance that would enable them to afford standard housing are now receiving it. This situation compels continuation of the Credit and approval of improvements needed to increase its impact.

Since created in 1986, the Credit has emerged as the primary tax incentive for stimulating low-income housing production and rehabilitation. State agencies who are charged with allocating the Credit from an annual state allocation have witnessed the use of the Credit grow from 19 percent of the allocation available in 1987 to an estimated 60 to 70 percent of that available in the year just ending. Prospects for 1989 are for continued growth in the use of this resource, especially with the improvements to the program made by Congress in the Technical and Miscellaneous Revenue Act of 1987.

The Credit has an important role to play in a re-invigorated national housing policy in the years ahead. In order to fulfill this role and to build upon the foundation of growing success which the program has exhibited during the past two years, the Credit must: be in such demand as to fully use the volume allocated; achieve an extended duration of low-income use; work efficiently with tax-exempt bonds and other subsidies; be responsive to the development process; be viable in all types of markets; and meet the most critical housing needs of the State.

Findings of the Task Force

The Task Force concurs with the current unit set-aside requirements and tenant income limits. Credits should continue to be awarded only to eligible units and for a minimum 15 years compliance period. This 15 year compliance period should be extended where possible. The Task Force recognizes that the Credit alone cannot ensure project feasibility, except under special market conditions and circumstances.

The States play a valuable role in administering the program, but increased flexibility is needed in allocating Credits to a project so that only the amount of Credit needed to ensure viability is received.

The Task Force believes that no unnecessary obstacles should hinder project sponsors from including a mix of low-income and market rate tenants in a project as long as the minimum set-aside for low-income households is honored.

After frequent changes in the tax treatment of low-income housing in recent years, statutory stability is needed to encourage developer and investor participation. Moreover, the full set of regulations should be implemented promptly.

Finally, the Task Force recognizes that the Credit can be helpful in addressing the preservation of the Federally assisted low-income inventory. However, it would be inappropriate to rely solely or substantially on the Credit for this purpose.

Recommendations of the Task Force

First and foremost, the Credit should be made permanent.

A. Affecting the Duration of Low-Income Use

A.1 To encourage extended low-income occupancy, the Task Force recommends that:

- during the initial 15 years, a regulatory agreement ensure low- income use, but within that period, investors may dispose of their ownership interest only to a new owner(s) who "steps into their shoes" for compliance purposes,
- owners may sell the project at market value at any time after 15 years as long as low-income compliance continues for whatever time remains in the period beginning at the end of the initial 15-year period and extending for 15 additional years,
- if unable to transfer for market value, the owner may notify the State Credit allocating agency and sell the project at original gross equity amount with consideration for outstanding debt as long as low-income compliance continues for whatever time remains in the period beginning at the end of the initial 15-year period and extending for 15 additional years, and
- if no purchaser is willing to pay either market value or the original gross equity, the owner(s) may sell the property for highest and best use.

A.2. To facilitate below-market purchase options to non-profits, such options should be allowed at the time of development and owners transferring to non-profits or tenant cooperatives at year 15 should be relieved of tax liability on transfer.

B. Affecting the Types of Projects Eligible

B.1. To limit Credit use with acquisitions, the Task Force recommends that no acquisition credit be allowed unless substantial rehabilitation also occurs.

B.2. "General Public Use", "Significant Services", and "Transient Use" should be redefined such that:

- the term "general public use" is synonymous with compliance with federal fair housing laws
- low-income units in owner-occupied quadruplexes, triplexes, and duplexes should be eligible for the Credit,
- the reference to "significant services" should be eliminated and medical facilities made specifically ineligible, while projects in which non-medical services are provided should qualify for the Credit if the cost of these services is separable from debt service and operating costs, and
- Single Room Occupancy units involving transient use should qualify for

the Credit if rent and income requirements are met.

B.3. The Ten Year Holding Period rule should be amended:

- to allow a waiver if HUD or the allocating agency certifies that the sale would prevent a default or conversion to market rate use,
- to remove through rehabilitation a health or safety threat,
- to prevent default of Federally assisted housing to a State housing agency, and
- to prevent default on housing on which the mortgage originates from the Federal government or is Federally insured or guaranteed, but which receives no Federal assistance (as defined under IRC §42),

In addition, an exception to the 10 year limitation should be allowed for units which were formerly owner-occupied.

C. Affecting the Application of the Credit to a Project

C.1. To facilitate optimum use of the Credit and ensure an appropriate Credit based subsidy for each project, the Task Force recommends greater discretion in setting the Credit Rate, such that:

- a Credit of up to 70 percent present value may be used for new construction or substantial rehabilitation,
- a Credit of up to 30 percent present value may be used for the acquisition portion of projects involving both acquisition and rehabilitation,
- a Credit of up to 100 percent present value may be used to achieve deeper targeting, make the program viable in high cost areas, target distressed low-income communities, or achieve specific goals set forth in the annual state plan approved by the Governor,

Further, no reduction in the Credit rate should be required where other public subsidies are used, including tax-exempt bonds.

C.2 To encourage the greatest use of the Credit to meet state housing needs, the State allocating agency should be required to devise public allocation plans and administrative guidelines governing use of the Credit and establish a process for analyzing each project to establish the amount of Credit it would receive.

C.3. To limit the "soft" costs associated with the Credit, the Task Force encourages allocating agencies to work with for-profit and non-profit developers and investors to establish industry standards of reasonableness for "soft" costs for use in allocating the appropriate amount of Credit to a project .

C.4. To bring the allocation of the Credit into conformity with standard real estate practice, the Task Force recommends that the IRC §42 should clearly state that allocations and compliance are based on projects rather than buildings. In addition, units located on scattered sites which are commonly owned and financed should be treated as a project.

C.5. To clarify an important point of action in the allocation process, the IRC § 42 should clearly define "Placed-in-Service" and ensure that all eligible costs associated with a project, including those expenditures properly charged to the capital account of a project that are incurred by the end of the first year of the Credit period may be included in basis.

D. Affecting Marketing Limitations to Investors Using the Credit and Financings

D.1. To expand the pool of individual investors in the Credit, the Task Force recommends that taxpayers using the Credit may reduce their tax liability up to $20,000, plus 20 percent of the liability over that amount.

D.2. To remove a major restriction on non-profit debt, the Task Force recommends that the 15 year repayment requirement on non-profit debt be removed and that below-market loans by qualified non-profits should not be recast by discounting to present value the debt service payment in order to isolate the cost of interest reduction for tax purposes.

D.3 To remove unnecessary impediments to transfers of ownership, the recapture of the Credit on sale of interest should be amended to permit individual investors in a partnership to sell their interest if no more than 50 percent of the interest in the partnership is sold within a one year period.

D.4. To ensure equity participation by financial institutions, no changes in federal regulations should inhibit banks and other financial institutions from making equity investment in real estate, including Credit projects.

D.5. To increase the availability of debt financing for Credit Projects, Fannie Mae should be encouraged to provide a market for Credit related debt financings. The Federal Reserve should also use its educational and information capacity to increase bank participation.

E. Affecting Project Feasibility and Management

E.1. To reduce financial uncertainty and risk, the Task Force recommends that the method for determining rents be revised so that rents charged on a unit are based on the number of bedrooms. A range of household sizes per unit based on the number of bedrooms should be established as a basis for setting the allowable rent. The allowable rent could not exceed 30 percent of the mean of the household sizes allowed in a given sized unit.

E.2. To remove a threat to the financial viability of a project should area median incomes decline, a rent floor based on the initial rents charged and below which rents cannot drop is recommended.

F. Affecting Program Administration

F.1. To ensure full use of available Credit authority, the Task Force recommends that States be allowed to carry-forward any unused State allocation for one year, with any Credit that is not used at the end of the carry-forward year going to a national pool for re-allocation.

F.2. To facilitate developer involvement, the Task Force recommends that the project carry-over created in the Technical and Miscellaneous Revenue Act of 1988 be made permanent and that this provision be extended to tax-exempt bond financed projects.

For the full report and further information contact:
NATIONAL COUNCIL OF STATE HOUSING AGENCIES
444 North Capitol Street N.W., Suite 118
Washington, DC 20001
(202) 624-7710

ABOUT THE AUTHOR

JOSEPH GUGGENHEIM is a housing and development consultant in Washington, D.C. Active in the field since 1965, he has been in a leadership role for most of that time.

As a consultant, he has designed and implemented financing strategies and carried out development of government-assisted housing for private property owners and non-profit sponsors. He also has done policy studies, research, and program design work for local government and national and local non-profit organizations.

He has worked in the public and in the for-profit and non-profit private sectors. In an appointed position at HUD, he played an instrumental role in many of the new federal initiatives in housing and urban development from 1977 to 1981. As Housing and Community Development Director for the city of Camden, New Jersey, he stimulated revitalization projects, developed new funding sources, and revamped existing programs.

Earlier, he pioneered housing advocacy efforts at the state and regional level in Detroit, Michigan, resulting in major state legislation and in changes in housing policy affecting Detroit's suburbs. He has spoken before numerous conferences, college groups, public bodies, and organizations in many parts of the country.

His work has resulted in awards and honors from a number of civic and professional organizations. A recent full-scale development effort won an award of merit from the Association of Local Housing Finance Agencies.

He has been retained as a consultant to provide advice and assistance on low income housing development and use of the tax credit to a variety of developers, attorneys, accountants, lenders, non-profit organizations, and government agencies in 25 states and the District of Columbia.

He has lectured and conducted training on the low income housing tax credit at a variety of conferences and seminars in a number of cities across the country.

He is also active in carrying out low income housing development projects using the tax credit and other forms of governmental and private assistance for profit-motivated and non-profit owners in Washington, D.C. and other cities in the nation.

He recently completed a study outlining a strategy to stimulate the development of permanent low income housing for the city-wide Task Force for the Homeless in Atlanta, GA.

He currently participates in an advisory committee formed under the auspices of the Treasury Department to provide recommendations and assistance to the Internal Revenue Service in developing regulations and otherwise administering the low income housing tax credit program.

He is the author of an article on "Policies and Strategies for Developing Low Income Housing", which was published jointly in 1988 by the U.S. Dept. of Housing and Urban Development and the Howard University Partnership Institute; articles on "Using the Low Income Housing Tax Credit to Help Produce Affordable Cooperative Housing", and "Using Tax Credits: Financing Rehabilitation"; and other publications and articles.

He is available to assist clients -- private developers, government agencies, and non-profit organizations -- in working with the tax credit program and on other aspects of housing and development.

FILL IN THIS FORM IF YOU--

-- WANT TO KEEP ABREAST OF FUTURE DEVELOPMENTS REGARDING THE LOW INCOME HOUSING TAX CREDIT.

-- WOULD LIKE FURTHER INFORMATION ON THE SUBJECT.

___ I would be interested in purchasing periodical updates or supplements to Tax Credits for Low Income Housing, covering Treasury regulations and rulings, new income limits, legislative developments, etc.

___ I would be interested in learning about particular projects which used the tax credits.

___ I would be willing to make available summary information about a project I am involved in which uses the tax credits.

___ I would like to talk to Joe Guggenheim about employing his consulting services.

___ I know other persons, organizations who should get information about this book (list below or use separate sheet)

___ I have comments, suggestions, criticisms below (or on separate page)

Name & Title ____

Organization ____

Address ____

City/State/Zip ____________________________ Phone ________________

Send to: SIMON PUBLICATIONS, P.O. Box 70425 Southwest Station,
Washington, D.C. 20024-0425

Comments or Other Names:

NEED MORE COPIES OF THIS BOOK FOR YOUR LAWYER, ACCOUNTANT, LIBRARY, FIELD STAFF, ASSOCIATES, CLIENTS, BOARD MEMBERS?

KNOW SOMEONE ELSE OR SOME OTHER ORGANIZATION THAT MAY BE INTERESTED IN THIS BOOK? PASS ALONG OR COPY THIS ORDER FORM FOR ADDITIONAL COPIES OF:

TAX CREDITS FOR LOW INCOME HOUSING

Please send me _________ copies of Tax Credits for Low Income Housing at $32.95 each, plus shipping charges. (D.C. Purchasers: Add $1.98 sales tax per copy) — Book Total ________

Shipping charges: $2.25 for 1–2 copies; $3.25 for 3–5 copies; $4.25 for 6–10 copies. — Shipping Charge Total ________

My payment is enclosed (check or money order). — GRAND TOTAL ________

Name & title:________________________________

Organization:________________________________

Mailing address:________________________________

City, State, Zip________________________________

(Discount for more than 10 copies available on request)

Make checks payable to SIMON PUBLICATIONS

Send to: SIMON PUBLICATIONS, P.O. Box 70425, Washington, D.C. 20024–0425